Nobody's Perfect

NOBODY'S PERFECT
A New Whig Interpretation of History

ANNABEL PATTERSON

Yale University Press   New Haven and London

Published with assistance from the Mary Cady Tew Memorial Fund.

Printed in the United States of America

Library of Congress Cataloging-in-Publication Data
Patterson, Annabel M.
Nobody's perfect : a new Whig interpretation of history /
Annabel Patterson.
p. cm.
Includes bibliographical references and index.
ISBN 0-300-09288-1 (cloth : alk. paper)
1. Great Britain—Historiography. 2. Historiography—Great Britain—
History—17th century. 3. Historiography—Great Britain—History—
18th century. 4. Great Britain—Intellectual life—17th century.
5. Great Britain—Intellectual life—18th century. 6. Political science—
Great Britain—History. 7. Whig Party (Great Britain) I. Title.
DA1 .P38   2002
941.007'2—dc21
2002006398

A catalog record for this book is
available from the British Library.

10 9 8 7 6 5 4 3 2 1

This book is dedicated to Jason Endicott.

CONTENTS

Acknowledgements

This book engendered itself around the chapter on Reynolds, which at one stage in my thinking was to have been part of a politically inflected study of the portrait in early modern Europe. For its new shape I have to thank, first, the hostile responses of two anonymous art historians to a long chapter on portraits of Melanchthon, and then my growing realization of how costly and painful is the task of acquiring many illustrations and the permissions to reproduce them. My respect for art historians has grown accordingly. But before the portrait project was disassembled I benefited greatly from the encouragement and help of my colleagues Christopher Wood and Julia Marciari-Alexander, as also from that of Ronald Paulson and Claude Rawson. The rest of the new book seemed to sprout *sua sponte* from my chance discovery of John Almon, a piece of work if ever there was one, and so in a sense I owe most to him. But the Beinecke Library, with its ever courteous and helpful staff, were what made the discovery of Almon (and the remarkable prints from the *Political Register*) fruitful and sustainable. Other friends whose wise advice or generous listening I wish to record include Isobel Armstrong, David Bromwich, April London, Harold Love, Joseph Roach, and Blakey Vermeule, all eighteenth-century mavens, whereas I am a rank intruder in this century; John Shawcross, who corrected my knowledge of editions of Milton for the chapter on Burke; Dayton Haskin, who was blessedly keen on the chapter on Thompson's 1776 edition of Marvell's works; and Simon Schama, who turned out to be another proponent of the whig interpretation of history. Finally, the book owes its appearance to my friend and arbiter, Jonathan Brent of Yale University Press, who liked it from the title onwards. Let us hope he is not secretly thinking, as Marvell did about Milton's whig interpretation of history in *Paradise Lost*, "I liked [the] project, the success did fear."

For we have not as yet completely forgotten what we still remember to have forgotten. Therefore, what we have completely forgotten we cannot even look for if it is lost.

—St. Augustine, *Confessions*

Nobody's Perfect

Introduction

This book will probably be seen as the sequel to my *Early Modern Liberalism;*[1] that is to say, it carries the story of liberal thought (and its eventual transmission to America) from seventeenth-century England through to the end of the English eighteenth century. Most of the men introduced or reintroduced here— John Almon, Edmund Burke, James Barry, Edward Thompson, Thomas Erskine, and (for a while at least) William Wordsworth —thought of themselves as continuing the work of Milton or Locke or Marvell or Algernon Sidney in the field of political thought. In conviction they were akin to Thomas Hollis, the Whig entrepreneur in the field of transmitting liberal ideas who was one of the heroes of *Early Modern Liberalism.* Indeed, some of them knew him.

If it were possible to aim at still larger game, however, this book does so. Rather than merely recuperate liberalism through its founding fathers, an act of refurnishing the public memory, I hereby offer a challenge to one of the reigning conventions of the modern Anglo-American academy. I propose to reinstate a "whig interpretation of history," in defiance of the historiographical orthodoxy that declares such an interpretation archaic and procedurally mistaken. This orthodoxy is most often associated with the name of Herbert Butterfield, from his early tirade *The Whig Interpretation of History* (1931), a general essay on historical method; but another kind of demolition had occurred a few years earlier in eighteenth-century studies, specifically, in Sir Lewis Namier's paradigm-shifting *The Structure of Politics at the Accession of George III* (1928). It is no coincidence that one of the great whig historians whose view of the eighteenth century Namier supplanted was Thomas Erskine May, whose two-volume *Constitutional History of England since the Accession of George III* appeared in 1861–63. Thomas Erskine May was, of course, named after Thomas Erskine, the great barrister whose whig interpretations of history are the subject of my penultimate chapter.

To show how the supposed demise of the whig interpretation is today taken for granted, one has only to turn to Kevin Sharpe's series of proposals for the new millennium, *Remapping Early Modern England* (Cambridge, 2000). There, in his opening chapter, Sharpe filled in the middle stages of the historiographical story between the early "whig" historians and memoirists—John Rushworth, Edmund Ludlow, Gilbert Burnet, John Oldmixon, Laurence Echard, Rapin de Thoyras, James Ralph—and the later ones, Thomas Babington Macaulay, Samuel Rawson Gardiner, and Wallace Notestein. Sharpe observed, as I will, too, that the first attack on the whig interpretation came remarkably early, from the "Tory philosopher David Hume" (p. 5), whose stated agenda was to replace a partisan historiography with an objective one. It was the political resurgence of the Whig party in the context of the first Reform Bill, Sharpe continued, that required Hume's rebuttal by Macaulay. Moreover, to bring the story up to date, Sharpe implicitly acknowledged that the most recent heirs of Namier and Butterfield, themselves the heirs of Hume, have been the "revisionist" historians of early modern England today, Conrad Russell, Mark Kishlansky, and of course himself. While restating and supplementing Butterfield's critique of whig historiography, Sharpe, however, announced the demise also of that very revisionist history of which he had been a spokesman, prophesying the arrival of still further advances, if only we could move from narrowly political to broadly cultural analysis. He therefore, self-admittedly, brought the idea of progress back into the picture, "re-inscrib[ing] a teleology, a Whig history," and raised the question of whether any and all metanarrative about history "is not open to such a charge" (p. 37).

Yes, probably; but unlike Sharpe, I see this less as a charge to which one must plead guilty and more as a deep reassurance. But before proceeding to the pros and cons of any whig historiography, we need to deal with potential confusions in terminology that may already have surfaced in this conversation. In my usage, as distinct from Sharpe's, "whig" uncapitalized refers *either* to a particular bias in historical theory or practice, *or* to a matching set of political views that might be held at any time, from the mid-seventeenth century till now. "Whig," however, refers to a member of a political party, group, or faction prepared to use that name. Although what became the Whig party emerged in the 1670s under the leadership of Anthony Ashley Cooper, earl of Shaftesbury, the formal opposition between Whigs and Tories was primarily an eighteenth-century phenomenon, and it caused as many problems of definition as it solved. Here, for example, is the account of the muddle that had developed by the accession of George III, as seen from the contemporary perspective of Horace Walpole. Undoubtedly biased in favor of whig ideals, and largely written well after the events related, Walpole's *Memoirs of the Reign of George III* nevertheless gives a picture of the breakdown of the two-party system, and the problems of terminology, that is worth recuperating:

> Though Grenville and the Duke of Bedford had always called themselves Whigs, and the *Chancellor Northington really was one,* yet Lord Bute had left the standard of prerogative in the Court, and

his successors had relaxed none of those high-flown doctrines. Nothing could be more despotic than Grenville's nature. Bedford was drawn by the Duchess and Rigby to adopt any principles, however contrary to his opinion, that favoured her love of power, or Rigby's rapacity: and Lord Mansfield retained great weight in a cabinet so framed to embrace boldly any arbitrary measures that he was always ready to suggest and always afraid to execute himself. On the other hand, the Opposition, though headed by Newcastle, who had sailed with every current, and though composed of great and proud families, dated from the stand they had made, or by resentment had been forced to make, to the Favourite's [Bute's] plan of extending the prerogative. Lord Temple stood on no ground but popularity; and the cast of Mr. Pitt's life, contrary to his temper, had thrown him too on the affections of the people. The crisis I am going to describe, broke these ill-consolidated connections into several factions; and though one of those factions adhered more steadily to their professions than the rest, the subsequent contests were rather a struggle for power, than the settled animosity of two parties, though the body of Opposition still called itself Whig, an appellation rather dropped than disclaimed by the Court; and though the real Tories still adhered to their old distinctions, while they secretly favoured, sometimes opposed, the Court, and fluctuated according as they esteemed particular chiefs not of their connection, or had the more agreeable opportunity of distressing those who supported the cause of freedom.[2]

This passage has the advantage of being deliberately summative. Walpole is instructing his readers about the state of the government in 1765, at the time when the instability he describes was about to be exacerbated by the "crisis" provoked by the arrest of John Wilkes for the authorship of *North Briton,* no. 45. His analysis also has the merit of showing us, in his own response, that extreme cynicism about individuals is compatible with a strong commitment to "whig" ideals, which Walpole did not think outmoded or naive, merely outmanoeuvred.

From the perspective of twentieth-century hindsight, the eighteenth century was the period in which the idea of "party" itself became discredited, not only because, under Walpole's father, Sir Robert Walpole, as Whig prime minister, the Whigs began to behave like Tories and some Tories like principled Whigs, but also because in the next reign George III decided to rule without political parties. Whether *he* did so cynically, or because of the influence of Lord Bute on his early education, or for genuinely idealistic reasons (perhaps inspired, ironically, by the *Idea of a Patriot King,* the product of that least-disinterested of all political theorists, Henry St. John Bolingbroke), has been one of the central topics of debate. But the young king's stated policy of creating administrations across what might have been, or might have become again, party lines was itself, as it were, a form of revisionism, ostensibly intended to replace factionalism with a meritocracy, but in the views of some, only creating more faction. It certainly had the effect of increasing the role of self-interest in politics, as men jockeyed for places for themselves or their friends and refused to work with temporary enemies. George III later described this situation in very different terms, taking personal credit for what he saw as a more stable situation: "I . . . put an end to those unhappy distinctions of party called Whigs and Torys by declaring I would countenance every Man that supported my Administration & concurred in that form of Government which had been so wisely established by the Revolution.[3] But the difference between this rosy view of his administration and that of at least some of the Whigs can be seen in a cartoon, *The R——l [Royal] Dupe,* almost contemporary with it, five years into the reign (Figure 1). It was printed in John Almon's *Political Register* for February 1770. Here the king sleeps in his mother's lap, while Lord Bute steals his sceptre from behind, and Henry Fox, portrayed *as* a fox, picks his pocket. The royal statement of policy certainly *sounds* more idealistic than does Walpole's, and the cartoon explains why: the king has been sleeping on the job.

It has been claimed that one of Lord Bute's manoeuvres was to place in the hands of the young George III a copy of David Hume's *History of England.* The first volume of this work, *Containing the Reigns of James I and Charles I,* appeared in 1754, with a second volume, dated 1757, bringing the story of the seventeenth century up to the Revolution of 1688. In 1759, Hume took the story back through the Tudors, and in 1762, from Julius Caesar to Henry VII. Hume has been seen as the first of those who attacked the whig interpretation of earlier English history. At the center of the controversy he caused was his dislike of the *method* of tracing the benefits of the present English Constitution back into the past and finding its origins in an "ancient constitution" instead of in the settlement of 1688–89; while at the same time his emphasis on the role of accident in history depreciated that of character and principle.[4] It was this aspect of Hume's revisionism that drove Catharine Macaulay to write in 1763 her own interpretation (both Whig and whig) of seventeenth-century history, where the heroic model of causation was emphatically reinstated, though in rather too pious a style. And it was Hume's attack on ancient constitutionalism that caused Thomas Jefferson to replace Hume's *History* as the

Figure 1. *The R——l [Royal] Dupe.* By John Jones? *Political Register,*
February 1770. Courtesy of the Beinecke Rare Book and Manuscript
Library, Yale University.

textbook at the University of Virginia with John Baxter's *New and Impartial History of England* (1796).[5]

But as Victor Wexler has shown,[6] Hume did not originally conceive of his project as an attack on the theory of the ancient constitution, with its veneration of Magna Carta and its obsession with the antiquity and power of the House of Commons. Instead he began with the more local issue of the bias against the Stuart monarchs that had animated the Whig historians who preceded him, retelling the story of their reigns in what he claimed was a more objective, less partisan way. His major instance of a "Whig historian" seems to have been Paul Rapin de Thoyras, a French Protestant refugee who in 1700 was granted a pension by William III to write his *Histoire d'Angleterre*. But as Hume's project grew, and as the clamor of protest against *his* interpretation of Stuart history affected sales, his idea of what constituted the "whig" interpretation acquired careerist dimensions. In *My Own Life*,[7] he recounted the reception of the first volume: "I was assailed by one cry of reproach, disapprobation, and even detestation; English, Scotch, and Irish, Whig and Tory, churchman and sectary, freethinker and religionist, patriot and courtier, united their rage against the man who had presumed to shed a generous tear for the fate of Charles I and the Earl of Strafford." Hume felt himself hard done by; and in later editions he actually decreased what there had been in his work of moderate criticisms of Charles I and his father.

In a passage concluding the volume of the *History* which dealt with Charles II and James II, Hume explained his motives in a rather revealing formulation:

> The whig party, for a course of near seventy years, has, almost without interruption, enjoyed the whole authority of the government; and no honours or offices could be obtained but by their countenance

and protection. But this event, which . . . has been advantageous to the state, has been proved destructive to the truth of history, and has established many gross falsehoods. . . . And forgetting that a regard to liberty, though a laudable passion, ought commonly to be subordinate to a reverence for established government, the prevailing faction has celebrated only the partisans of the former, who pursued as their object the perfection of civil society, and has extolled them at the expense of their antagonists, who maintained those maxims that are essential to its very existence. But extremes of all kinds are to be avoided; and tho' no-one will ever please either faction by moderate opinions, it is there we are most likely to meet with truth and certainty.[8]

While the last part of this paragraph expresses an admirable principle of mediation, seeking the middle ground between opposed biases, the center clearly states that the "laudable passion" for liberty ought "to be *subordinate* to a reverence for *established* government," and the beginning admits, perhaps unconsciously, to motives external to political theory. As Wexler's biographical introduction shows, Hume believed that the Whigs "held a stranglehold on places, positions and literary taste" in a world in which he personally had struggled without success for place and respect (p. 8). When he was finally, in his forties, elected to the position of Keeper of the Library of the Faculty of Advocates in January 1752, he not only had the resources to write his *History*, he had accumulated some of the animus he needed to see the project to completion.

As distinct from this characterological explanation, it has been argued by Nicholas Phillipson that Hume *had* to write the kind of history he gradually wrote, because he had already worked out, at the level of political and moral theory, a commitment to absolute monarchy as the guarantor of peace and stability. He was, in other words (though Phillipson does not put it like this) a more genial version of Hobbes. For Hume, Bolingbroke's attempt to dispense with the two old parties and create a new, fluid coalition of anticorruption reformers was a major theoretical mistake, and one that threatened merely to reintroduce faction in a new form:

> In translating the metaphysical language of the *Treatise* [*of Human Nature*] into a party political language, Hume had to make it clear that the most "natural" form of government was one that was simple, not mixed; regular, not uncertain in its operations; and supported by opinion which was shaped by considerations of interest and habit rather than by abstract reasoning about the principles of government. In his essay "That Politics May Be Reduced to a Science" he laid down the central principles . . . : that the constitution of mixed monarchies were more prone to faction and civil disorder than simple forms of government; and that hereditary monarchy was to be preferred to elective monarchy, aristocracy or republics, all of which encouraged faction. For civilized polities were governed by laws, not men, and only absolute sovereigns whose power was undivided and whose authority was undisputed could hope to govern by rules and squeeze corruption and faction out of the political system in the process.[9]

This remarkable return to a theory of absolute monarchy would naturally recommend itself to George III.

But neither a Hume who grew increasingly embittered against

the Whigs for reasons of personal ambition, nor a Hume who followed the logic of his theory of human nature through to a desire to set back the political clock, seems quite adequate to the present study. For between these two there stands, in a posture of insecurity and negotiation, the Hume whose own uncertainties and conflicting imperatives are constantly revealed in his style, so that the nuances he inserts into his accounts—for example, of the debates on the Petition of Right in 1628—and the vibrations we can hear in his judgements—for preeminent example, of the executions of Lord Russell and Algernon Sidney in 1683—made it possible for later and less subtle thinkers to ignore the signs of the "good" Hume and focus, even to misrepresentation, on the "bad" one. It should not be forgotten that Hume, in his history of Charles I's reign, relied explicitly upon the compilations of that old republican John Rushworth, along with Whitelocke's *Diary* and the *State Trials*, and he even cited Thomas May's *History of the Parliament of England* (1647), the work for which May was regarded as a traitor in royalist circles.

Given that debates on the validity of the "whig interpretation" began in the reign of George III, it is perhaps not surprising that *modern* attacks upon it originated in eighteenth-century historiography. Sir Lewis Namier began *The Structure of Politics* with a clear statement of his ethical premises, at least as they affected his view of the eighteenth century and have been affecting accounts of it ever since: "After a century of Parliamentary contests over causes which had moved the conscience of men and for which they had died on the scaffold and the field of battle, fifty years later the nation was at one in all fundamental matters, and whenever that happy but uninspiring condition is reached, Parliamentary contests lose reality and unavoidably change into a fierce though bloodless struggle for office. In a House dominated by party organisations such struggles assume the decorous forms of wholesale transactions glorified by the mutual loyalties and the common joys or sorrows of the contending teams. In the eighteenth century the transactions were carried through individually or by small groups, and were therefore as sordid as solitary drinking."[10] This is a striking opening, and its quality of contemptuous overstatement might have been evident from the first; but the forcefulness of Namierism, and the brilliant new documentation it brought to the political process, largely obscured the attitude that underpinned it. John Brewer, whose *Party Ideology and Popular Politics at the Accession of George III* can reasonably be seen as the first major theoretical challenge to Namier, reminds us that this attitude is itself ideological. As Brewer put it, in one of the clearest summaries of the historiographical debate that the ordinary reader is likely to find, the pre-Namieran view of eighteenth-century politics "has an epic quality about it":

> Politics is envisaged as a struggle between conflicting principles which are not only professed but believed. The forces of progress battle with the forces of reaction. The political actors have coherent intentions and seek rational ends. When we observe men disputing matters of principle we are able to see what politics is about. The pursuit of sincerely held beliefs is a strong motive in politics. Tory historians' views tend, however, in a diametrically opposite direction. They start from the premise that politics is about power—its acquisition, exercise and retention. Professions of principle are secondary; they merely serve the purpose of providing basic political instincts with an air of legitimacy. They act, in other words, as a species of *ex post facto* rationalization: as Namier put it, "what matters most [in politics] is the underlying emotions, the music, to which ideas

are a mere libretto, often of a very inferiour quality."
It follows from this that talk about the constitution
of political ideas is frequently cosmetic and has little
or no effect on the course of politics; the only occasions on which such ideologies might affect political
actions is when the agent credulously believes that
he says and acts because he genuinely holds that belief.[11]

What Herbert Butterfield took from Namier, and general-
ized to all historical periods, was this strain of anti-idealism.
Namier's introduction of the eighteenth century, as quoted
above, distinguished it from the more principled seventeenth
century, when crisis required men to act and suffer conscientiously. But Butterfield attempted, in this early and shortsighted
work, holistically to banish the thought that the world we in-
habit today is a better one than it would have been without the
efforts of principled individuals. In *The Whig Interpretation of
History,* Butterfield's version of this argument was that history
moves as a result of unpredictable convergences or collisions of
interests, rather than being driven by programs; hence the very
idea of *forward* movement or progress is a fantasy, in Butterfield's words, "a mental trick," caused by reading the past in the
light of the present. This is the delusion claimed by Butterfield
to be the province of whig historiography, the belief in progress,
and hence in "progressive" ideas, which is now almost universally laughed out of countenance.

In Butterfield's classic little essay, written in 1931, significantly
before the impact of Naziism on world history, the focus was on
what he claimed to be a mistake of historical reasoning:

It is part and parcel of the whig interpretation of
history that it studies the past with reference to the
present; and though there may be a sense in which

it is inescapable, it has often been an obstruction to historical understanding. . . . Through this system of immediate reference to the present day, historical personages can easily and irresistibly be classed into the men who furthered progress and the men who tried to hinder it; . . . the historian . . . will imagine that he has discovered a "root" or an "anticipation" of the 20th century, when in reality he is in a world of different connotations altogether, and he has merely tumbled upon what could be shown to be a misleading analogy. *Working upon the same system* the whig historian can draw lines through certain events, some such line as that which leads through Martin Luther and a long succession of whigs to modern liberty; and if he is not careful he begins to forget that this line is merely a mental trick of his; he comes to imagine that it represents something like a line of causation. The total result of this method is to impose a certain form upon the whole historical story, and to produce a scheme of general history . . . all demonstrating throughout the ages the workings of an obvious principle of progress, of which the Protestants and whigs have been the perpetual allies while Catholics and tories have perpetually formed obstruction.[12]

I make so bold as to say that Butterfield was here himself guilty of making a misleading analogy. His essay began by asserting that it is the chief job of the historian to stress the *unlikeness* between the past and the present, to stomp on "those very analogies which we imagined to exist," in other words, to exercise the true historical imagination against the temptation of presentism. But presentism—finding our own concerns in past societies or finding them lacking—is a very different conceptual mistake, if it is one, from a belief in progress, which allows us to acknowledge that modern society is *better* than pre-modern—more comfortable, more efficient, and infinitely more just to the majority of its members. There is indeed an analogy between these two kinds of reasoning—both read the past in terms of the present—but that is the only likeness between them.

But whether or not Butterfield actually confused the two, he most strongly believed at this stage that the mistake whig historians had made in the past and should be prevented from making in the future was to attribute these improvements, at least in political history, primarily to rational human efforts. To record who, specifically, made those efforts, and who resisted them, was indeed part of whig historiography; and one of the most puzzling aspects of Butterfield's argument is his failure to acknowledge that certain reform milestones in British political history were *undeniably* initiated and fought for by determined individuals, often sensing that the moment for them was finally propitious. So obsessed was Butterfield (despite being an active Methodist) with what he saw as the overvaluing of the Reformation as a move forward—the "but for Luther" story of modernization—that at this early stage of his career he could see only its persecutory consequences and not the slow achievement of toleration and the secular state.

Another paragraph in Butterfield's essay brings us closer to Namier, though not to the full Hobbesianism of the Namierite position. This was his theory of how Britain acquired its supposedly enviable Constitution. The whig historian, wrote Butterfield: "is apt to imagine the British constitution as coming down to us by virtue of the work of long generations of whigs and in spite of the obstructions of a long line of tyrants and tories. In reality it is the result of the continual interplay and perpetual collision of the two. It is the very embodiment of all the balances and compromises and adjustments that were necessitated by this interplay. The whig historian is apt to imagine the British constitution as coming down to us safely at last, in spite of so many vicissitudes; when in reality it is the result of those very vicissitudes of which he seems to complain. . . . In the most concrete sense of the words our constitution is not merely the work of men and parties; it is the product of history" (p. 41).

Here the grand view obliterates the significance of particular reforms and campaigns. Later in this Introduction I will identify some of the constitutional and legal changes that were, if not exclusively, unquestionably the direct results of individual effort and sometimes personal heroism.

Butterfield's attack on the whig interpretation of history was something of which, in the middle of the Second World War, he dramatically repented. In 1944 he published *The Englishman and His History*, another brief and ideologically candid book that diametrically reversed and did penance for his former position — without acknowledging that it *was* his position. By now, Butterfield was prepared to define the "whig" interpretation as the "English" interpretation, fully absorbed into the country's public culture and capable of inspiring the great speeches of defiance and resistance to Nazi Germany of 1940. He observed that "one man in the 18th century wrote essays on English history so full of the song of liberty that he has been called the founder of the whig interpretation; yet he was none other than the politician Bolingbroke, notorious in his day and ever since as the wildest and wickedest of tories. The tories in fact do not escape the whig interpretation, though they may try to undermine it and they play tricks with it at times.[13] Butterfield observed that "there is not anything worth the name of the 'tory interpretation of English history,'" though perhaps he would have changed his mind about this had he lived another twenty years. "It is not necessary or useful to deny that the theme of English political history is the story of our liberty; . . . it will always be true that in one important aspect—in yesterday's meaning of the term at least—we are all of us exultant and unrepentant whigs. *Those who, perhaps in the misguided austerity of youth, wish to drive out that whig interpretation . . . are sweeping a room which humanly speaking cannot long remain empty*" (pp. 3–4; italics added). Butterfield therefore illustrates poignantly one of my own propositions, that political history makes no sense unless we make room in our interpretations for honest changes of mind, as well as dishonest ones. Nevertheless, the *name* of Butterfield remains indissolubly attached to that early essay, whose brevity and overstatement made it a magnet for subsequent writers, while its stigmatic effect on the term "whig" has been even more durable than Butterfield's views on historical method. Meanwhile, Namierism, in the broader sense, as the belief that self-interest is *the* ruling political motive, is continually fortified by observation of contemporary political behaviour.

I raise my own standard on the premise that every historical period contains its own mixture of actors who are moved primarily by principle, those who are moved primarily by self-interest, and some highly interesting combinations of both. I also believe that, in the eighteenth century, both numerically and qualitatively, *more* principled persons chose to call themselves Whigs than chose to call themselves Tories. Some, like the young and overexcited Wordsworth, even chose to call themselves democrats.

A "whig" interpretation of eighteenth-century history, however, will not rely on the hopelessly porous and shifting nature of political allegiances, nor need it necessarily embroil itself in the debates, strenuously conducted at the time and into the nineteenth century, as to whether political parties were a benign or a malign force in government. Instead, it defines "whig" as a term, if not synonymous, then certainly cognate, with "liberal," and for purposes of studying the later eighteenth century, perhaps of greater merit and interest. Especially when the Whig party under George III disintegrated into factions, variously associated with the Bedfords, the elder Pitt, with Grafton, Grenville, Rockingham, or with Fox (to name only a few of the subcombinations), it became necessary for men (and for the occasional vocal and public woman) to dig beneath labels that had grown misleading for the principles that had given rise to them. This was essentially the motive behind both Edmund Burke's *Thoughts on the Causes of the Present Discontents,* also a response of early 1770, *and* Catharine Macaulay's strictures upon it.[14]

Second, having mentioned Butterfield's change of direction, and intending to focus on other eighteenth-century turnabouts, most important that of Burke himself, I want to explain now my main title, *Nobody's Perfect.* This is intended to stand for a humanist historiography which can mediate between idealism and realism (as distinct from cynicism) as standards for assessing the past. A new whig interpretation of history can, I suggest, be erected only on the basis of an attitude of tolerance towards human inconsistency, and on the observable fact that people whose lives have been dominated by principle will often, at some stage, make moves that show them to be captives of self-interest in one of its most naked forms. One of the greatest and most indefatigable Whigs of the period, Charles James Fox, converted initially from the other side. William Pitt the Elder, the "Great Commoner," was thought to have deserted the people by accepting a title and retiring to the House of Lords. To take a much less well known example, Sir James Macintosh, lawyer, historian, and member of the House of Commons, first enthusiastically supported the French Revolution, vehemently answering Burke's *Reflections* in his *Vindiciae Gallicae* (1791), then repented of that book and became Burke's eulogist. John Almon, the ardent whig polemicist and publisher, was accused towards the end of his life, when he was in straitened financial circumstances, of negotiating for a stipend from the Tory ministry of William Pitt the Younger. Thomas Erskine, who sacrificed his position as attorney general to the Prince of Wales (the future George IV) in order, on principle, to defend Thomas Paine from a charge of seditious libel, subsequently acted as prosecutor against a wretched bookseller who had simply distributed Paine's *Age of Reason*. The smear of sexual impropriety made the populism of John Wilkes into something of a liability for his Whig supporters in high places. In our own day, the presidency of William Clinton, both in itself and in its Hollywood reincarnation, *Primary Colors*, makes an interesting analogy. But imperfect agents of principle do not render principle itself nonexistent or nonviable. On the contrary, their behaviour tends to clarify principle's longevity and rigour.

Edmund Burke himself put an aspect of this problem with exemplary clarity at a very early stage of his career, when publicly defending the Rockinghamites against a spokesman for the Grenville administration. In his *Observations on a Late State of the Nation* (1769), he wrote: "I believe the instances are exceedingly rare of men immediately passing over a clear marked line of virtue into declared vice and corruption. There are a sort of middle tints and shades between the two extremes; there is something uncertain on the confines of the two empires which they first pass through, and which renders the change easy and imperceptible. There are even a sort of splendid impositions so well contrived, that, at the very time the path of rectitude is quitted for ever, men seem to be advancing into some higher and nobler road of public conduct. . . . [F]ew are the steps from dereliction to persecution."[15] This canny observation applies, with a dreadful retroactive irony, not only to Burke himself as he came to excoriate the Reverend Richard Price and the Dissenters who welcomed the French Revolution, but also to William Pitt the Younger, whose own proposals for a reform of the franchise in the early 1780s were repudiated by himself in the 1790s, a reversal that led directly to the infamous Treason Trials of 1794. And in my last chapter I deal with the notorious transformations that overtook Samuel Taylor Coleridge and William Wordsworth, both of whom started as ardent supporters of the French Revolution and opponents of Pitt but changed their tune. Why they did so is a more complicated issue than why Pitt changed his, and it is also a literary issue.

A sophisticated and therefore seductive version of this same historiographical assumption—that the political psyche is more labile than rigid—was defined by Mark Philp in his essay "The Fragmented Ideology of Reform."[16] Starting with the "deep and obvious divisions in the ranks of those sympathetic to reform" in the last decades of the eighteenth century, Philp maintains that both reformers and loyalists changed and developed their theoretical positions in response to the arguments and events of the decade. Burke wrote in response to the French Revolution, Paine developed his principles in response to Burke, John Thelwall came to a full realization of what were the "just and inalienable rights" of human beings by reviewing the "abstract and difficult propositions" of political theory as a prisoner in the Tower, awaiting his trial for treason. Lability can be within the sphere of principle itself. What we get from Thelwall, writes Philp, "and from many others on both sides, is a sense of the period as transforming or traumatising people so as to produce highly individual personal and intellectual responses, rather than a pattern of simple conformity to a creed." Hence (though not solely hence) the splintering of the reform movement, the split in the Whig party itself, the tensions between Grey's Friends of the People and the extraparliamentary organisations for reform, few of which agreed with each other!

I do not wish to be caught in the folly of assuming that the term "principle" applies only to what I call "progressive" principles—those that did, in fact, gradually help to lead us from the world of anciens régimes to that of modern democracies. As Butterfield himself observed, that was another of the mistakes of the old whig historians: "It seems to be true," he wrote in 1957, "that the Whig historians will tend to assess the virtues of the Rockinghamites by their ideals, but still may be content to measure the followers of Lord North only by their interests—a procedure which is not improved if the opponents of the Whigs merely reverse the formula."[17] To move the argument on to the 1790s also requires the capacity to see both sides of the question. Despite the legendary status that the Treason Trials have assumed in subsequent historiography, and the legal folly of trying under a medieval treason statute a modern political movement, it is possible to see why Pitt's government panicked at what they thought was a national conspiracy to change the Constitution on the model of the French Revolution.

In arguing for a new, less stubbornly partisan but still "whig" interpretation of history, which acknowledges both the existence of principled conservativism and the flawed careers of true progressives, I want also to introduce another, semicomic notion by which Butterfield's original hypothesis may be countered. History, if one wants to adhere to that grand abstraction, does move forward, but it tends to do so in a one-step-backwards, two-steps-forward dynamic. The whigs of the eighteenth century, whether they were Old, new, true, Grenvillite, Rockinghamite, Foxite, really independents, or republicans in or out of the closet, did not agree with Sir Lewis Namier that England was now "one in all fundamental matters," nor did they see the state of the nation as a "happy but uninspiring condition." On the contrary, they firmly believed, some of them more firmly than others, that either the changes of the Revolution of

1688 had not gone far enough, or they were being silently reversed. As Catharine Macaulay's preface to her *History* put it: "[T]his [Court] faction has not only prevented the establishing any regular system to preserve or improve our liberties; but lie at this time [the 1760s] in wait for the first opportunity which the imperfections of this government may give them to destroy those rights, which have been purchased by the toil and blood of the most exalted individuals."[18] And in 1790, responding both to the policies of the younger Pitt and to Burke's *Reflections on the Revolution in France*, Joseph Towers, an inveterate pamphleteer, made the claim that while France and America had learned liberty "from the Lockes and the Sidneys of England, unhappily, at a period when English writers are illuminating the world, and contributing to its emancipation from tyranny, much of the antient spirit of liberty appears in England itself to be evaporated, and we seem in this respect to be greatly degenerating from our ancestors. A spirit of court servility, and an implicit confidence in the minister, without any just grounds, have lately become so prevalent, that there is too great reason to apprehend, that we have lost much of that vigilance in the support of public freedom, which is essential to its preservation."[19] And like Macaulay, Towers would take issue with the first of the historians to deliberately challenge the whig interpretation of history, David Hume, whose *History of England*, it was claimed by John Almon, was deployed in the instruction of George III by Lord Bute.

This backwards slippage was particularly true in the area of law and jurisprudence. John Almon and others were convinced, for example, that Lord Chief Justice Mansfield was putting the chariot of law into reverse by the doctrines he pronounced about the limited role of juries in libel cases, of which the century, symptomatically, had dozens. But it would not be until 1792 that Charles James Fox in the Commons and Lord Camden in the Lords were able to get passed a new Libel Act moving protections for the freedom of the press not only back to where they had been before Mansfield's supremacy, but a little bit further forward. In that campaign, Thomas Erskine's impassioned defence of Thomas Paine's right to have written the *Rights of Man* was a crucial piece of propaganda. Likewise, the practice of issuing general warrants for arrests—warrants that did not specify the name of the person nor the offence charged—was rendered politically embarrassing by a huge parliamentary debate in 1764, which lasted for about two years. The issue was raised to consciousness by the arrest of Wilkes under a general warrant, and it was widely argued in both houses that the practice was illegal, an opinion that eradicated general warrants even though the Whigs never managed to pass an act outlawing them. John Almon argued in the press that the dangerous legal measure had somehow slipped beneath the scrutiny of those who constructed the 1688–89 Constitution.

In another arena, Almon, Wilkes, and others were convinced that the old rules which prevented public knowledge of what went on in parliamentary debates were wrong and needed to be challenged. Thanks to them, in 1771 the Commons were strategically embarrassed into permitting, as a de facto event, the reporting of their doings in the daily newspapers. The whole area of press freedoms received more sustained attention and support from the Whigs in the eighteenth century than in the seventeenth, and Erskine, their great champion in the courts, saw himself as working in the intellectual tradition of John Milton, whose *Areopagitica* he liberally quoted during his defence of Paine.

The greatest challenge to political thought, however, was surely England's relation to its American colonies, as focused precisely on the old seventeenth-century issue of taxation. And it is important to see that the stance men took in the 1760s and 1770s regarding America was one of direct application of a constitutional principle—no taxation without representation—to a part of the system, one that was threatening to break off its metonymic relation to the whole. In contrast, the crisis caused in England by the French Revolution was merely crisis by analogy —the fear that the new French system of republicanism would spread across the Channel. When Burke defended the colonists in his famous speech *On Conciliation* in 1774, he, too, defended them on principles which would appear to have been officially recognized as victorious in 1688, although, as the present conflict showed, there had been serious backsliding in the nation's (and the king's) thinking subsequently. In the seventeenth century, Burke implied (though he was not chronologically precise): "They took infinite pains to inculcate, as a fundamental principle, that, in all monarchies, the people must in effect themselves mediately or immediately possess the power of granting their own money, or no shadow of liberty could subsist. The Colonies draw from you as with their life-blood, these ideas and principles. Their love of liberty, as with you, fixed and attached on this specific point of taxing. Liberty might be safe, or might be endangered in twenty other particulars, without their being much pleased or alarmed. Here they felt its pulse."[20] It was not Burke's fault that this argument, and all subsequent arguments for conciliation, failed.

For the test of principled action (especially when it takes the form of speech) can never be exclusively, or even primarily, political achievement. When the Rockingham administration repealed the Stamp Act in 1766, they accomplished something temporary, a slight political advantage, to be rendered nugatory ten years later, when the Declaration of Independence was signed. But the principle of *representation* was now in the public sphere; and, as John Brewer has argued, the defence of the colonists now bounced back and sparked a movement for better political representation at home.[21] In 1776, John Wilkes introduced into Parliament (of course unsuccessfully) a bill for "a just and equal Representation of the People of England in Parliament." By 1782, William Pitt the Younger, of all people, was arguing for parliamentary reform. Bill after bill, proposal after proposal, the idea of reform was rejected in Parliament. Then the French Revolution intervened, to render change even more suspect—and even more desirable among the disenfranchised. In 1794 there were mass meetings of the London Corresponding Society lobbying for reform—meetings that resulted in the treason trials of Thomas Hardy, John Horne Tooke, and John Thelwall. This was the one step backwards—reviving the bad old days of constructive treason jurisprudence that preceded the 1688 Revolution and surely contributed to it. One falls back *pour mieux sauter,* as a whig interpretation of history would prefer to see it. But even though Thomas Erskine achieved the acquittal of Hardy, Tooke, and Thelwall, in part by arguing that nothing they were working for had not previously been proposed by the duke of Richmond and by William Pitt himself, it was a long step backwards. It was not until 1832 that the first Reform Bill finally passed both houses of Parliament. That Lord John Russell, the architect of the first Reform Bill, was self-consciously descended from Lord William Russell, a 1683 victim of the doctrine of constructive treason in the hands of Chief Justice Jeffreys, was no coincidence.

Let us recall for a moment Butterfield's statement in *The Whig Interpretation of History* as to how we get change. The whig historian, he charged, "is apt to imagine the British constitution as coming down to us by virtue of the work of long generations of whigs and in spite of the obstructions of a long line of tyrants and tories. In reality it is the result of the continual interplay and perpetual collision of the two. . . . [The whig historian] does not see whig and tory combining in virtue of their very antagonism to produce those interactions which turn one age into another. He does not see that time is so to speak having a hand in the game, and the historical process is working upon the pattern which events are taking" (pp. 41-42). Now, on the grand scale of abstraction, of course this last sentence is true; but what it chooses to omit are the individual components of the constitution, such as the much vaunted protection of habeas corpus, that which protects the citizen from arbitrary imprisonment. The legal doctrine of habeas corpus had long existed in common law (actually since Magna Carta) as a prerogative writ, whereby someone imprisoned could legally request to be brought into court in person so that a judge might determine whether his imprisonment was legally justified. It could easily be undermined, however, by deliberate delay on the part of a judge, or circumvented outright, as, for example, when Charles II's government imprisoned Sir Thomas Vane in the Scilly Isles instead of in London. In 1679 it was impressively strengthened by statute (31 Charles II, c.2), when its chief architect was the leader of the nascent Whig party, Anthony Ashley Cooper, earl of Shaftesbury. During the eighteenth century there were constant attempts by Tory governments to turn back the clock, using political unrest as the justification: during the Jacobite rebellion of 1745, when Lord Mansfield spoke in favor of suspension; during the war with the American colonies, when a partial suspension of habeas corpus for enemies of the state was legislated in February 1777, over the protests of the remaining handful of Whigs in Parliament, including Charles James Fox and Lord Camden. At this time the radical artist James Barry enrolled the visual arts in defence of liberty, creating an extraordinary print which we will examine in detail in Chapter 3, but which had habeas corpus as one of its visual and textual symbols. Significantly, he would reissue this print during the anti-Jacobin panic of the 1790s, when Pitt suspended habeas corpus protections for eight years.[22] Another suspension would be legislated in 1817, when Radical agitation over the Corn Laws was used as the pretext. Even in America, habeas corpus was suspended during the Civil War by an 1863 act of Congress requested by President Abraham Lincoln, and the constitutional debates on the issue were intense. These are some of the vicissitudes that Butterfield, "in the misguided austerity of youth," saw as benign forces, like wind and water, slowly creating the political landscape of the future.

David Hume took up the issue of habeas corpus in a way that allows for some theoretical subtlety. In his account of the reign of Charles II in the *History of England,* Hume observed the passage of the statute strengthening the common law procedure, but he started his brief account with a sturdy preamble, full of whig inflections:

> Arbitrary imprisonment is a grievance, which, in some degree, has place almost in every government, except that of Great Britain; and our absolute security from it we owe chiefly to the present parliament [that of 1679]; a merit which makes some atonement for the faction and violence into which their prejudices had, in other particulars, betrayed them. The great charter had laid the foundation of this valuable part of liberty; the petition of right had renewed and extended it; but some provisions were still wanting to render it complete, and prevent all evasion or delay from ministers and judges. The act of *habeas corpus*, which passed this session, served these purposes. By this act it was prohibited to send any one to a prison beyond sea. No judge, under severe penalities, must refuse to any prisoner a writ of *habeas corpus*. . . . [E]very prisoner must be indicted the first term after his commitment, and brought to trial in the subsequent term. And no

> man, after being enlarged by order of court, can be
> recommitted for the same offence. (8:106-7)

"This law," continued Hume, "seems necessary for the protection of liberty in a mixed monarchy; and as it has not place in any other form of government [of course he knew nothing of the American constitution], this consideration alone may induce us to prefer our present constitution to all others." But here comes the other side of Hume, the side that infuriated many of his original readers: "It must, however, be confessed, that there is some difficulty to reconcile with such extreme liberty the full security and the regular police of a state, especially the police of great cities."

The phrase "extreme liberty," especially as applied to so modest a protection as habeas corpus, belongs to the other side of the political spectrum; and it was certainly on the basis of public security that Pitt, and later Robert Jenkinson, accomplished its suspension. A new whig historian will see the trajectory of such a protection as a bellwether or, perhaps, as a canary in a mine; *whenever* arguments for public safety are used to abrogate civil liberties, we are in danger of moving backwards.

Finally, at the level of historical method, this book is manifestly not written by a historian, but by someone who attempts to combine the techniques of the historian with those of the literary scholar, a task pioneered by James Boulton in his important study *The Language of Politics,* which dealt in detail with the most influential ideological statements of Burke and Paine.[23] To a lesser extent I also encroach on the jealously guarded territory of the art historian. Chapter 5, on the career of Sir Joshua Reynolds and its role in the long historiographical debate (was Reynolds a Whig iconographer, or an apolitical painter for whom success meant everything?) deals directly with the portrait, an appropriate subject for a study that focuses on the individual, on names, faces, motives, and personal narratives. But the eighteenth century is also the great age of political prints, and several of these, like *The Royal Dupe,* will figure as evidence. In this area, Kathleen Wilson's *The Sense of the People* is an essential guide and corrective, especially for the earlier part of the century, with which I barely deal.[24] Her account of how the Whigs used the popular media of pamphlet and print in the Succession crisis that brought about Hanoverian rule establishes the context for the work of John Almon, the subject of my first two chapters, who combined in one person the function of publisher, bookseller, and Opposition pamphleteer, while initiating the use of political prints as a regular feature of the *Political Register.* One of the striking characteristics of eighteenth-century cartoons that Almon exploited is the collaboration of image and text, an absorption into a lively new context of the explanatory titles or mottos derived from the emblem tradition. Eighteenth-century purchasers of prints literally *read* their meaning; and to understand a major statement like James Barry's *The Phoenix,* they needed to have read a good deal beside.

This book privileges reading, and hence of course writing, over archival research. Therefore the published work, or the recorded speech, is more central to its argument than correspondence (the great tool of Namierite history), though letters also count considerably. In Chapter 2 the literary technique of close reading is brought to bear on John Almon's famous *Letter Concerning Libels,* whose constant revisions from edition to edition constitute evidence: about authorial intentions, authorial fears, and changing circumstances. In Chapter 3, Edmund Burke's speech *On Conciliation,* which was carefully prepared for publication by Burke himself, is shown to be a masterpiece of literary quotation and adaptation. In Chapter 5 a scholarly *edition*—in this case Captain Edward Thompson's 1776 edition of the works of Andrew Marvell—appears from its list of subscribers to

A whimsical Account of the present Corps of British Writers.

SIR,

IN ancient history we read a deal about the *Macedonian phalanx*, and of their wonderful achievements and strength of parts; but I don't recollect that I ever knew amongst this *cemented* body of bullies a clever Fellow—that is to say, a wit, or an Author: And therefore I hold this *phalanx* at a cheap rate; and I think cut three divisions of *marines* would have trimmed their jackets any day in the week, in any place between this and the Streights of *Thermopyle*. And give me leave, Mr. Printer, to tell the world, that we have, in and about this town, a *phalanx* more formidable than ever the *Macedonian madman* led into the field; fellows that will flash and cut with ten times the keennefs of that military body. I therefore have sent you their names and characters, their influences, inclination, and the powers of their weapons; and beg to distinguish this terrible corps by the titles of the *Bull Dogs*, the *White Boys*, and the *Sawneys*.

The English Phalanx, or the Bull Dogs.

Names.	Occupations.	Party.	*lb. oz. qrs.	Poetic.	Prosaical.	Both or neither.
Catharine Macaulay,	Not a Sempstress,	Republican,	44 1 3	—	Yes.	
John Wilkes,	A Gentleman,	Anti-Ministerial,	45 0 0	—	Yes.	
Doctor Johnson,	Once a vender of Books,	Ministerial,	42 1 0	—	—	Compound.
Doctor Franklin,	Priest,	Ministerial,	16 0 3	—	—	Compound.
Doctor Langborne,	Ditto,	Ditto,	5 0 1	—	—	Neither.
Doctor Mason,	Ditto,	Ditto,	17 0 2	Yes.	—	
Doctor Gray,	Ditto,	Ditto,	16 0 1	Yes.	—	
Leonidas Glover,	Merchant,	Anti-Ministerial,	24 0 0	Yes.	—	
David Garrick,	Merchant,	Patentee,	43 1 0	Yes.	—	
George Colman,	Called to the Bar,	Ditto,	42 0 3	—	Yes.	Dramatic Compound.
— Hoole,	Clerk of the India-House,	Mum,	8 0 0	Yes.	No.	
						Names.

* Weight in the literary scale, two ounces to the pound, paper weight.

Figure 2. *A Whimsical Account of the Present Corps of British Writers. Political Register*, 1770. Courtesy of the Beinecke Rare Book and Manuscript Library, Yale University.

Names.	Occupations.	Party.	lb. oz. grs.	Poetic.	Prosaical.	Both or neither.
Underwood,	Was a Student,	Ministerial,	0 0 3	No.	No.	Jumble.
—— Keith,	A Gentleman,	Dubious,	11 1 0	Yes.	No.	
Barnaby Greene,	A Brewer,	Republican,	35 1 0	Yes.	Yes.	
George Stevens,	A Militia Officer,	Not material,	0 0 1	No.	No.	Light.
G. A. Stevens,	Any thing,	Ministerial,	14 1 0	—	Yes.	Whimsical Mixture.
—— Ansty,	Gentleman,	Anti-Ministerial,	36 0 1	Yes.	—	Droll.
Samuel Foot,	A Flesh Mirrour,	Patentee,	39 0 3	—	Yes.	Fun without Fallacy.
Edward Thompson,	Sailor-Man,	Republican,	22 1 0	Yes.	Yes.	And Ovidian.
—— Read,	A Rope-Maker,	Tyburn,	5 1 1	No.	No.	Neither.
John Hall,	Gentleman,	Anti-Ministerial,	21 0 0	Yes.	—	Fabulous.
Mrs. Brookes,	} Ladies	} Masculine	7 0 0	—	Yes.	Romance.
Miss Carter,			24 0 0	Yes.	No.	Classic.
Mrs. Lennox,			12 0 0	No.	—	A Female Quixote.
Mrs. Griffiths,	} ——	} ——	9 0 0	No.	Yes.	Platonic.
Mrs. Montague,				No.	Yes.	
Mr. Shepherd,	Priest,	Ministerial,	20 0 1	Yes.	Yes.	Didactic.
Mr. Horne,	Ditto,	Anti-Ministerial,	29 0 3	No.	No.	
William Kenrick,	Brass-Rule-Maker,	Ditto,	2 0 1	Yes.	Yes.	
Paul Whitehead,	Gentleman,	Ministerial,	31 0 0	No.	Yes.	
William Whitehead,	Laureat,	Ditto,	16 0 1	Yes.	No.	
Lord Lyttelton,	——,	Anti-Ministerial,	32 0 0	Yes.	No.	
Horace Walpole,	A Printer,	Heterogeneous,	12 0 3	—	—	Both and neither.

Names.

Names.	Occupations.	Party.	lb. oz. grs.	Poetic.	Prosaical.	Both or neither.
John Jago,	A Parson,	Not known to himself,	0 0 1	No.	—	No. Neither.
Mr. Cumberland,	L'Homme de Cour,		0 0 2	No.	—	A little
Scot,	Priest,	Ministerial,	19 0 0	—	Yes.	Old Slyboots.
JUNIUS,	Trimming,	Anti-Ministerial,	45 0 1	—	Yes.	Yes.

The Irish Phalanx, or the White Boys.

Names.	Occupations.	Party.	lb. oz. grs.	Poetic.	Prosaical.	Both or neither.
Edmund Burke,	Gentleman,	Anti-Ministerial,	44 1 3	Yes.	Yes.	Sublime and Beautiful.
Arthur Murphy,	Clerk, Player, Lawyer,	Ministerial,	30 0 0	Yes.	---	
Doctor Goldsmith.	Bred to nothing,	A Doubt,	21 0 0	Yes.	---	My Shame in Crowds,
Hall Hartshorn,	Gentleman,	Anti-Ministerial,	22 0 0	---	---	
Hugh Kelly,	Wardrobe keeper to the Muses,	Ministerial,	21 1 3	Yes.	Yes.	
Doctor Sherridan,	An Orator,	Ministerial,	4 0 0	No.	No.	
Doctor Hiffernan,	A walking Pulse-feeler,	All Sides,	0 0 1	No.	No.	
Isaac Bickerstaff,	Was a soldier,	Pro or con.	19 0 1	---	---	Music and Drama.

The

The Scotch Phalanx, or the Sawneys.

Names.	Occupations.	Party.	lb. oz. grs.	Poetic.	Profaical.	Both or neither.
Hume }	Bred to the Kirk, —		40 0 0	---	Yes.	Hiftorical.
Home }			20 0 0	Yes.	No.	Neither.
Armftrong,	Surgeon		2 1 0	---	---	Between the two,
Macpherfon,	Schoolmafter	Minifterial	14 1 1	---	---	In Medio.
Dowe,	A Factor,		4 0 1	---	---	Neither.
Ogilvie,	A Minifter,		1 0 1	---	Yes.	
Whiteford	Merchant		5 0 0	---	---	Both, with Readinefs.
Doctor Campbell,	Phyfician		19 0 0	---	---	Iterum, iterumque.
Doctor Smollet,	Surgeon,		21 0 0	---	---	
Faulkner,	Purfer,		7 0 0	Yes.	---	

By this method we fee at one view the ftate of literature in thefe kingdoms; and every perfon may be able to judge of the power of party-writing—the fcale being at prefent 4oz lb. 1-half anti minifterial, and 395 lb. minifterial; difference 7lb. 1-half. Minifterial writers 24—anti-ditto 13—*Jacks of all fides* 17".

Thefe, Mr. Printer, are the principal men that occafion all this literary buftle; and, for the convenience of the public, I have remitted the account to you. Had fuch lifts been preferred fince the time of the old Grecian ballad-finger, they would have been an agreeable catalogue for the amufement of the ingenious.—For once I am ferious; and if any author is difpleafed with his weight, I beg he will inform me of his difcontents, by a card to the publifher, *and be fhall be weighed over again!*

I am, Gentlemen, your humble Servant,

PETER QUEER, Secretary, and Weigher.

(By order of the profeffors of Poetry, of the colleges of Oxford, Cambridge, Dublin, Glafgow, Edinbro', and Aberdeen,) have had major political significance. In Chapter 6 the speeches of Thomas Erskine for the defence are honoured both for their "whig" arguments and for their rhetorical strategies, which were unquestionably what saved the skins or reputations of Erskine's clients in most of his legendary cases.

And to give a sense of the importance of reading and writing in the political life of the eighteenth century, I want to close this Introduction by reproducing a document (Figure 2) published in Almon's *Political Register* in 1770, evaluating what some might call the mental world or the public sphere of the new Georgian regime. "A Whimsical Account of the Present Corps of British Writers" takes as its premise the notion that all writing in this period is to some extent partisan, and that writers have taken the place of the military—though a military divided into supporters of the current ministry and supporters of the Opposition. All these are to be not only counted, but *weighed*. Writers are assigned a weight in "literary pounds" and fractions thereof. The heaviest weight is Junius, who comes in at 45 pounds 1 oz., just above John Wilkes, at 45 pounds exactly, figures obviously resonant of the notorious no. 45 of the *North Briton*. I will leave my readers to work out the various levels of joke, only suggesting that they look out particularly for the names already mentioned here: in order of appearance, Catharine Macaulay ("Republican"), John Wilkes, Horace Walpole, Edward Thompson ("Republican"), [John] Horne [Tooke], Edmund Burke, and [David] Hume. Note that Walpole's party affiliation is defined as "Heterogeneous," rather than Whig, and that Burke at this stage (the stage of his *Thoughts on the Causes of the Present Discontents*, is known both as "anti-Ministerial" and as "Sublime and Beautiful," a double entendre too good to miss. Twenty years later his definition and weighting would have changed. Dr. Johnson ("once a vendor of Books" and "Ministerial") will appear in his ministerial colors in my third chapter.

The Scottish contingent makes the "ministerial" writers out-number the "anti-ministerial" by twenty-four to thirteen, with seventeen Jacks-of-all-sides; but when the tally is finished, the anti-ministerial writers outweigh their opponents by seven and a half pounds!

I

John Almon

In *Early Modern Liberalism,* I made this claim: when considering
the origins of the liberal political and social thought that today
we take for granted, our respect should be equally distributed between those who first formulated these principles and those who
subsequently transmitted them to the future—men like Thomas
Hollis, whose editorial efforts may have helped to educate a generation of late eighteenth-century Americans in seventeenth-
century liberal thought. John Almon, Whig bookseller of the
later eighteenth century, is another example of a neglected trans-
mitter, someone to whom we owe more than is known or remembered and whose reputation among those who have remembered
him has been probably unfairly tarnished. There may even be a
class prejudice against booksellers, as there certainly was in the
eighteenth century. Those who struggle to understand the unstable Georgian ministries and the personal inconsistencies of
great figures like Pitt and Burke are unlikely to care about a commercial entrepreneur. But Almon was considerably more than
a bookseller. Like Thomas Hollis, he believed in the power of
the printed word to make or prepare for political changes; but
instead of using his personal wealth to subsidize the reprinting
of the liberal classics, he became, though starting from nothing,
the greatest political publisher of his generation. Like Hollis, he
supported the American Revolution and saw to it that the colonists' perspective was made available to the English public; but
whereas Hollis kept a low profile personally, refusing to stand for

Parliament, Almon adventured his personal safety in the legal struggles of his day, combatting the dangerously elastic laws of libel with powerful theoretical arguments as well as by guerilla tactics.

Almon also got things done. His activities on behalf of the freedom of the press resulted in at least one major breakthrough in his own time. Not single-handedly, but definitely leading the attack, Almon established, against all parliamentary efforts to the contrary, the rights of London newspapers to publish the debates of the House of Commons. And among his vast body of publications, some of which he wrote himself, is the tract that deserves to stand as the eighteenth-century equivalent of Milton's *Areopagitica:* the *Letter Concerning Libels.* This remarkable pamphlet, which appeared in seven editions, the first in 1764, updated the problems of freedom of the press for a culture that had substituted for the expired system of licensing an arbitrary and highly politicized concept of libel.

Almon is also an example of that phenomenon in which a regenerate individualism should be particularly interested: the self-made man, who, as distinct from the self-fashioning one, creates himself from scratch *in defiance* of social norms. Without a dynastic leg to stand on, without money or connections, Almon made himself into an institution. Although he did acquire invaluable patronage from the Whig leadership, which ensured that his bookselling business flourished, it was native talent and indefatigable energy that made his considerable fortune. It was stubborn courage that then lost it. Horace Walpole complained that Almon was "reckoned to have made a fortune of £10,000 by publishing and selling libels." It is difficult not to see this as the complaint of a very wealthy aristocrat, whose wealth was entirely inherited, against the success of an upstart working-class businessman.

In terms of the material history of print, Almon was brilliantly

in advance of most of his contemporaries in grasping its structure conceptually, as well as in exploiting relatively new developments like the newspaper and the political cartoon. He intuitively understood publicity, distribution, and timing. He knew how to combine serious content with popular appeal. Almon also used his own quite serious brushes with the law to focus public attention on the law's abuses—a strategy he may have learned from John Lilburne, the great worker of the media in the mid-seventeenth century, whose career was well known to him. Perhaps because his own financial and even personal survival was at stake, Almon became a brilliant political writer in his own right. He had somehow acquired a literary education. And despite being unquestionably biased in favor of Whig writers, he was a refreshingly candid literary critic.

So who was John Almon, and why has nobody heard of him today?[1] These questions have already been partially answered by Deborah Rogers, whose pioneering biography, *Bookseller as Rogue,* appeared in 1986.[2] The title, taken from another sour remark of Horace Walpole's, seems slightly unfortunate if one is attempting to recuperate a figure from the past. Rogers apparently wrote under the shadow of a remarkable piece of character defamation, the chapter on Almon in Lucyle Werkmeister's study of the London press.[3] We will return later to the motives for Werkmeister's attack on Almon as a striking instance of how the present can blacklist the past. Nevertheless, Rogers recreated for modern readers the broad outlines of Almon's career and retrieved in an appendix a huge list of works issued under his imprint, which gives us not only the shape and color of his project, but also some sense of his extraordinary energy and persistence. The list is somewhat inflated by the fact that in the later eighteenth century it was common for several booksellers to distribute the same work; but even so, it is clear that Almon's efforts on behalf of what he saw as his cause vastly exceeded in scale those of radical Whig publishers of the late seventeenth and earlier eighteenth centuries such as the two John Darbys, father and son, or Richard and Anne Baldwin, or Francis "Elephant" Smith.[4]

John Almon was an enterprising orphan from Liverpool, who, at the age of twenty-two, having lost both parents and his older brother, and having briefly tried the life of a sailor, moved to London. Having found employment as a journeyman-printer with John Watts, he took quickly to the world of the printed word. In 1759, his first year on the job, he published a curiously backhanded defence of Lord George Sackville at the battle of Minden, *The Cowardice of a Late Noble Commander Examined,* which attracted public attention to Sackville and his subsequent court-martial and which ran to two editions. This drew Almon to the attention of Charles Green Say, the printer and owner of the liberal *Gazetteer,* who hired him to compete against Oliver Goldsmith, writer for the *Public Ledger.* For Say, Almon wrote a series of articles on contemporary politics under such self-explanatory pseudonyms as "Independent Whig" and "Lucius [Junius Brutus]." He also wrote a defence of William Pitt's administration, broken off in 1761 by Pitt's resignation over the ending of the Seven Years' War, an essay that Almon shrewdly dedicated to Pitt's brother-in-law, Richard Grenville, Earl Temple.[5] The result was that Temple sent for him, took him into his favor and under his patronage, and introduced him to many of the leading Whigs, including Pitt himself, the duke of Newcastle, the duke of Devonshire, the marquis of Rockingham, and the about-to-become-notorious John Wilkes. In the autumn of 1763, with Temple's encouragement and financial support, Almon resigned from his job at the *Gazetteer* and started his own business as bookseller and publisher.

1763 was a red-letter year in the old Whig historiography, since it featured a major legal and parliamentary debacle, one that helped to crystallise the deeper differences between groups whose ideological boundaries had been blurred, deliberately, by George III's determination to govern without recourse to political parties. The story of the notorious number 45 of the *North Briton,* which contained an attack on the king's speech at the end of the spring session of Parliament, has been told many times, most fully perhaps by Peter Thomas in his biography of Wilkes.[6] The origins of the offending article were these. The royal speech of closure, to be delivered on April 19, was by convention undebatable; but the day previous to its public presentation Prime Minister George Grenville had, as a courtesy, sent a copy to his brother, Lord Temple, and he and Pitt were discussing its offensive qualities when Wilkes happened to visit. Together they agreed on the strategy whereby the speech would, in effect, be debated in public by way of the *North Briton,* the journal that Wilkes and Charles Churchill had founded as an antidote to the pro-Bute *Briton.* According to Thomas, Wilkes was the sole, though anonymous, author, but Temple and Pitt undoubtedly agreed on the content. The king took the article, which appeared on April 23, as a personal insult. On April 26, Lord Halifax, secretary of state, signed a general warrant for the arrest of "the authors, printers and publishers of a seditious and treasonable paper." A general warrant is one where no individual suspects are named, and its dubious legality as a procedure led to a major legal and constitutional debate which could only, both in the short and in the very long term, embarrass the government. Forty-five persons were arrested, including Wilkes, who, after a series of dramatic manoeuvres on both sides, was discharged by Chief Justice Charles Pratt, on the grounds that libel was not a breach of the peace and that his parliamentary privilege had been infringed. Both Pratt and Wilkes thereby became heroes of the Londoners, who demonstrated effusively in their support. A series of court cases awarded damages to those who had been so rashly arrested; but meanwhile the government was determined to pursue Wilkes on the libel charge.

As Almon would later candidly object, Wilkes irresponsibly played into his enemies' hands, and deeply embarrassed his supporters, by republishing the offending issue of the *North Briton* at his own private press, set up for the purpose; he also printed an obscene parody of Pope's *Essay on Man*. This, though intended only for private circulation among like-minded friends, fell into the hands of Lord Sandwich, who in a cabinet shuffle over the summer became the northern secretary of state. When Parliament reconvened in November, there was a double attack on Wilkes: in the Commons it was finally voted that parliamentary privilege did not extend to cover seditious libel; in the House of Lords, Sandwich read aloud parts of the *Essay on Woman*, which was voted a "scandalous, obscene and impious libel." That Sandwich would forever after be tagged with the name of Jemmy Twitcher, thanks to a saucy topical allusion in a performance of *The Beggar's Opera*, was small comfort to the Opposition. On December 1, the Lords accepted a proposal from the Commons that *North Briton*, no. 45, should be publicly burned by the common hangman. On December 6, Wilkes's action for trespass in relation to the search of his house and seizure of his papers resulted in a verdict by Pratt that general warrants were illegal when used as an excuse for widespread searches, especially against printers. Meanwhile, Wilkes had been summoned before the Commons to answer the charge that he was indeed the author of *North Briton*, no. 45, and after several days of evasion, pleading ill health, he decided to flee to Paris. In his absence, on January 19, Wilkes was expelled from his parliamentary seat.

This extremely truncated account of the affair of *North Briton,* no. 45, is a necessary introduction to John Almon's role therein. In the first place, as Wilkes's personal friend and ally, Almon had been a crucial go-between in the flurry of action that began with Wilkes's arrest. Having by chance arrived at Wilkes's house at that very moment, Almon was able to take a message to Temple, asking him to arrange for a writ of habeas corpus. He then communicated steadily with Wilkes in France, keeping him fully informed about political events and especially about Temple's reactions. Far more important, however, were Almon's public gestures on Wilkes's behalf. Beginning in the early spring of 1764, he published a series of pamphlets linked by a dramatic fictional premise. First came *A Letter to the Public Advertiser* from someone who called himself "Candor," whose strategy was that of total reverse irony; that is to say, he presented himself as a defender of the government's actions in the Wilkes case, and in particular of Lord Mansfield, Lord Chief Justice, on whom he lavished obsequious compliments, declaring him a successor to George Jeffreys, who had held the same office in the 1680s: "In short, the language of Law, touching Libels, was, in the Court of King's Bench, the same before the Revolution as it is now. And Lord Jeffreys and Lord ******* not only concur in sentiment, but in expression" (p. 9). Since Jeffreys, as Candor reminded his readers (p. 8), was the notorious judge who had condemned to death Lord William Russell and Algernon Sidney, cases that became part of the ideology of the revolution, not many of Candor's contemporary readers could have missed the irony; but reverse irony is an unreliable tool, as witnessed by Defoe's *Shortest Way with the Dissenters.*

Perhaps initially to avoid the possibility of misprision, of having Candor's opinions be taken as genuine support for

Mansfield's jurisprudence, Almon published a second attack on Mansfield's doctrine about libels, self-dated October 17, 1764. As Robert Rea points out, this had originally been advertised by Almon as a second *Letter from Candor*, but during the printing process the pseudonym was changed to "Father of Candor"; the title was also expanded to give, as it were, a table of contents: *An Enquiry into the Doctrine, Lately Propagated Concerning Libels, Warrants, and the Seizure of Papers; with a View to Some Late Proceedings and the Defence of Them by the Majority; upon the Principles of Law and the Constitution. In a Letter to Mr. Almon from the Father of Candor.* Rea suggests that the change of pseudonym was made "as an added note of mystery and with an eye to greater sales"; but he does not articulate the important point that the two pamphlets must have had a single author.[7] The seven subsequent editions, with their fame already established in advance, used a slightly more economical title, *A Letter Concerning Libels, Warrants, the Seizure of Papers, and the Sureties for the Peace of Behaviour.*

Rogers makes virtually no comment on the contents of the *Letter,* which is understandable, given her belief that Almon was merely the publisher. She repeats various competing hypotheses as to its author: the *Gentleman's Magazine* assigned it to Pratt, Walpole to John Dunning, who with Sergeant Glynn had defended Wilkes, and the old *Dictionary of National Biography* offered Temple.[8] She does not mention that Robert Watt in the still contemporary *Bibliotheca Britannica* (1824) had assigned it to Almon himself; and she claims that Almon, in his end-of-the-century reminiscences, proposed a collaboration between Pratt (now elevated to Lord Camden) and Dunning. This is not what Almon in fact wrote; in his review of the career of Lord Mansfield (in which he several times mentions the *Letter* as one of the most important documents of the time!), Almon noted that Dunning had "burst out with astonishing splendour" when attacking Mansfield's use of a writ of attachment, "which gave rise to the report that he was the author of the tract" that had devoted so much energy to the same issue. "By many people the tract was supposed to be written by Lord Camden," Almon continued. "It certainly contained the whole of his Lordship's doctrine concerning libels. *There was a third gentleman concerned.*"[9] On the basis of this odd remark, an admission of inside knowledge that remains teasingly enigmatic, and a great deal of other evidence from Almon's publications, I shall argue here that the *Letter* and its sequel were an unequal collaboration between Camden and Almon, with Camden supplying the references from legal history and Almon doing all the actual writing (and rewriting). Nothing in the records of either Camden or Dunning suggests that they were capable of this rhetorical tour de force, whereas Almon's conduct of the *Political Register,* the journal he started in 1767 upon the demise of the Rockingham ministry, clearly evinces such skills.

The other vital matter not mentioned by either Rogers or Rea is that, for the second edition through the fourth, the *Letter* was strenuously revised and expanded. I shall address its complex evolution in the next chapter, after having here explained its consequences to Almon and completed the tale of his incendiary career. The immediate result of the *Letter* was that Almon was prosecuted as its publisher in the Court of King's Bench. Indeed, Mansfield may well have made the assumption I am making here, that Almon was considerably more than the publisher. He was tried by writ of attachment, without a jury—precisely that abuse of the law that Dunning would "burst out" so splendidly against.

We need a little more chronological and technical detail. The first edition of the *Letter* was dated October 30, 1764. In Almon's *Memoirs,* written in 1789–90, when he was an outlaw in France, he observed: "The friends of the Yorke family [i.e. of the previous attorney general, Charles Yorke] took public notice of it, by writing against it in the newspapers; but the person who was most offended with the pamphlet was Lord Mansfield. At the instance of his Lordship, a prosecution was instituted by the Attorney-General (Sir Fletcher Norton) against the publisher, not in the common way by indictment or information, but by motion in the court of king's bench, for a writ of attachment for contempt."[10] The "contempt" of court invoked was a single paragraph in which the *Letter* had complained that Lord Mansfield had altered the record in the libel case of John Wilkes for *North Briton,* no. 45. But the real reason for Mansfield's outrage was a catalogue of abuses in his jurisprudence that the *Letter* had offered in the form of hypotheses or conditional clauses, which thereby rendered them harder to prosecute. For example, the *Letter* had imagined: "If any Chief Justice should, by solemn but unnecessary givings out from the Bench, endeavour to blast the repute of Juries with mankind, by pronouncing that the trial by jury would be the very worst of all, were it not for the controuling power of judges, by the award of new trials and the reconsideration of verdicts. . . . [I]t would, indeed, be very unhappy for the subjects of this country, if there were a man to whom any one of these things were applicable; and the Lord have mercy upon the nation, if a time should ever come, when they shall all center in one and the same man." This catalogue of abuses was actually expanded in the second edition of the pamphlet, also dated October 1764. But it was not until January of the following year that the Crown moved against it. On January 23 there were a series of depositions from press spies who said they had obtained copies of the *third* edition from Almon's shop in Piccadilly, and Almon was charged with contempt on January 25. The case finally went to court on May 1. Sergeant John Glynn, who shared the defence with Dunning, clarified what was principally at stake with a splendidly ironic disclaimer: the pamphlet could not possibly contain a "portrait of an original, [Mansfield], it deviated so far from the likeness of any chief justice, particularly the present one." One might reasonably suppose that this disingenuous statement only rendered the *Letter*'s offence more egregious.[11] Thanks to a technical mistake in the writ, however, whereby Wilkes's name had been put in the title of the case instead of Almon's, the trial dragged on until, in July, George Grenville's government was dissolved and Rockingham became prime minister. Unsurprisingly, Rockingham, now the head of a somewhat more coherent and party-minded Whig junto,[12] insisted that the charges against Almon be dropped.[13]

WORDS AND IMAGES: *THE POLITICAL REGISTER*

The Rockingham ministry was itself dissolved a year later, trapped by its own inconsistencies with respect to the American colonies. But Almon became, if anything, more of an independent activist. In 1767 he began publishing the *Political Register*, a monthly periodical which combined reviews of recent books (many of them written by Almon himself) with letters to the editor (many of them evidently written by Almon to himself), satirical cartoons, and occasional poems. The preface to the first volume set out the agenda: to raise the political consciousness of the nation. "The people of England, it is generally observed, are, of all nations in the world the most addicted to Politics. The fact is certain and the reason of it is evident. The English government is universally allowed to be one of the freest that ever yet existed; and it will be found to be a maxim that will for ever hold true, that the more free is the government, the more fond are the people of Politics. . . . [This] ought surely . . . to be not only indulged, but in the highest degree encouraged. To direct the people, therefore, in the study of Politics, and to explain to them the conduct, the views, and principles of those who undertake the government of the state, seems a task not unworthy of a lover of his country; and such is the chief design of the *Political Register*."

Despite its claim to be offering political education in a broadly patriotic manner, the *Register* was unmistakably Whig in tone, and it alternated between high seriousness (as in the preface) and various levels of satire. The satirical component was driven home by the presence of fiercely oppositional political cartoons created by John Jones, an artist almost unknown today, but who in 1792 would become official engraver to the Prince of Wales.[14] In Almon's *Memoirs*, written in political exile and published in 1790, he remarked especially on this feature of the *Register:* "Mr. Almon having a taste for caricature prints, he indulged this humour occasionally, in several satirical prints, prefixed to the monthly numbers; some of which were much admired."[15] This suggests that, at the very least, Almon took a strong interest in the caricatures and may have helped to design them. According to Dorothy George, Almon was the first to publish a monthly magazine illustrated by satirical engravings, and he started a new fashion.[16]

The prints in the *Political Register* offer an interesting qualification to the standard view of Georgian visual political satire as offered by Dorothy George and Herbert Atherton. In that view, although each new crisis in government generated a shift in satirical subject matter—the Excise scheme, the Jacobite rebellion of 1745, the Wilkes affair, the trouble with America—the visual vocabulary and spirit of the prints were extremely repetitive. The preoccupation with Lord Bute (the boot) as favourite lasted for a decade after his resignation in 1763. George's descriptions, print by print, become involuntarily tedious. Atherton had his own theory: "The basis [of the imagery] is stubborn and permanent discontent: the unchanging anti-court, anti-ministerial bias that viewed all authority with suspicion or contempt. . . . Raised from this basic attitude was a superstructure of issues—a programme of sorts—concerned with political corruption, constitutional purity, ministerial oppression (particularly as it applied to trade and to the press), national betrayal, and foreign subversion. . . . What genuine crises there were . . . were either manufactured or distorted. . . . These explosions were often like profound eruptions, coming from the substrata of simple prejudices in the public consciousness: nativism, xenophobia, adamantine hatreds shaped long ago." But Atherton also makes the point that eighteenth-century prints were the heritage of seventeenth-century ideology: "Semi-coherent beliefs, intellectual hand-me-downs to the untutored, fast becoming banalities—they remained common currency in the political lore. [T]hey were vestiges of half-forgotten struggles, the experiences of previous generations. . . . The remnants of worn-out convictions sometimes force an unreal construction on new activities."[17] It is not hard to see in each commentator, though differently expressed, a lack of sympathy for the printmakers, who, they agree, were almost invariably Oppositionist. George notes some four hundred anti-Bute prints, as compared to four in his defence (p. 121).

The prints for the *Political Register* are an exception to part of this critique (the charge of lack of inventiveness) and a riposte to the other part (the distaste for "worn-out convictions"). First, they avoid some of the most tiresome symbols, such as the boot for Bute (though not the fox for Henry Fox). They also completely eschew the scatology that attacked sensibility with broad bottoms and excrement. Third, some had a strongly literary component. Thus the first volume (for 1767) contained, as an introduction to the August number, an image of Lord Bute as Samson, naked except for a kilt and Scotch bonnet, pulling down the pillars of the constitution (Figure 3). The pillars are identified respectively as *Magna Charta, Revolution 1688,* and

Samson pulling down the Pillars.

Hitherto...... I have perform'd.
Not without Wonder :
Now...... such other trial
I mean to shew you of my strength, yet greater,
As with amaze shall strike all who behold,
This utter'd, straining all his nerves he bow'd,
As with the force of winds and waters pent,
When Mountains tremble, those three massy Pillars
With horrible convulsion to and fro

He tugg'd, he shook, till down they came, & drew
The whole roof after them, with burst of thunder
Upon the heads of all who sat therein;
Lords, Counsellors, or Priests,
Their choice nobility, & flow'r, not only
Of this but each Philistine City round,
Met from all parts,
Samson with these immix'd, inevitably
Pull'd down the same destruction on himself.

Samson Agonistes!

Accession of the House of Brunswick. The statue of Liberty on the pediment topples with the building, as do church and state, accompanied by Lord Chief Justice Pratt, recently made Lord Camden, and the archbishop of Canterbury, Thomas Secker. Behind Bute fall, among others, George III, preceded by his crown, and William Pitt, now earl of Chatham, preceded by his signature crutches. Underneath the print, to nail home its venerable message, are eighteen lines (ll. 1640–58) from Milton's *Samson Agonistes* (slightly adjusted for the purpose), concluding with the warning that Samson/Bute will inevitably "pull down the same destruction on himself."[18] Admittedly this print is belated, in the sense that five years have elapsed since Bute's resignation. But the very emphasis on *structure,* on a complex architectonic design, suggests that constitutional theory is far from an obsolete hangover from the preceding century. Milton's conceptions are potent and memorable. Even Bute himself is a relatively dignified figure.

This was entirely consistent with the aims of the *Register* when Almon started it. The first instalment began with an essay, "Remarks on the Principles of the British Government Addressed to the Guardians of the Constitution" (pp. 1–8), a predictable piece of Whig political theory. Its attention to current disputes can be seen in the "Continuation of the Notes on the Works of the Late Mr. Churchill," an ostensibly literary and memorial enterprise consistent with Almon's role as the publisher of Charles Churchill's poetry. The article, however, really deals in large terms with the politics of art and specifically with the recent involvement of William Hogarth in party politics. Its topic was the famous satirical portrait of John Wilkes produced

Figure 3. *Samson Pulling Down the Pillars.* By John Jones? *Political Register,* 1767. Courtesy of the Beinecke Rare Book and Manuscript Library, Yale University.

Figure 4. *John Wilkes, Esq.* By William Hogarth. Courtesy of the Yale Center for British Art, Yale University Art Gallery Collection, Gift of Allen Evarts Foster, B.A.

by Hogarth and published in May 1763 (Figure 4). The intent of the portrait was to counteract Wilkes's sudden development into a popular hero, thanks to his temporary rescue in the Court of Common Pleas by Chief Justice Pratt. Churchill had written before he died an "Epistle to William Hogarth" protesting his conduct, and this was Almon's excuse for his "Continuation."

Today's readers can learn a great deal by comparing the story that Almon[19] tells here in the *Register* with the traditional view of art history, in which Hogarth used to be presented as the victim of Wilkes's malice. To that end I shall quote Almon's version almost in its entirety. Its brilliant mixture of politics with psychology, and indeed with theories of representation, is inseparable from its length:

> Mr. Hogarth had for several years lived on terms of friendship and intimacy with Mr. Wilkes. . . . A friend wrote to him [Wilkes], that Mr. Hogarth intended soon to publish a political print of the *Times*, in which Mr. Pitt, Lord Temple, Mr. Churchill and *himself*, were held out to the public, as objects of ridicule. . . . Mr. Wilkes . . . remonstrated by two of their common friends to Mr. Hogarth, that such a proceeding would not only be unfriendly in the highest degree, but extremely injudicious; for such a pencil ought to be universal and moral, to speak to all ages and all nations, not to be dipt in the dirt of the fashion of a day. . . . An answer was sent, that neither Mr. Wilkes nor Mr. Churchill were attacked in the *Times*, tho' Lord Temple and Mr. Pitt were, and that the print would soon appear. A second message soon after told Mr. Hogarth, that Mr. Wilkes would never think it worth his while to take notice of any reflections on himself, but when

his friends were attacked, he then found himself
wounded in the most sensible part, and would, as
well as he could, revenge their cause; adding, that
if he thought the *North Briton* would insert what
he should send, he would make an appeal to the
public on the very Saturday following the publication of the print. The *Times* soon after appeared
[on September 7, 1762], and on the Saturday following, no. 17 of the *North Briton*. If Mr. Wilkes
did write that paper, he kept his word better with
Mr. Hogarth than the painter had done with him.
(p. 288)

Whatever we may think of John Almon, he was capable of ar-
ticulating high ideals—in this case the ideal of an art designed
"to speak to all ages and nations, not to be dipt in the dirt of
the fashion of a day"—precisely that problem that has by now
rendered Georgian satirical prints almost illegible and to some
distasteful. But Almon is also concerned with personal ethics, an
issue brought home by the *literary* vocabulary he used to describe
the making of the notorious caricature: "When Mr. Wilkes was
the second time brought from the Tower to Westminster-hall,
Mr. Hogarth *skulked* behind in a corner of the gallery of the court
of Common Pleas, and while the lord chief justice Pratt, *with the
eloquence and courage of Old Rome*, was enforcing the great principles of Magna Charta and the English Constitution, while
every breast from his caught the *holy flame of liberty*, the painter
was employed in caricaturing the person of the man, while all
the rest of his fellow-citizens were animated in his cause" (italics added). But the drama of courage and cowardice, principle
and interest is a rhetorical feat, one which can easily be reversed
by the other side; more intriguing is what follows: an analysis
of the very nature of caricature, and the uneasy bases—mean-

ness, hyperbole, exaggeration of physical and hence involuntary characteristics—on which it sometimes rests.

> The print of Mr. Wilkes was soon after published, *drawn from the life by William Hogarth.* It must be allowed to be an excellent compound caricatura, or a caricatura of what nature had already caricatured. I know but one short apology to be made for this gentleman, or, to speak more properly, for the *person* of Mr. Wilkes; it is, that he did not make himself, and that he never was solicitous about the *case* of his soul (as Shakespeare calls it) only so far as to keep it clean and in health. I never heard that he once hung over the glassy stream, like another Narcissus, admiring the image in it, nor that he ever stole an amorous look at his counterfeit in a side mirror. His form, such as it is, ought to give him no pain, while it is capable of giving so much pleasure to others. I believe he finds himself tolerably happy in the clay cottage to which he is *tenant for life,* because he has learned to keep it in pretty good order. (pp. 288–90; italics original)

This is very elegant and rather moving, considering that Wilkes had a terrible squint, one of nature's more insidious inequities, the eyes being so focal in human communication. It is also disingenuous, since (as Almon would complain in later versions of the *Letter Concerning Libels*) Wilkes "did himself all that his severest enemies could wish, to turn his own case into ridicule, and to let the people see . . . that he had too much levity and viciousness of natural constitution, to make the good of his country the rule of his conduct in any one action of his life" (7th edition, p. 39). But as an item to which contemporary readers might turn as they leaf through that instalment of the *Political Register,* it would have considerable drawing power, narrative skill, inside information on a recent press duel, and some shrewd thoughts on the relation of personal good looks or their absence to social and political success.

In the following year's issue, for 1768, there was a predictable, topical emphasis on the Middlesex election scandal and the massacre in St. George's Fields. A different kind of tactic, however, is evinced in a "letter to the editor" in the April instalment. The author has sent Almon "a Copy of Lord Molesworth's valuable Preface to Hotoman's *Franco Gallia* (a book that is now become extremely scarce) which I have taken from the Second Edition, printed in the Year 1721: But the Preface was written in 1705" (p. 281). This letter provides the excuse for the *Register* to reprint the entire preface (pp. 281–96), which just happens to contain a definition of a true Whig. The task of reprinting the old Whig classics (Thomas Hollis's mission) was evidently also part of the *Register*'s agenda.

In the November instalment, by similar token, there is a long quotation (p. 280) from Algernon Sidney's *Discourses on Government*, recently reedited by Thomas Hollis and published by Andrew Millar, in a sumptuous royal quarto, in 1763.[20] The passage in question, for which Almon provided a page reference that matched Hollis's edition (p. 214), was one in which Sidney had focussed (prophetically, since he was about to become a victim of jurisprudence run amok) on the abuses of the legal system in late Restoration England, whereby "the law is made a snare" for the subject. One can see why Almon had sought this passage out. Also in the November issue was a long retrospective essay on the Wilkes case, featuring a Hollis-like politico-literary gesture: "Mr. Wilkes's friends have the comfort of finding that he possesses peace and fortitude of mind, that he does not *bate a jot of heart or hope, but still bears up and steers right onward*. He might add that all he has suffered, has been 'In liberty's defence,

his noble task/Of which all Europe rings from side to side'"
(p. 269). Culturally literate members of his readership would
immediately recognize these quotations from Milton's sonnet
to Cyriack Skinner describing his blindness not as a curse for
his regicidal allegiances but as a reward for his writerly services
to the Commonwealth. First published in John Toland's *Life
of Milton* in 1698, a work itself recycled by Hollis in 1761, this
sonnet was one the four Commonwealth sonnets that Milton
himself did not dare to publish during his lifetime. Revived as a
tribute to John Wilkes, the lines take on a new lease of political
life. A counterportrait of Wilkes, to undo the Hogarth cartoon,
made a similarly learned point (Figure 5).

The *Political Register* was a risky venture. Almon also tells us
in his memoirs that "some circumstances obliged Mr. Almon to
abandon it, after he had finished the second volume." A footnote adds: "A monthly publication was indeed continued for
some time afterwards, under the *same name;* but Mr. Almon had
no concern in it." So what were those circumstances? Almon
tells us:

> One . . . was printing in one of the numbers, "An
> eighteen day's journal of Lord B's visits to Miss V. in
> Sackville-Street and to Carlton-house." This gave
> great offence; and though it was a paper upon which
> no prosecution could be instituted, yet it was of
> such a nature, as could not fail bringing on the pub-
> lisher the most severe resentment, at the first op-
> portunity; however frivolous or trifling the osten-
> sible cause might be. The other circumstance was
> of a nature still more private. It was the publica-
> tion of a plan for augmenting the army in Ireland. It
> was the [King's] own plan, written by himself. He
> shewed it only to General Harvey, at the Q[ueen]'s

IOHN WILKES
ELECTED KNIGHT OF THE SHIRE FOR MIDDLESEX
ON THE XXVIII. OF MARCH, MDCCLXVIII
BY THE FREE VOICE OF THE PEOPLE.

Figure 5. *John Wilkes, Elected Knight of the Shire for Middlesex on the 28th March, 1768. Political Register, 1768.* Courtesy of the Beinecke Rare Book and Manuscript Library, Yale University.

H[ouse], who made some corrections in it, but did not take the paper away. In a few days it was printed in the *Political Register,* as corrected. The day after the publication, the King sent Mr. Barnard, jun. to Mr. Almon, to know how he obtained that paper? Mr. Almon declined, in the most respectful terms, giving an answer to the question. But he rightly foresaw, that this refusal would inevitably draw on him [Lord Mansfield?]. And therefore, with the view of deprecating such consequences, he discontinued the publication. In a short time, this apprehension was verified, in the prosecution of Mr. Almon for selling one of Junius's letters. (pp. 47–48)

As Rea explains, in July 1768 publication was transferred to Henry Beevor in Little Britain.[21] But whatever the business or legal pretexts Almon arranged to keep him in the clear from 1768 onwards, we can be reasonably sure that he did have *some* concern in the subsequent volumes through 1777, since the tone and format, including Jones's cartoons, became, if anything, more forceful, and references to Almon's adventures were ubiquitous.

Almon's behaviour vibrated between caution and rashness, with a strong strain of outright defiance. His activities had been noticed by George III himself; but rather than lying low, he continued to be associated, directly and indirectly, with the most intense provocations. We now come, therefore, to the second stage of Lord Mansfield's revenge, which Almon claimed in his *Memoirs* to have anticipated. On December 19, 1769, Junius's famous letter directly attacking George III (no. 35) appeared in the *Public Advertiser,* edited by Henry Sampson Woodfall. It was quickly reprinted, as Rogers observes, in virtually every newspaper and magazine in the country.[22] The attorney general, William de Grey, however, brought libel charges against only six publishers. Of these, only four were brought to trial. Of the four, only Almon was convicted. His trial, moreover, was the first of the series. He was tried on June 2 in the Court of King's Bench before Lord Mansfield himself, before a special jury, whereas the other three defendants were subsequently tried in the Guildhall before sympathetic London juries and acquitted.[23] It was a face-to-face confrontation between Almon and Mansfield. On his conviction, Almon was sentenced to pay a modest fine but was required to post £800, four of his own and four from guarantors, to insure his good behaviour for two years.

In terms of legal history, however, Almon's case was tied to that of Henry Woodfall, the original publisher of Junius's letter, for it was in relation to Woodfall that Mansfield was compelled to articulate his reactionary doctrine that in cases of libel juries were permitted to give a verdict only on the fact of publication (or sale), and it was entirely the province of the judiciary to pronounce on the criminality of the content. In *Rex v. Woodfall*, moreover, he tangled with the jury, who brought in a defiantly evasive verdict, "Guilty of printing and publishing *only*," and were strongly rebuked for obstructing the law. So unpopular was Mansfield's doctrine in this case that he felt obliged to provide a justification of it for the House of Lords; but in an extraordinary display of pusillanimity, he merely delivered his rationale in the form of a written statement and refused thereafter to answer questions about it on the floor.

At this point in Almon's story, a strange glitch occurs in Deborah Rogers's account. Convinced that the two-year financial restraint on Almon's behaviour must have been a decisive disincentive, she argues that, until the expiration of his sentence, Almon abandoned political publication and devoted himself instead to literature—as if the two were immune from each other. She stressed his anthologies of verse, *The New Foundling Hospital of Wit* (1768–96) and *An Asylum for Fugitive Pieces* (1776–

85).[24] There are several problems with this argument. One anthology was started prior to his trial, and both continued long after the restraints on him expired; it is therefore difficult to see them as temporary, prudent substitutes for overt political commentary. Second, there is plenty of political satire and commentary in those anthologies, if anyone cared to ferret it out. Most important, however, as soon as his trial was over, Almon calmly published *Another Letter to Mr. Almon, in Matter of Libel,* which was self-dated August 5, 1770; and the following year a second edition of this sequel appeared, as did the seventh edition of the original *Letter. Another Letter* was attributed by Rogers to Camden on the basis of a guess by Edmund Burke;[25] but the arguments for attributing the first *Letter* to Almon can be repeated here, with a twist. If Almon were merely the publisher, he was clearly risking his bond. If he were the author (and I shall show in the next chapter that he surely was), he was determined, like Milton, to "steer right onward" in his attack on contemporary libel law. This was not to adopt a low political profile. Addressing *Another Letter* to himself and referring in it to his own case in 1765 was more like thumbing his nose.[26]

Whether or not it could be laid at his door, the *Political Register* carried on Almon's campaigns. Thus volume 7, the first of two volumes for 1770, contains an account of Almon's trial for selling the issue of the *London Museum* in which was contained Junius's fateful letter to the king; a review of *Another Letter to Mr. Almon, in Matter of Libel,* where the reader is told that "[i]t is hardly possible to bestow too great an encomium on this elaborate treatise" (p. 311); and an eloquent print based on *Macbeth,* in which the self-explanatory caption reads: "Round about the Cauldron go,/In the Tortur'd Printers throw" (Figure 6). In the center right the attorney general holds a volume entitled "Junius," his follower holds one named "Almon," and other legal "witches" hold the names of Woodfall and Charles Green Say, all of whom

Figure 6. *Round About the Cauldron Go.* By John Jones? *Political Register,*
June 13, 1770. Courtesy of the Beinecke Rare Book and Manuscript
Library, Yale University.

are to be thrown in the cauldron of libel law; at their feet is a torn Magna Carta, two books, entitled *Prerogative of the Crown* and *A List of Pensioners on the Irish Establishment,* and a roll marked *Mansfields Min[istry]*. On the left is seated George III on his throne, directing the procedures.[27] The index to the volume further interprets the image: "September, the Attorney general and the Ministry in the act of witchcraft, represented in the tragedy of Macbeth, throwing certain papers into a Cauldron, *they become fascinated into libels*" (italics added).

THE PUBLIC'S RIGHT TO KNOW

Nor was it cautious of Almon to spearhead, in 1771, the defiance by the London newspapers of the House of Commons, a defiance which established for the first time the right of the press to publish parliamentary debates. Peter Thomas gives John Wilkes virtually all the credit for this great reform.[28] Thomas mentions Almon only in passing, as someone who unfairly claimed credit for what he calls "The Wilkes Coup of 1771." Rogers, however, attributes the coup to Almon, as did D. Nichol Smith before her. It was definitely Almon who had laid the groundwork for the confrontation, since he had started providing anonymous reports of the debates, three times a week, in the *London Evening Post* as early as 1768, thereby defying the parliamentary bans of 1728 and 1738. Other newspapers copied the practice. In 1771, the Commons precipitated a crisis by taking action against the printers of eight newspapers, including the *London Evening Post* and its printer, John Miller. In Almon's *Memoirs* there is a nonchalantly comic account of what followed:

> A plan of resistance was settled by Mr. Almon and Miller. Mr. Wilkes, and some others of the city magistrates were consulted. When the messenger of

the House of Commons came to take Miller into custody, a constable was ready; and the messenger was carried before the Lord Mayor, charged with an assault, as had been pre-concerted. Mr. Wilkes and Mr. Oliver were also at the Mansion-house. The assault was proved, and the messenger was admitted to bail. The Lord Mayor (Mr. Crosby) and Mr. Oliver, being members of parliament, were committed to the Tower; but Mr. Wilkes brought further disgrace upon the House of Commons. They did not know what to do with him. At length they contrived an expedient as cowardly as it was contemptible. They made an order for him to attend on the 8th of April; and then adjourned to the 9th of April, to avoid their own order. During the debates upon this subject, which were very warm, several gentlemen, who were magistrates, declared they would act in the same manner in all such cases hereafter, and if any printers brought the messengers of the house before them, they would commit those messengers. Parliament now finding its own impotency in this business, abandoned the whole question entirely. (p. 120)

From the perspective of 1790, however, Almon added an important rider to this triumph: "The court . . . have taken their revenge in another way, for they have laid heavy imposts upon these printers in consequence, and newspapers are now become an important article of the revenue."[29]

Just how important to Almon, ideologically, was the project of making Parliament's doings available to the public can be learned from one of the many promotional sales catalogues he attached to his books and pamphlets. Especially useful in this context is the catalogue appended to a 1774 pamphlet on the struggle over the colonies.[30] It began with the announcement that "speedily will be published" the "tenth and eleventh volumes of the Debates and Proceedings of the House of Commons, which complete that Work to the Dissolution of the late Parliament, on the first of October, 1774." This promise was followed by a typographical pointing hand drawing our attention to a polite warning: "Those Noblemen and Gentlemen, who are in possession of any of the former Volumes of this Work, are desired to complete their Sets as soon as possible, because there will be no more detached Volumes sold when the present impression is disposed of." The next catalogue item was the "just published . . . nine former Volumes of this Collection." One could buy the eleven-volume set "neatly bound and lettered" for £3.6. Next followed the *Protests of the House of Lords,* a two-volume set, and the *Debates and Protests of the Irish Commons.* And Almon offered the whole set of sixteen volumes for £5, "bound, gilt and lettered." In case one should be hesitating over the price, the catalogue added: "This Set of Books is one of the most useful and proper to be placed in a Gentleman's Library, it being allowed to contain the truest History of the present times."

The next item, an advance notice that Almon was planning a similar account of debates and proceedings in the Lords from 1772 to 1774, is worth citing as evidence of how he acquired his information: "As it is not known that any Account of the Proceedings of the House of Lords during the Period, was taken, it is humbly requested of any Gentleman, who may be in Possession of any Speeches, Papers, or other Materials proper for the Work, that he will be so obliging to communicate them to the Publisher, who will make any Compensation required." In his *Memoirs,* Almon recorded that when he had first determined to "make the nation acquainted" with the proceedings in Parliament, a decision made in the immediate aftermath of the massacre at St. George's Fields, "he employed himself sedulously, in obtaining from different gentlemen, by conversation at his own house, and sometimes at their houses, sufficient information to write a sketch of every day's debate"(p. 119). Putting these two statements together, we can deduce that Almon had a network of friends in both houses of Parliament who shared his views of the public's right to know and the obnoxious effects of secrecy. His energetic presence at the Coterie, the Whig club that met at Wildman's tavern from 1764 onwards, had given him access, on unusually equal terms, to most of the Whig leaders in Parliament, including Newcastle, Grafton, Rockingham, and Burke; and Temple may have been in active collaboration on the debates.

The same catalogue advertised Almon's *Collection of Interesting Political Tracts*, published in 1773, containing, it need hardly be said, both the *Letters Concerning Libels* and a *Collection of Interesting Letters from the Public Papers*, including that very tract whose scarcity and importance Almon had noted in the *Political Register*: "Franco Gallia. Written in Latin by Francis Hotoman. Translated into English by Lord Molesworth, with his Lordship's Preface." This item was also set off by a typographical pointing hand, calling our attention to "an Observation in Kennet's Register, which Lord Somers has taken for his motto to his collection of Tracts, 'That the Bent and Genius of the Age is best known in a free Country, by the Pamphlets and Papers which daily come out.'" At Almon's press, evidently, the genius of the age was not going unsupplied.

In Almon, business acumen was inextricably mixed with principle. And there is something else we can learn from this catalogue. Almon obviously regarded the dissolution of 1774 as the end of an era; and so it proved, since the North ministry was returned with a secure majority, and the Rockingham group lost seats. The country turned its attention from issues of freedom of the press to the American crisis. From late 1774 to 1781, when Almon left London on account of his wife's fatal illness, he somewhat shifted his priorities. From 1764 onwards, when he published James Otis's *Rights of the British Colonies Asserted and Proved,* he had already become one of the primary outlets whereby the English public could hear the American point of view. In 1767 he had published the first English edition of Benjamin Franklin's testimony before the House of Commons on the repeal of the Stamp Act. But from 1774 onwards, he was in direct communication with Franklin, who sent him for publication *An Appeal to the Justice and Interests of the People of Great Britain, in the Present Disputes with America,* and advised his colleagues also to send Almon their tracts. From 1775 until his premature retirement in 1781, when he sold his business, Almon put out a new series, *The Remembrancer,* to provide a permanent record of all commentary on the American Revolution he thought worth saving for posterity. Though it did include some pro-North arguments, the series was preponderantly pro-American. Once again, Almon was the major conduit for Whig or liberal thought on the issue. In 1776 he published four editions of Thomas Paine's *Common Sense.* In his *Memoirs,* Almon complaisantly reported an anecdote testifying to his new reputation. The duke of Grafton had been called on in the Lords to give some statistics about the strength of the English and American armies: "[T]he Duke replied that he did not know; but those who wanted such information, might probably obtain it by applying to Mr. Almon." "Whether his grace meant this as a sneer," Almon added, "or an acknowledgment of Mr. Almon's intelligence, is not now material. It certainly was a confession that ministers knew nothing of the state of their enemy" (p. 93).

After the sad hiatus caused by the death of his wife in 1781, Almon could not stay silent long. In order to take care of her in the country, he had sold his business in Piccadilly. But in 1784 he returned to London and married the widow of William Parker, owner and printer of the *General Advertiser,* a coup which provided him with a new outlet. Whether or not the duke of Grafton had sneered at his pro-American activities, this phase of his career was certainly stigmatized, both by his contemporaries and by his modern assessors. He was attacked in the *Morning Post* by the Reverend William Jackson for making a mercenary marriage and for using the *General Advertiser* to curry favor with both parties. In the late twentieth century Jackson's charges were restated at length, and evidently believed, by Lucyle Werkmeister, who regarded Almon, as a mere bookseller, as naturally committed to his own profit and therefore unable to maintain the standards of party loyalty assumed by newspaper publishers and editors.[31] This odd criterion, whereby Almon was excoriated for his various attempts to survive financially in a particularly dark and difficult period of his life, was consequently echoed by Rogers, using terms like "double-dealing" and "duplicity."[32] Here is a clear example of how the twentieth-century academy demands higher standards of behaviour and consistency from the past that it takes for granted in the present.

Almon was accused by Jackson (who was himself a ministerial writer and therefore scarcely disinterested) of having written in support of the new administration of William Pitt the Younger, and by Werkmeister and Rogers of then having defended himself against the charge of trimming "by publishing two libels" on Pitt in the *General Advertiser,* on October 20 and 27, 1785. These "libels" consisted of sentences which *nearly* accused Pitt of stockjobbing—that is, profiteering—from the peace with the

Dutch. As the prosecutor observed, the language was oblique enough to avoid a direct accusation, though as it turned out, the mere presence of the opprobious term "stock-jobbing" in close proximity to Pitt's name was deemed enough to lay charges. This was a full year after Jackson's accusations, so the notion that Almon was "forced to choose sides" only by Jackson's charges, even if true, seems bizarre. That he would take so indirect a route to align himself with the Opposition he had so energetically supported for thirty years is incredible. Almon himself, in the account of his trial which he published as an appendix to his *Memoirs,* steadfastly denied any responsibility for the offending paragraphs, claiming that "he was totally ignorant and innocent of the two publications; he was in the country at the time the libels were printed, he had no knowledge of them at the time, and the first moment he knew that Mr. Pitt was offended, he instantly contradicted the paper" (p. 241). Of course, we do not have to believe him; but nor do we have to believe his political enemies.

It also seems extraordinary that Pitt, whose father had patronized Almon and been well supported by his press and his pen, should have overreacted in this way, claiming damages of £10,000, which, if awarded, would obviously have done far more than bankrupt Almon. The threat can be construed only as *in terrorem,* directed against any and all who might publish critiques of ministers. And by challenging Almon in a civil suit, the political implications of the action were usefully, from the ministry's perspective, obscured. It seems far more likely that someone powerful had objected to the *General Advertiser*'s having been taken over by so famous a Whig entrepreneur and was alarmed by Almon's return to the scene. The spring of 1784 had seen the rout of the Coalition as a direct consequence of the defeat of Charles James Fox and his East India Bill in December of the previous year, after which the king had dissolved the government. Now, on February 20, 1786, Almon was to be tried, once again, before Lord Mansfield and a special jury at Westminster Hall. The symmetry with his previous contests with Mansfield is striking.

Also striking is his choice of defence attorney. For this would be one of the earlier trials conducted (and won in principle) by Thomas Erskine, already a famous and extremely expensive lawyer, who in 1783, thanks to Lord Mansfield, had been given the right to wear a silk gown. Erskine was a friend and protégé of Mansfield; he was, however, an enemy of Pitt and hence one of "Fox's Martyrs," the group of Whig members of Parliament who had lost their seats in the 1784 election. Almon could not have afforded the 300 guineas that Erskine was now entitled to charge for a special retainer. Possibly Erskine worked on this case pro bono. Quite apart from its intrinsic interest in Almon's story, we owe to Almon's *Memoirs* the only record of Erskine's speech for the defence, which resulted not only in Almon's conviction for publishing the libel but also in a reduction of the damages to £150 plus costs. In addition to preserving the shorthand record of Erskine's defence, Almon included Lord Mansfield's conduct of this case in his *Biographical . . . Anecdotes,* so that we can see the two diametrically opposed attitudes to libel law once more set in high relief.[33]

We will return to Thomas Erskine in Chapter 6. Meanwhile, the penalties Almon was accruing over his career were escalating in seriousness. Starting in 1765 with a fortunate escape (over the first publication of the *Letter Concerning Libels*), backing off from the *Political Register* in 1768, undeterred by the small fine and large surety imposed in 1770, he was now required to pay a total of £300 in damages and costs, a painful outlay for someone who no longer had the large, steady income of a publisher. After 1784 there are only a handful of his imprints, most of those in collaboration with J. Debrett. Significantly, these were either light literary works—the comic opera *Robin Hood* of Leonard McNally, for example, which Almon printed in 1784 and again in 1787—or Frederick Pilon's *The Fair American*, another comic opera that he printed in 1785; or they were reports of minor court cases, such as *The Trial of a Cause between Miss Mellish, Plaintiff, and Miss Rankin, Defendants, from Notes Carefully Taken in Court* (1785). Not much here to entice a large market.

And then came Almon's last court case of his own, and his most devastating penalty. In October 1788, as Almon put it in his *Memoirs*, "a violent fever seized upon the King's intellectual powers" (p. 135). On November 18 there appeared in the *General Advertiser* a brief paragraph insulting the king, and the attorney general, Alexander Wedderburn, moved against Almon by ex officio information, exactly that method against which the *Letter Concerning Libels* had been so instructively and eloquently opposed. Though the paragraph had appeared in other newspapers, only Almon was prosecuted. He complained, naturally, that he had been "ensnared" by an anonymous writer who had contributed the paragraph but now disappeared from view. In view of the nature of the libel, "a spirited defence was deprecated" (*Memoirs*, p. 140); his case was poorly handled, and there were marshalled against him the Prince of Wales's own lawyers, one of whom was Thomas Erskine! His rescuer in 1786 was now, two years later, on the other side. Almon was convicted, and an appeal to the prince was unsuccessful. Sentencing was delayed, and its likely severity widely discussed. In his *Memoirs*, Almon reported (with persuasive local color) what was being threatened: "Some days after the trial, Mr. Almon happened to meet in the street (between Clare Market and Lincoln's Inn) one of the principal law officers of the crown, who . . . assured Mr. Almon, that he should press for the severest punishment, and in particular, for the pillory" (p. 142). Almon accordingly fled to France, where he lived as an outlaw. Early in

1791 he returned to England. In early 1792, his anecdotal biography of Pitt's father, earl of Chatham, was published, and on the strength of this pro-ministerial offering Almon surrendered to the authorities and spent a year in prison.[34] In April 1793 his outlawry charge was reversed on a technicality.

It was during his exile in France, therefore, that Almon wrote his *Memoirs,* published in London, anonymously, and with no publisher named. He tells his story throughout in the third person, creating a fictional Editor, a strategy not unusual in eighteenth-century memoirs, but in this instance especially prudent. It is impossible to agree with Rogers's suggestion that Almon wrote this book "to ingratiate himself with the Government" (p. 99); while at every turn he exculpates himself, he consistently portrays himself as the victim of a vicious political campaign. The epigraph on the title-page, said to be Lord Courtenay's motto, was "Ubi lapsus? Quid feci?" or "Where was the fault? What did I do?"—scarcely an apology. The opening advertisement addresses itself particularly to "the Gentlemen of the Law," who are invited to find therein "some useful hints, and perhaps instruction, on a point of infinite importance to Public Liberty." What point that was is left inferential. But we can be certain what it was by reading the notes that Almon appended to his account of "the madness of King George" and his embroilment in its whirlpools. Having just asserted that Almon was invariably loyal and polite to the Crown, especially during this crisis, the *Memoirs* add the following: "Informations *ex officio* have always been held odious, and their legality is more than doubted. It has been disputed but not decided. All the books agree that the practice of filing them is a manifest violation of the rights of the subject. They are a relic of the Court of the Star-Chamber, and ought to have been abolished with that Court, but the Commons in their precipitation to destroy the Court itself, overlooked this instrument of it" (p. 139). The Editor then cites the remarks of Andrew Hamilton,[35] the defence lawyer in the American trial of J. P. Zenger, to the effect that: "The practice of information for libels, is a sword in the hand of a wicked King, and an arrant coward, to cut down and destroy the innocent; the one cannot because of his high station, and the other dares not because of his want of courage, revenge himself in another manner." And here is Almon's summation: "There have been more informations against libels in the reign of George the Third, than during the reign of any of his predecessors. From the accession in the year 1760, to the year 1790, the number of informations against Printers and Booksellers is incredible. . . . A subsequent age cannot offer the occurrences of the present reign in proof of constitutional integrity" (p. 139).

This helps to explain Almon's frequent promotion, in retrospect, of the *Letter Concerning Libels,* which he describes elsewhere in the *Memoirs* as "that celebrated and much admired pamphlet" (p. 73). Likewise, in his *Biographical . . . Anecdotes,* published in 1797, he inserted into his life of Charles Townshend the following excursus, attached to his mention of Townshend's *Defence of the Minority* and its ministerial answer, *A Defence of the Majority:* "This answer gave rise to one of the best, most able, and most constitutional legal tracts, that has been written in the English language, since the days of Lord Somers. It was entitled, 'A Letter concerning Libels . . .' The Ministry did not attempt to answer this work. It was invincible. Lord Mansfield felt himself severely hurt by it, and he prosecuted the printer" (1:79). It is to that "invincible" argument that we will shortly turn, looking forward to the pleasure of identifying its author as Almon himself and hence recognizing the statement just quoted as one of the most amusing pieces of self-promotion in the history of advertising.

But there is one last piece of evidence that Werkmeister cites as proof of Almon's perfidy. In 1793 there appeared an anonymous pamphlet, *The Causes of the Present Complaints Fairly Stated and Fully Refuted*. Echoing the title of Burke's *Causes of the Present Discontents,* this was in fact of a piece with Burke's *Reflections,* a reaction against the French Revolution and the activities of the London Corresponding Society, specifically an argument that reform of the franchise was unnecessary. For some reason, never explained by Werkmeister, this was attributed to Almon, though there is not a trace therein of his zesty style and command of examples from the past.[36] And meanwhile he was working on his *Biographical, Literary, and Political Anecdotes* and his editions of Wilkes and Junius, all of which asserted and confirmed the "Revolution principles" by which his long and tempestuous career had been driven. He died in December 1805, just having finished his work on Junius and with no trace remaining of the great fortune he was reported to have amassed when unofficial publisher for the Whigs or their separate factions. There is no evidence for Robert Rea's assessment that "as his wealth increased he grew more and more conservative"; rather, the record shows a degree of political intransigence, and a level of energy in maintaining and publicising it, that exceeded almost all of his contemporaries.[37]

2

Reading the *Letter*

A (SHORT) CHAPTER OF ITS OWN

The *Letter Concerning Libels* was, I have suggested, the successor
to Milton's *Areopagitica* in an era that was learning how to live
without licensing. Here I hope to demonstrate that John Almon
was not only the publisher of the *Letter* but its author, reviser,
defender, and advertiser—a project that engaged him for over a
decade. We need here an essentially literary practice, the practice
of "close reading," the patience to attend to textual details, especially the detailed strategy of revision, as also the arts of allusion,
innuendo, and quotation. But the discipline involved should not
obscure an important and pleasurable finding. If John Almon
was a second John Milton, he was surely one with a better sense
of humour.

Perhaps the best way to begin is to return to the fictional exchange between the "Father of Candor" and his "son," identified
in the previous chapter as being two versions of the same person. Remember that the primary strategy of Candor had been
total reverse irony, whereby that was ostensibly praised which
was actually deprecated. But would everyone have been aware
that this was not, in fact, a ministerial publication? Could you, as
a reader in 1764, be certain that Candor meant the exact opposite
of what he wrote in the following "attack" upon civil liberties
and the freedom of the press? "[A]s the end of all Law is substantial Justice, if That be obtained, in spite of old rules or old
cases, Is it not so much the better for the subject? [E]specially
if it be compassed in less time, and in a more summary way. . . .

I hope for the peace of the community . . . that unlearned men will . . . cease to reflect upon government, or the ways of administration and publick justice. In God's name, what business have private men to write or speak about publick matters? Such kind of liberty leads to all sorts of license and obloquy, the very reverse of politeness; and the greatest man, be he ever so cautious, if such things are endured, may be traduced."[1] A similar exegetical insecurity arises from Candor's pretended support for Lord Mansfield's known dislike of jury trials:

> I would with great deference presume to ask, Why we should not grow wiser than our forefathers in law, as well as in other parts of science, after repeated experiments; and as new lights arise, correct our old prejudices, and even our old constitution, where expedient or necessary? In the name of common sense, What Gentleman would not rather have his cause tried intirely by men of science, (I mean the Judges who are named by the King at the recommendation of the Ministry, that is, of the first people in the kingdom) than by illiterate Country-fellows, common shopkeepers, or aukward Country Gentlemen, who may probably never have seen a Court? . . . [W]hen once we have got rid of Juries in concerns of property, we shall soon come to do without them in concerns of life and limb: And, till then we shall never have the Crown-trials properly managed, let Judges take what pains they will. (p. 43)

This Swiftian stance prepares the way for the gravitas of Candor's Father's letter, which purports to be a form of corrective: "Sir, Some weeks after my son's sending you *A Letter to the Publick Advertiser*, I was surprised with the sight of a pamphlet* wherein a contrary doctrine in very material points is conveyed, altho' I cannot say directly affirmed; from which last circumstance I guess it to be the work of some daring and enterprizing Attorney, here and there retouched by his superior. Be this as it may, I think it not improper to consider what has been advanced by this extraordinary writer, altho' I shall go more at large than he has done into the subject, *and even differ in some things from my son himself, whose notions in several respects are too novel and modern for my approbation*" (p. 1; italics added). A footnote identified the offending pamphlet as *A Defence of the Majority*, a ministerial answer to Charles Townshend's *Defence of the Minority*, the issue in question having been the debate in the House of Commons on the legality of General Warrants.[2] On February 14, 1764, at a late stage in the previous year's fracas over *North Briton*, no. 45, a motion stating their illegality had been made by Sir William Meredith and seconded by Sir George Savile.[3] The debate became so complicated (given that it was also to be decided in the courts) that the sides were drawn up on a motion for postponing a decision! As Horace Walpole put it, the vote on this issue, 207 for the government, 197 for the Opposition, was "a triumph in parliamentary cases little preferable to a defeat; so strong had been the alarm on seizing [Wilkes's] papers, and so evident was it that the Ministerial majority had been the work of venality against conviction."[4]

Not choosing to mention this first stage of this sequence, Candor's father presents the *Defence of the Majority* as the first aggressor; and at this stage he seems to have believed that its author, introduced as a "daring and enterprizing Attorney," was Charles Yorke, the current attorney general, whose shadowy "Superior," then, would be Lord Mansfield. The enemy is referred to throughout as "the Attorney," and in his *Memoirs*, Almon had observed that "friends of the Yorke family" were "exceedingly offended" (p. 18). Later, however, Almon learned, and reported in his life of Townshend, that the real author was no lawyer, but the private secretary of George Grenville—Charles Lloyd,[5] who was more than once employed as a polemicist.[6] Almon's first supposition, however, accounts for the extended (but syntactically devious) attack on Lord Mansfield mentioned in the previous chapter.

In addition to thus personifying his opponents, the "Father of Candor" also creates dramatic characters for both himself and his "son," based on the premise that Candor's youthful errors will herein be corrected by the wisdom of his elderly parent. There is a deep political allegory resident in this ploy. By "novel and modern" the *Letter* refers to Candor's ironic declaration that the time has come to do away with obsolete and clumsy aspects of jurisprudence like the jury trial and to expedite matters by giving the Chief Justice huge executive powers. The "Father's" elderly status aligns him with the old legal protections of the subject, from Magna Carta to habeas corpus, indeed, with what is sometimes described as the ancient constitution.

A good deal of rhetorical energy is deployed, also, on the subject of rhetoric:

> The Attorney begins like himself, by reproaching others with "wretched quibbling upon words, misrepresentation, ignorance, blundering and falshoods," and then represents himself and his friends as "reasoning men, of knowledge, integrity and ability,"[7] but I suspect nevertheless, from the sophistry and refinement one now and then meets with in his argumentation, that he has had the assistance of another man "who has been taught to think himself a Statesman, and who would be too happy to be able to think himself a minister," and to whom I shall only say, as he loves a classic,

Vane Ligur, frustraque animis elate superbis,
Nequicquam patrias tentasti lubricus artes.

(pp. 1–2)

This premise, that the unevenness of style in the government pamphlet suggests collaboration, introduces literary standards of communication that are driven home by the cheeky quotation from Virgil, *Aeneid*, 11:715–16.[8] The allusion to a man "who has been taught to think himself a Statesman" is a weapon stolen from the enemy, a quotation from the *Defence of the Majority*, where it was originally part of an attack on Sir George Savile, the seconder of the Opposition's original motion. Now it is swung against the unnamed "Superior," whom Almon guessed, incorrectly in one sense, to be Lord Mansfield.

In this first edition, the remaining paragraphs of self-introduction continue the task of establishing an appropriate tone and rationale, explaining, in effect, the genre of the pamphlet:

> The Attorney, however, I must say, has ventured to assert in print, what I do not remember to have heard any one gentleman avow in parliament, and for that reason, among others, has attracted my notice and indignation. . . . I shall not treat the subject in the perfunctory manner he has done, nor intirely pursue his method, and therefore shall only advert to what he has said as he happens to fall in my way. Indeed, the discourse of late has run so much upon libels, warrants, and resolutions of parliament, that every body's thoughts have been naturally and involuntarily turned to these points. For my own part, I shall endeavour to offer what I have to say with clearness, and according to law, altho' it is long since I have quitted the bar, and to express myself with that freedom and plainness which becomes the

member of a free state. I do not think myself at liberty to scan the private actions of any man, but have a right to consider the conduct of every man in public; and to approve or to condemn his doings as they appear to me to be calculated, either for the good or the hurt of his country. [In atchieving this, I am well aware that I shall run counter to many fashionable doctrines; but my age exempts me from any particular delicacy or false complaisance in that respect. Nevertheless I should not peradventure have gone so far as I have done, were it not by way of gentle and indirect remonstrance to my son, who seems to be somewhat infected by the general turn of the times, maugre the legal education I have given him.] (pp. 2–3)

This is not, then, to be an "answer" as such to *A Defense of the Majority,* nor is it to proceed, as in animadversions, as a point-by-point refutation. Nor is it to descend to ad hominem argument. Rather, the *Letter* will assume the responsibility of the public intellectual, who has "a right to consider the conduct of every man in public" as it affects the general welfare and the health of the constitution.

An effective and genial self-introduction, one might very well think. How interesting, therefore, to discover that, from the second edition onwards, most of these moves were gradually deleted. In the second edition, also dated 1764, and advertised on the title-page as "much improved," the drama of father and son, ancient and modern, is much reduced by the omission of the sentences between square brackets in the last paragraph cited above. But the sardonic personification of the Opposition is retained and actually enhanced. After the ironic pretence that he is not impugning the public integrity of either the attorney or his superior, he adds, intriguingly: "altho' I remember that one of them, during the last rebellion, would never in his public speeches venture to call the rebel army any other than the *Highland Army*, for fear, I presume, of spoiling his fortune, in case it succeeded" (p. 6). This was probably an allusion to Lord Mansfield, who as a member of Parliament for Boroughbridge, Yorkshire, had delivered a speech on February 18, 1744, arguing for the suspension of habeas corpus for the impending Jacobite invasion.

By the third edition, however, not only the specious claim of avoiding personal reflections but the personal insinuations themselves have vanished. The tone becomes one of lofty detachment. The dramatized enemy couple, master and servant, have almost, but not quite, disappeared. What remains is the mode of self-authorization: "Indeed, the discourse of late has run so much upon libels, warrants, and resolutions of parliament, that every body's thoughts have been turned to these points. Now, I do not think of myself at liberty to scan the private actions of any man, but have a right to consider the conduct of every man in public; and to approve or to condemn his doings as they appear to be calculated, either for the good or the hurt of his Country." The matured *Letter* thus announces itself less as a contemporary intervention in the politics of the 1760s and more as a transtemporal statement of principles—principles which, from the perspective of the *longue durée*, are manifestly Whig or liberal.

Historiography

But some inarguably radical statements were apparently, in the interim, thought better (or worse) of. In the first edition, there was a revealing excursus on the use of history and the extent to which historiography is ideologically inflected:

It would, in my poor opinion, be of infinite use to young men of fortune, beginning the great world, who may hereafter be ministers of state, to read attentively the reign of Charles the 1st, in the annals of Frankland, the diary of Rushworth and Whitelocke; and, even the causes of the troubles of his government, with the best apology that could be made for them, as set forth by a divine-hereditary-right-man, lord Clarendon; together with Ludlow and the Parliamentary History for that period. They would soon perceive what mighty ill consequences flow from small beginnings, and particularly, from right not being to be had for the subjects in courts of justice. I think, the perusal of these writers, with Hooker, Milton, Sidney, Locke, Burnet, and the common memoirs of the publick proceedings for 12 years before the coronation of William the 3d, will be of more service and information, in the study of the rights of the people, and the prerogative of the crown, than all the revolutions of the Jesuit d'Orleans, or the conceits of Mr. Hume, altho' they both express themselves well, and the former (altho' the professed advocate for the Stuart family) was the first writer of English history, put into a certain most amiable Prince's hand by a certain person, and the latter is, I know, a favourite author, writes prettily and ingeniously, notes the progress of arts and sciences, refines on common matters, and will for ever amuse by the new and fanciful turn he gives to every thing his pen touches. Whether he be or not really happy in his conjectures, sound in his judgment and faithful in his narration, qualities, however[,] requisite in a historian, that are notwithstanding less brilliant and striking than paradox and novelty, the salubrious fountains from whence our modern British historian derives his indifference about religions, or rather his ridicule of every protestant, when opposed to the catholic faith, as well as his indifference about politics, or rather his ridicule of all Commonwealthsmen when opposed to Royalists. (pp. 65–66)

This passage is a paradigm of classical Whig thought. Let us start where it ends, with a scathing attack on the historiography of David Hume, whose revisionist account of the reigns of James I and Charles I had appeared in 1754. But preceding the attack on Hume (who would also be the target of the *Letter*'s later supplements) is a veritable catalogue of the Whig canon. Thomas Frankland's *Annals of King James and King Charles I* is, admittedly, eccentric in that canon. Frankland, "impostor and annalist," as the old *Dictionary of National Biography* introduced him, published his history of the first two Stuarts anonymously in 1681, in the context of the Exclusion Crisis. Although it is largely a collection of parliamentary speeches and state documents, its stance is unmistakably royalist and Anglican. John Rushworth's *Historical Collections of Private Passages of State, 1618–1648,* on the contrary, had first been published in 1659 with a dedication to Richard Cromwell. Bulstrode Whitelocke, who had assisted Rushworth in compiling his sources, not only kept an important diary but wrote his own *Memorials of the English Affairs; or, An Historical Account of What Passed from the Beginning of the Reign of King Charles the First, to King Charles the Second* (1682), another work published in the heat of Charles II's struggles with the Whigs over his brother's rights of succession. The *Memoirs* of Edmund Ludlow the regicide had been edited by John Toland in 1698 and reprinted by A. Millar in

1751. Gilbert Burnet's *History of His Own Time*, posthumously published in 1724, was the memoir of a man whom James II had sought to have extradited from Holland and tried for treason. The names of Hooker and Clarendon, authors, respectively, of *The Laws of Ecclesiastical Polity* and *The History of the Great Rebellion,* are invoked, typically, as authorities whom all sides might claim, though Clarendon's objectivity is that of "a divine-hereditary-right-man" (p. 65). As for "Sidney, Milton, Locke," these were the political theorists whom the eighteenth-century Whigs had adopted as forefathers—not properly speaking, of course, but as sources of historical information.

In the second, "much improved" edition this highly provocative list of authorities vanishes. In its place we find merely this: "It would, in my poor opinion, be of infinite use to young men of fortune, beginning the great world, who may hereafter be ministers of state, to read attentively the first 15 years of the reign of Charles I. and the 12 years immediately preceding the Revolution. They would thereby perceive, what mighty ill consequences flow from small beginnings, and particularly, from right not being to be had for the subject in courts of Justice" (p. 54). But later the author seems to have repented of this self-censorship as too rigorous. Evidently he realized the truncated version contained no directions at all as to how to understand the political history of the previous century and might even have opened the road to Hume. From the third edition onwards, the advice to the ministers of the future was "to read attentively the first fifteen years of the reign of Charles I, and the last sixteen years before the Revolution, in the original diaries, annals, memoirs, tracts, and in the parliamentary and contemporary histories *of those days*" (p. 65; italics added).

It is hard not to believe that these changes were motivated by caution. Perhaps Almon already anticipated the prosecution that began in January. This hypothesis is strengthened by another related cancellation. As part of his closing remarks, the author of the *Letter* had reminded his readers that the unusual length of this pamphlet was absolutely necessary "to vindicate the laws and the constitution from the attack made upon both by *The Defence of the Majority,* {which (to use the words of old Milton), "As it is a particular disesteem of every knowing person alive, and most injurious to the written labours and monuments of the dead, so to me it seems an undervaluing and vilifying of the whole nation"}" (pp. 132–33). This sentence from Milton derives from the *Areopagitica,* Milton's attack on the licensing system which the new Commonwealth had adopted from the Stuarts it replaced; it comes from that section of Milton's pamphlet where he sums up the personal humiliations for the author, the cultural losses for the state, and the invariably politically motivated arbitrariness of licensing.[9] If one recognized the source of the quotation, it would stand as an indictment of a political system that had learned to use the libel laws to create even greater threats for the writer or publisher, who could not tell in advance what would bring down on him the wrath of the government, nor the scale of the punishments he would incur. But in the second edition, the allusion to Milton and *Areopagitica* simply disappear.

In Almon's *Memoirs,* there is another important quotation from *Areopagitica.* It is introduced in a particularly Almonesque way, as a tease, a hint, a half-avowal, a semi-disclaimer. In giving his own account of his trial in 1770, he added in a long footnote a letter "written by the author of that celebrated and much admired pamphlet, for which Mr. Almon was before prosecuted, viz. The Letter on Libels, Warrants, the Seizure of Papers, &c." This letter, which is signed "Phileleutherus Anglicanus," defended Almon and specifically deplored Lord Mansfield's decision to set aside the affidavit of John Miller, a young lawyer who had testified that Almon had refused to sell him a copy of the

London Museum until Junius's letter had been deleted. The letter ends: "In fine, if once directions or instructions in point of law touching the fact in criminal trials are not to be left to the judgment of the jury, in the words of *Milton,* 'Law and compulsion grow fast upon those things which were governed heretofore by exhortation,' and the liberty of the press will be but a name."[10] Neither of these quotations from *Areopagitica,* though apt for the new occasion, are obvious choices or rhetorical flourishes; each would require its quoter to have true familiarity with Milton's argument. I claim that the same person chose both, that Phileleutherus Anglicanus in 1770 is also the author of the putatively anonymous *Memoirs* in 1790 and, as *he* tells us, also the author of "that celebrated and much admired pamphlet" around which Almon shaped his career, revising, reprinting, and praising it to the last.

OBSCENITY

There are also some signs of extreme caution with respect to matters sexual—a caution, no doubt, induced by the fate of John Wilkes and the disreputable *Essay on Woman.* Towards the end of the first edition, the *Letter* contained the following remarkable blend of social satire and its opposite, a normative statement of principles:

> I have dwelt thus at large upon the matters that compose this letter, because I am fully persuaded that the happiness both of King and Subject depends upon a due observance and reverence of the laws, and because I am willing, in particular, that my son should have an opportunity of perusing by himself my notions in this respect, when I shall be dead and gone. Young men, I know, are apt to be

led away by the turn of the company they happen to fall in with, to admire the splendor and pomp of great men, and to swallow their doctrines too; and to regard every thing like opposition as the effect of mere party or personal disappointment, and for that reason to laugh at all discourses upon liberty and the constitution, in the lump, as antiquated stuff, fit for no gentleman of the world to trouble his head about. Whereas, when he has lived as long as myself, he will see the necessity, every now and then, of bringing things back to their principles, and that there is nothing so mean, so corrupt, and so unprincipled, but what he may find some courtier of title, in a laced coat, and a gilt chariot, with a princely carriage and numerous retinue, will submit to do, in order to keep with the minister of the day, and be spoke to at St. James's. He will discover that those polite gentlemen who are of the *bon ton* and set the mode or true taste for the rest of the world, are as ignorant about the subject matter of this letter, as children. In short, a real acquaintance with the history of this country, and an insight into the constitution, by a general view of its laws, can only be had by a good deal of pains, reading and inquiry, and the reflection of a good understanding upon the whole. They are neither to be picked up in the streets like a girl of the town, or at routs, nor even at Arthur's or Wildman's, nor are they to be had of a French or Italian master, or at a toyshop, nay not by confirmation from the hand of a Bishop, or even the hand of a Minister. It is infinitely easier to turn a polite period, in a letter about nothing, or to say a very genteel thing, than to think justly and speak clearly, upon any subject of importance. Knowledge is not, that I know of, to be had by inspiration, excepting, perhaps, sometimes in religion; and yet, unless a man really understands the matter in question, I do not see how he can, at any time, deal with a bold, dexterous fellow, that has an interest in deceiving him. . . . Of this, however, I think every Englishman may be assured, that the two real pillars of our constitution are Parliaments and Juries, and that, in order to be what they ought to be, the former must be independent of the Crown, and the latter of the Judges. (pp. 116–17)

Returning to his theme of youth versus age, cynicism versus educated belief, the author of the *Enquiry* laid himself on the line; yet in the next edition he though better of this passage and, with the exception of the "two real pillars of our constitution," replaced it with a long attack on class and privilege. What induced him to do so? Perhaps it was the allusion to prostitution in the center. Perhaps it was the descent into social satire.

But whatever the motives for specific excisions, the overall evidence of revision in different editions of the *Letter* indicates long-term solicitude—an attention to nuance and effect that would scarcely be exercised by anyone other than its author. To comment only on what was excised would be misleading. The improvements and enlargements advertised on subsequent title pages speak to the substantially increased legal and historical documentation that also came with second (or later) thoughts. Almon thought these supplements so important that he twice published them as a separate document.[11] A close reading of all the editions, however, shows that Almon did *not* republish all of his additions. Those he selected as necessary reading had a strong constitutional content or reemphasized the legal issues

inherent in the Wilkes affair. Other alterations were introduced
silently. And sometimes these emendations tell us more about
the *process* of revision than those that Almon subsequently insisted his customers should notice, and indeed purchase.

Here I shall display, in its various stages of growth, one of
the essay's central arguments, that proceeding against putative
"libels" by an "information" of the attorney general, rather than
indictment by a grand or petit jury, is a constitutional outrage,
reminiscent of the practices of the now abolished Star-Chamber.
Since the argument is so central to the case of John Wilkes and
subsequently to Almon's, how it grew is worth our sustained attention. First came the *Enquiry*'s version:

> By the old constitution, and afterwards by Magna
> Charta, no man could be put upon his trial for any
> offence, until a grand Jury had found a bill of indict-
> ment, or of their own knowledge, made a present-
> ment thereof; and then the person so charged, was
> to be tried upon that indictment or presentment by
> a petit Jury of his Peers. By degrees however, and
> by virtue of particular statutes, crimes against the
> peace became presentable by conservators or justices
> of the peace, and the persons accused were to be
> tried thereupon by a petit Jury. In process of time,
> some few offences under special acts of parliament
> came to be prosecuted by information; and, in some
> very enormous cases, the court of *King's bench*, upon
> motion in open court supported by affidavit, and op-
> portunity given to the party charged to defend him-
> self, would sometimes grant leave for filing an in-
> formation. A Jury was afterwards to try the truth
> of every such charge. But, Henry the 7th, one of
> the worst Princes this nation ever knew, procured an

act of parliament which, after reciting many defects and abuses in trials by Jury, and pretending a remedy for the same, gives a summary jurisdiction to certain great officers of state, taking to their aid a bishop, to summon, try and punish, of their own mere discretion and authority, any persons who shall be accused of the offences therein very generally named and described. In short, the court of Star-chamber is, by this act, so enlarged in its jurisdiction, that it may be said to be erected, and both grand and petit Juries in crown matters are in great measure laid aside, as the Attorney-general now brings every thing of that sort before this court, which, by its constitution, never can make use of either. In lieu of an indictment or presentment of their peers, or informations by leave of the King's-bench after hearing both parties upon affidavits, people of all degrees are now put on their trial by a charge framed at the pleasure of the Attorney-general, called an information, and filed by him without even the sanction of an oath, or the leave of any court whatever; and the Star-chamber decide thereupon most conscientiously, but as most true courtiers would wish to do, without the intervention of any Jury at all. The faces of the subject are so ground by this proceeding, that every body at length is alarmed, and the people in struggling with the crown happening to get the better, the patriots of the time seized an occasion, towards the latter end of the reign of Charles the First, to extort from that martyr to obstinacy, an act for the abolition of this most oppressive and intolerable jurisdiction. But, by some fatality or other, the method of proceeding by an Attorney General's in-

formation, filed at discretion without oath, an offspring of the Star-Chamber, was over-looked and
suffered still to remain, and the use that is now commonly made of it, every body knows. It is reported,
however, that my Lord Chief Justice Hale had so
little opinion of the legality of this kind of informations that he used to say, "If ever they came in dispute, they could not stand, but must necessarily fall
to the ground."* Indeed, there is this very dreadful
circumstance attending this mode of prosecution,
that as the Attorney-General can file an information for what he pleases, and the Crown never pays
any costs, so it is in the power of this Officer of the
law to harrass the peace of any man in the realm,
at his pleasure, and put him to a grievous expence,
without ever trying the matter at all, and without
any possibility of redress or retaliation. Most Booksellers and Printers know this very well, and hence
so few of them can be got to publish any stricture
whatever upon any Administration, [dreading this
arbitrary scourge of the Crown, and regarding the
same as a perpetual injunction, and as terrible as a
drawn sword suspended by a thread, hanging over
their heads.] (pp. 5–6)

In the second edition, these last clauses, represented here as
within square brackets, were omitted; but in their place appeared
a very particular illustration:

This very game was played with a late Vice-Chan-
cellor of Oxford, when L.H. [Lord Hardwicke] was
of the Cabinet, and the head of the law. The Attorney General filed an information *ex officio* and
after putting the Doctor to a vast expence, entered

a *nolle prosequi* [I will not prosecute]. Soon after he filed another information for the same offence, and, when a like expence was incurred, entered another *nolle prosequi*. In short, this politico legal game was had resort to, because there was no evidence to convict, and was dropped and renewed in order to oppress, to the extreme charge of the worthless Doctor, and to the infinite discredit of a moderate King. During the reign of this Law-Lord, the same Star-chamber weapon was frequently brandished, like Medusa's head, to terrify and benum individuals. A secret and efficacious method of preserving the peace! Many an useful publication has been nipped in the bud by an information *ex officio* (that great suppressor of truth) and by the gripe of its executioner, that enemy to light, the messenger of the press. (p. 8)

This addition survived into the later editions, though in the fifth edition the saucy phrase "This very game was played" was replaced by sober statement; and new material was inserted between it and the quotation from Lord Chief Justice Matthew Hale (at the place marked above by an asterisk). More research had turned up a resolution moved by Sir George Treby and apparently passed in the House of Commons on February 2, 1689, that informations in King's Bench be done away with. This occurred, according to the *Letter*, "immediately after the revolution, when members of parliament were actuated by the genuine and pure spirit of liberty, before the hope of administration, or the lust of power, had debauched their minds." Ex officio informations, however, not only continued to be used, but "may, in time, become an ordinary engine of Administration, as much as any Gazette or common courier" (p. 8). And, after his statement about the well-understood threat this practice posed to book-sellers and printers, the fifth edition added a paragraph expati-ating on its persecutory potential and suggesting legislation to subject the attorney general to full liability for costs. The entire process illustrates the stages of rethinking and of new research into past and recent legal history that tied the era of Charles I and the Star-Chamber to the present, with the alleviating mo-ment of the 1688 Revolution seen as brief and vulnerable.

And since we are investigating here the collaboration between literature and politics, some highlighting of the *Letter*'s style is in order. Calling Charles I "that martyr to obstinacy" is a brilliant revision of the royalist trope of the royal martyr. Cut-ting the "drawn sword suspended by a thread" over the heads of booksellers seems a rhetorical loss; but if we look more care-fully we can see that for the "arbitrary scourge of the Crown," Almon later substitutes a brilliant negative parallelism: "to the extreme charge of the worthless Doctor, and to the infinite dis-credit of a moderate king." This alteration effects the separation of George III from the policies of his ministers, Mansfield espe-cially, even as it requires the reader to focus on the Pope-like subtlety of the second phrase.

LIBELS, STYLE, AND THE FAILURE OF LITERARY IMMUNITY

What is a libel? Anything the government takes into its head to dislike, according to the *Letter*. What makes this interpretive practice even worse? The use of general warrants (already de-scribed in the Wilkes case); the government's assumed powers of forced entry and seizure of private papers (also deployed in the Wilkes case); the use of close imprisonment (of which Wilkes was also a victim) and attempts to circumvent habeas corpus; the doctrine of innuendo, whereby the government decodes the identity of persons left unnamed or half-named in text under dispute; and the instructions given to juries, whereby they are deprived of any right to decide whether the import or intent of a text was libellous and only permitted to decide on whether the person charged was in any way responsible for it. All of these abuses were rigorously analysed and decried, with the weight of the *Letter*'s critique invariably falling on, or returning to, the legal and constitutional issues.

Literary quality or intention makes no difference, as it sometimes had, at least in theory, in the seventeenth century: "If a man was now to publish an ode, like that of Mr. Pulteney to Lord Lovel, 'Let's out for England's glory,' inviting any courtier to join in measures of opposition to the administration, and it was writ with half the spirit and beauty, it might, for aught I know, be capable of an information *ex officio* as a libel, altho' no man turned of thirty, I suppose, would think any placeman could be moved thereby to oppose the court, and quit any part of his finery, for the sake of being called a patriot, or for any pleasure he could have from holding seditious discourses." So it went in the first edition (p. 24); in the second, it read "for the sake of *being* a patriot" (p. 23), and the last clause, which had undermined the integrity of the sacrifice, was itself sacrificed. The invocation of William Pulteney, earl of Bath, was, however, more than an attempt to theorize the literature-politics divide, for Pulteney had been one of the cofounders of the Patriot party, a reform movement within the Whigs under Walpole; a mainstay writer for the *Craftsman;* and the author of a successful political song, "The Honest Jury; or, Caleb Triumphant," on the 1729 acquittal of that journal's publisher in a libel case. In 1771, perhaps feeling that the allusion had become obscure to readers of the seventh edition of the *Letter* appearing in that year, Almon would republish this ode in his *New Foundling Hospital for Wit.* The stanza in question reads:

The cries of an insulted land,
Redress of injuries demand
Let's out for England's glory!
I'm ready to take part with you,
And am become a patriot too,
But neither Whig nor Tory.[12]

It is important to reiterate at this point that the only person who would obviously be interested in reprinting the *Letter* in 1771 was Almon himself, in the context of his 1770 trial over the publication of Junius's letter. The same must apply to the 1770 republication of Candor's *Letter to the Public Advertiser*; to *Another Letter to Mr. Almon*, published both in 1770 and 1771 at Almon's press; and to *A Second Postscript to . . . a Letter to Mr. Almon*, self-dated November 25, 1770, five days after the judgement came down against Woodfall; and especially to the P.P.S added on November 28, when "word was brought" to the author of the judgement against Almon, the good behaviour recognizance of £400 which ironically punished him for the complaints about that procedure levelled in the original *Letter* of 1765. This tangle of dates and cross-references is a symptom of a vast, watchful energy and of a huge personal investment in the issues at stake, requirements that disqualify both Camden, now distracted by parliamentary business in the Lords, and Dunning, who had actually acted as counsel for the Crown in Almon's trial in 1770!

And in the postscript to the postscript to *Another Letter* there is the unmistakable touch of Almon's irony, directed once again at his old foe Lord Mansfield. He invents the notion that his case was so good that Lord Mansfield himself would have found him innocent, had he been present. It was, therefore, "to be sure most exceeding unlucky that his lordship should *happen*, as the newspaper relates it, *to slip out of court but three minutes after* this poor bookseller was called up. It was unfortunate for both. I can only wish now that the record *together with the affidavits and the judges notes of the trial* could some how be brought or sent for by the lords and undergo a parliamentary review. The defendant would there be sure at least of Lord Mansfield's doing him justice."[13] Thus the drama of cowardice is documented for posterity; but after Mansfield's death in 1793, Almon would get *his* revenge, without the need for irony. In his three-volume *Biographical, Literary, and Political Anecdotes,* published in 1797 as his retrospective account of the Georgian era and his personal swan song, Almon devoted the most space to a hostile biography of Mansfield. Early in this life Almon reminded us once again that "Lord Mansfield was exceedingly hurt by a tract of great celebrity, entitled 'A Letter on Libels and Warrants'" (1:241), and the last event described is his conduct of Almon's trial for libel in 1686!

Here are Almon's two assessments of the man:

> It has been the great felicity of Lord Mansfield's reputation, that his conduct has generally been viewed on the favourable side only. . . . If the *whole* of his conduct had been fairly and impartially examined, it would in many points have brought to our remembrance the conduct of those learned chiefs, Tresylian, Keyling, Scroggs, Jefferyes and some others. (1:228–29)

> Of his Lordship's political opinions and conduct, it would have been happy for his country if they had been founded in those just principles of all government, which make the honour of the state and the interests of the people perfectly the same. His political ideas were like those of Lord Bute; they were contracted, splenetic, and tyrannical. No bet-

ter proof need be given than his memorable apostrophe in the House of Lords, in the year 1774, upon the Boston Port Bill. . . . His Lordship said, "the sword was drawn and the scabbard thrown away. We had passed the Rubicon;" alluding to Caesar's march to Rome. This was not less a prophetic and dreadful denunciation to the interests of Great Britain, than the inscription on the bridge over the Rubicon was to the fate of Caesar, and the liberties of Rome. (1:357–58)

Thus Almon takes us forward to Mansfield's role as chief hawk (after George III himself) in the American crisis, and hence to our next chapter.

3

Inventing Postcolonialism

BURKE'S AND BARRY'S *PARADISE LOST*
AND *REGAINED*

Edmund Burke is perhaps the most demanding subject for consideration under the motto "Nobody's perfect" that the eighteenth century provides. I refer to what is often called the Burke problem—the vexed relation between Burke's defence of the American Revolution in the mid-1770s and his attack on the French one in the early 1790s. This trajectory from undeniably liberal principles to an eloquent but extreme conservativism has naturally been celebrated by as many or more as have regretted it. It has been "explained" in psychological terms,[1] as the not-inconsistent behaviour of someone who was always "a believer in political and constitutional balance";[2] and as the frustrated response of a man whose talents were never rewarded by any significant public office and whose influence in the House of Commons had waned significantly after the death of his patron, Rockingham, in 1782, when Burke was no longer seen as "the mouthpiece, and perhaps also the brain, of one of the wealthiest landowners under the crown."[3] But the overall effect of the Burke problem in our own academic culture has been to privilege his *Reflections on the Revolution in France* as an intellectual event and rhetorical performance in whose shadow the speech on conciliation of the American colonies, delivered in the House of Commons on March 22, 1775, and extraordinarily celebrated in its own time, has rather languished. The central myth of the *Reflections,* that the French Revolution destroyed beauty, order, and custom to no good purpose, has effectively and affectively prevailed over the central myth of *On Conciliation,* which this chapter will offer to restore.[4]

Until the later twentieth century, *On Conciliation* must have been one of the best-known and best-conserved political speeches of all time. Published on May 22 by J. Dodsley, who had five years earlier published five editions of Burke's *Thoughts on the Causes of the Present Discontents,* it went through three English editions in 1775 and was also published in New York that year by James Rivington. This was no accident. The Opposition party in the Commons—usually known as the Rockingham Whigs—were always depressingly in the minority. Burke, as a member of that Opposition, knew in advance that his proposals would be voted down and that the main purpose of his speech was to consolidate pro-American feeling in England at large (of which there was very little) and to reassure the American leaders that they had articulate support in the mother country. Since then, the speech appeared not only in editions of Burke's collected works but in a chain of separate editions in both countries, some of these explicitly for use in schools. By 1895 it had evidently become a classic in the United States; by the 1990s it was a forgotten one.[5]

Perhaps this also stemmed from the way *On Conciliation* had been adopted in America. Thomas Jefferson had, naturally, purchased the New York edition of 1775 and placed it among his huge collection of tracts on Anglo-American relations.[6] But from 1895 onwards it was deployed either as a paradigmatic oration for the rhetorical instruction of advanced students or as the occasion for inculcating an important block of Anglo-American history. But somehow the two sides of this endeavour, the structural-textual and the historical-contextual, have not enlightened each other. We can see that this speech (even more than *Thoughts on the Causes of the Present Discontents*) crystallises the dilemma of the Rockingham Whigs, who with Burke as their Cicero attempted to define a cause around which they might rally; but the extraordinary tone of *On Conciliation* and its underlying myth have almost eluded us.[7] I call that myth, with Burke's authorization, *Paradise Lost*. Much later in his life, Burke would be scathingly associated with Milton's poem, when, after Rockingham's death in 1782, James Sayers published a cartoon showing Burke and Fox as Adam and Eve, excluded from Paradise, over whose locked gate is the sculptured, gloating head of William Petty, earl of Shelburne, to whom George III had offered the ministry (Figure 7). The historian F. P. Lock has suggested in his definitive new biography that "*Paradise Lost* more truly expresses Burke's plight in 1784," when the rout of the Fox-North Coalition in the election of that year completed the collapse of his political career, but in 1775 Milton's epic did not express his "plight" at all.[8] Rather, it represented his now fully developed philosophy of the Western empire, part tragic, part epic, part utopian foresight.

By 1775, Burke had *almost* reached the conclusion that the colonies, like Paradise itself, were effectively lost. He was trying to avert an event predetermined by precedent mismanagement, not to mention greed and stupidity. His argument was that George III and Lord North were attempting to punish heroic entrepreneurialism in the colonies and to wipe out resistance that was motivated, according to Burke, by essentially Whig principles; and one of his strategies was to marshall feelings, at the subliminal level, by casting his speech as a complex reworking of Milton's *Paradise Lost*. Far from being merely decorative, his allusions to Milton's poem constitute, as it were, a second-level hermeneutics by which we can understand why he delivered it and why he delivered it *then*. The role that the American colonies and the struggle with the mother country played in Burke's own intellectual and imaginative development (later to

Figure 7. *Paradise Lost*. By James Sayers. 1782. Courtesy of the Yale Center for British Art, Paul Mellon Collection.

be replaced by an equally idealistic but less realistic commitment to the Eastern empire) was more profound than we can deduce by merely following his arguments and identifying his positions. But we can get closer to plumbing its psychological and ideological depths if we attend to his invocations of Milton—already established, in Burke's 1757 *Philosophical Enquiry into the Origin of Our Ideas of the Sublime and Beautiful*, as the modern source of the Sublime.

Burke had a vast amount of Milton in his library. He had a precious copy of the 1691 edition of Bentley and Tonson's *Paradise Lost*, "adorn'd with Sculptures." He owned two copies of Newton's edition of *Paradise Lost*, the first published in Dublin in 1751 in two volumes, the second published in London in 1754 (erroneously cited as three volumes in the sale catalogue of his library). He owned a 1740 edition of Paoli Rolli's two-volume Italian translation,[9] as well as William Dobson's two-volume Latin-English edition, the volumes published in Oxford separately in 1750 and 1753. More significantly, he evidently recognized, as was rare in the eighteenth century, the whole Milton, the republican and regicide Milton, not just the author of the great poems, for he owned the 1753 edition of the prose works edited by Richard Baron, and, as a more specialized acquisition, the edition of *Eikonoklastes* produced by Baron in 1756. A still more telling item is John Toland's *Life of Milton* in the 1761 edition sponsored by Thomas Hollis, who sent Burke this copy in one of his famous red morocco bindings. Hollis at least assumed that Burke was an appropriate recipient of the Milton legacy.[10] As if this were not enough, Burke continued his Milton collection well past the era of *On Conciliation*, indeed, into the era of *Reflections on the Revolution in France*, for his library contained a 1793 edition of *Paradise Lost*, presumably purchased five years before his death.[11] Even in a collection as deep and as catholic in its tastes as Burke's (which was well supplied in the Whig classics of the seventeenth century), this cluster stands out as something special.

In 1775, so did *On Conciliation*. Naturally this was not the first time that Burke had delivered a major speech involving British policy towards the colonies. The first occasion was his *Observations on a Late State of the Nation,* Burke's response to William Knox, who had taken it upon himself to defend the policies of the Grenville administration, which had ended in 1765, and to argue that those of Rockingham's administration were plunging the nation into a financial recession. Burke's response, also published by Dodsley, appeared in February 1769, and in its last third it mocked Knox's proposals for raising £200,000 a year by some form of taxation of the American colonies.[12] This gave Burke the opportunity to review the history of the notorious Stamp Act, already repealed during Rockingham's brief administration, and to give a clear indication of his pro-American sympathies. The second occasion was Rose Fuller's motion of April 19, 1774, proposing the repeal of the tea duty, a motion supported by both the Chatham and the Rockingham wings of the Opposition but which would be characteristically defeated by a huge majority, 182 votes for the North administration, as against 49 for the other side.[13] Despite this legislative rout, Burke's speech made a lasting impression, primarily by virtue of its brilliant political character sketches: of Townshend and Grenville, now dead; of Chatham, Rockingham's rival for leadership of the anti-North parties; of Rockingham himself, who is presented as an ideal figure of rectitude; and, much more briefly, of General Henry Conway.

We should pause for a moment on these sketches because they evince Burke's extraordinary gift both for personalizing politics and for pressing beyond the local contingencies so beloved of Namierites to the broadest formulation of the issues. In the case of Grenville, presented as an honest and hardworking administrator, his failings consisted in too great a belief in the powers of regulation and in a certain jealousy of American success in the trade markets (2:432–33). In the case of Townshend, Burke delivered a devastating satire of his personality as the "delight and ornament" of the Commons, a phrase that rapidly acquires a dandyish inflection. Townshend "conformed exactly to the temper of the house; and he seemed to guide, because he was always sure to follow it." "He every day adapted himself to [its] disposition; and adjusted himself before it, as a looking glass." He so far avoided "the vice which is most disgustful" in politics, that is to say, obstinacy, that he changed his mind and his policies at the drop of a hat. "To please universally was the object of his life; but to tax and to please, no more than to love and be wise, is not given to men" (2:452–55).

In the case of Chatham, who was alive to hear of these criticisms, it was his cynical view of human nature, Burke suggested, that led him to construct an administration designed to substitute for probity and principle a system of checks and balances: "He made an administration, so checkered and speckled; he put together a piece of joinery, so crossly indented and whimsically dovetailed; a cabinet so variously inlaid; such a piece of diversified Mosaic; such a tesselated pavement without cement; here a bit of black stone; and there a bit of white; patriots and courtiers, kings friends and republicans; whigs and tories; treacherous friends and open enemies: that it was indeed a very curious show; but utterly unsafe to touch, and unsure to stand on" (2:450). This parody of nonparty government (which was also, probably, a parody of a similar architectural metaphor developed by Milton in *Areopagitica* to argue for the value of diversity of opinions)[14] simply led to chaos. "When his face was hid but for a moment, his whole system was on a wide sea, without chart or compass" (2:451).

One can already see, in this passage usually quoted for its political theory, the Miltonic talent for metaphor, never more obviously metaphorical than when employed in the immediate service of political theory, supposedly a purely rational discourse. In addition, the portrait of Chatham is introduced by way of a quotation from Lucan's *Pharsalia*, a text sharply appropriate to Burke's increasing conviction that the nation was engaging in a civil war with its colonies. In 1766 (though Burke does not give the date), "the state . . . was delivered into the hands of Lord Chatham—a great and celebrated name; a name that keeps the name of this country respectable in every other on the globe. It may truly be called, *Clarum et venerabile nomen / Gentibus, et multum nostrae quod proderat urbi.*'"

How many of Burke's audience or readers recognized this quotation from Lucan's epic, one must wonder, and of the handful that did, how many would have taken the trouble to trace these lines to their source in book 9, ll. 202–3, of the *Pharsalia*, where back in Rome Cato employed them in his lament for Pompey the Great, murdered in Egypt on Caesar's instructions? In the Loeb translation, they read: "His name is illustrious and revered among all nations, and did much service to our own State." But, Cato continued, "Sincere belief in Rome's freedom died long ago, when Sulla and Marius were admitted within the walls; but now, when Pompey has been removed from the world, even the sham belief is dead."[15] This was an extraordinary way to honor the elderly Pitt, who had been out of action through illness for three years and was now, as it were, to be buried alive in Burke's Roman analogy. This strategy of oblique criticism was enhanced by the hidden biblical quotation from Isaiah 54:8, "In a little wrath I hid my face from thee for a moment," which when used, as above, to describe the chaos that broke out when Pitt was disfunctional, not only made him an Old Testament deity but also, on too many occasions, an aloof and prickly one.

This demonstration of what Burke was about in his quotations should help to make plausible my account of an even more remarkable move, which was seemingly to praise but actually to destroy General Henry Conway, who was seated in the House and to whom Burke pointed on more than one occasion. Conway had been Rockingham's secretary of state during his brief ministry and had been given the distinction of moving the repeal of the Stamp Act in 1766. Burke recalled that moment as, ostensibly, one of glory:

> I remember, Sir, with a melancholy pleasure, the situation of the Hon. Gentleman who made the motion for the repeal; in that crisis, when the whole trading interest of this empire, crammed into your lobbies, with a trembling and anxious expectation, waited, almost to a winter's return of light, their fate from your resolutions. When, at length, you had determined in their favour, and your doors, thrown open, shewed them the figure of their deliverer in the well-earned triumph of his important victory, from the whole of that grave multitude there arose an involuntary burst of gratitude and transport. They jumped upon him like children on a long absent father. They clung about him as captives about their redeemer. All England, all America joined to his applause. Nor did he seem insensible to the best of all earthly rewards, the love and admiration of his fellow-citizens. *Hope elevated and joy brightened his crest.* (2:443)

Now, while this epic description might seem hyperbolic with respect to the person who, after all, had merely *moved* what turned out to be a highly popular repeal, there is something more than exaggeration in the quotation at which my citation pauses. These words come from Milton's epic and not, as one might guess, from the description of the Son's return to Heaven after his defeat of the fallen angels, but, the very opposite, from the description of Satan in the form of the serpent at the moment of his successful temptation of Eve. We need their fuller context also:

> Hee leading swiftly roll'd
> In tangles, and made intricate seem straight,
> To mischief swift. *Hope elevates, and joy*
> *Bright'ns his Crest,* as when a wand'ring Fire,
>
> Hovering and blazing with delusive Light,
> Misleads th'amazed Night-wanderer from his way
> To Bogs and Mires, and oft through Pond or Pool,
> There swallow'd up and lost, from succor far.
>
> (9:631–42)

Anyone who knew their *Paradise Lost* as well as did Burke must have himself become an amazed Night-wanderer at this moment, wondering where the *ignis fatuus* was leading. How was this sinister allusion to fit with what immediately follows, a comparison of Conway to St. Stephen at the moment of his stoning: "his face was as if it had been the face of an angel." But Satan, too, had had the face of an angel for some time after his fall.

One possible reaction to this disturbance in our readerly expectations is to say that it means nothing, that it *could* not mean what it seems to imply, that Burke was merely rolling familiar phrases around on his tongue, not stopping to consider what freight they carried with them. This seems unlikely, however, in that "Crest," though conceivably appropriate to the helmet of an ancient warrior, would surely have reminded Burke that its usage in Milton was part of an ornately visual description of a serpent, elsewhere described as bowing "his turret Crest" before Eve. What makes his allusion more suspicious, however, is the fact that before introducing it Burke twice referred to a rumour that Conway, even as he moved the repeal, "had another set of resolutions in his pocket directly the reverse of those he moved" (2:441). While ostensibly mentioning this rumour in order to discredit it, and asserting a moment later that "far from the duplicity wickedly charged on him, he acted his part with alacrity and resolution" (2:442), Burke may in fact, but very indirectly, have been seriously undermining Conway's integrity. In November 1770, indeed, he had attacked Conway in the House, an event which F. P. Lock reads as "part of a larger pattern of attacks on Conway, [which] suggests that their mere political differences, real as those were, were exacerbated by deep personal resentment."[16] And later, in November 1776, in a debate in the Commons moved by Lord John Cavendish and seconded by Burke on the impossible motion "for the revisal of all the Laws by which the Americans think themselves aggrieved," he attacked Alexander Wedderburn for *his* inconsistency in debate with an unmistakably Miltonic comparison: "On that memorable occasion he lay, like Milton's devil, prostrate 'on the oblivious pool,' confounded and astounded, though called upon by the whole Satanic host. He lay prostrate, dumb-founded, and unable to utter a single syllable, and suffered the goads of the two noble lords to prick him till he scarcely betrayed a single sign of animal or mental sensibility. Why, Sir, would he not be silent now?"[17]

In what follows, I shall argue that Burke's allusions to *Paradise Lost* in "On Conciliation" were not random memories but instead well-considered supports for his emotionally powerful philosophy of empire. It is worth pointing out that *On Conciliation,* like the other speeches published by Dodsley, is rhetorically polished to a high sheen and seems more fully premeditated than the two previous "American" productions; that Burke had announced his intention to present a bill at the opening of the session on November 30, 1774; that he had tried to introduce it on March 16, 1774, but it was mysteriously tabled until March 22; and that it was not published until May 22, so that he had two months to polish it still further. Unlike the two previous American speeches, it contains none of the obsessive concern with fiscal detail that might have distracted a reader outside the House, nor does it dwell obnoxiously on the inconsistencies of the Townshend and North policies. With one remarkable exception, it does not rely on ad hominem argument, however indirect, nor does it attribute the coming disaster to individual ministers. It eschews the individual political portraits of *American Taxation,* eulogistic, falsely eulogistic, or grandly retributive, and substitutes for them one of the most extraordinary accounts of national character, *American* national character, that either country had ever read. It was indeed an epic performance; Burke spoke for a full three hours. And the whole was placed within a grand adaptation of Milton's *Paradise Lost,* the premise being that there remained only the faintest chance that the story of England and its Western empire would turn out, instead, to be the story of *Paradise Regained.*

How soon could an attentive reader—a *very* attentive reader—have grasped this? Perhaps in Burke's opening moves. For after having explained the "providential favour" that has caused the Lords to return to the Commons "the grand penal Bill, by which we had passed sentence on . . . America," the great luck, as it were, of a second chance, he explained the nature of the challenge: "We are therefore called upon, *as it were by a superior warning voice,* again to attend to America; . . . surely it is an awful subject; or there is none so on this side of the grave."[18]

Only an ear tuned to Miltonic echoes, probably, would have caught that first echo, from the opening lines of *Paradise Lost,* book 4:

Oh for that warning voice, which he who saw
Th'Apocalypse, heard cry in Heav'n aloud,

Woe to the inhabitants on Earth! that now,
While time was, our first Parents had been warn'd.

(ll. 1-2, 5-6)

Of what should they have been warned? Of the approach of
Satan, winging his way towards the "new created World" intended to replace the space left in creation by the expulsion of
the fallen angels. Burke would certainly have been aware that
the New World of the American colonies was often described
in terms directly or mediately derived from Milton. The threat
to be averted was that the New World would also be corrupted.

But anyone who missed this, and most would, would also be
given a second chance at right reading when, following directly
on Burke's efficient and startling comparison between the volume of English trade to the colonies in 1704 and in 1772, he came
to the following long (and for purposes of quotation, indivisible)
passage:

> Mr. Speaker, I cannot prevail on myself to hurry
> over this great consideration. It is good for us to be
> here. We stand where we have an immense view of
> what is, and what is past. Clouds indeed, and dark-
> ness, rest upon the future. Let us however, before
> we descend from this noble eminence, reflect that
> this growth of our national prosperity has happened
> within the short period of the life of man. It has
> happened within Sixty-eight years. There are those
> alive whose memory might touch the two extremi-
> ties. For instance, my Lord Bathurst might remem-
> ber all the stages of the process. He was in 1704
> of an age, at least to be made to comprehend such

things. . . . Suppose, Sir, that the angel of this auspicious youth, foreseeing the many virtues, which made him one of the most amiable, as he is one of the most fortunate men of his age, had opened to him in vision, that, when, in the fourth generation, the third Prince of the House of Brunswick had sat Twelve years on the throne of that nation, which (by the happy issue of moderate and healing councils) was to be made Great Britain, he should see his son, Lord Chancellor of England, turn back the current of hereditary dignity to its fountain, and raise him to an higher rank of Peerage, whilst he enriched the family with a new one—If amidst these bright and happy scenes of domestic honour and prosperity, that angel should have drawn up the curtain, and unfolded the rising glories of his country, and whilst he was gazing with admiration on the then commercial grandeur of England, The Genius should point out to him a little speck, scarce visible in the mass of the national interest, a small seminal principle, rather than a formed body, and should tell him— "Young man, There is America—which at this day serves for little more than to amuse you with stories of savage men, and uncouth manners; yet shall, before you taste of death, shew itself equal to the whole of that commerce which now attracts the envy of the world. Whatever England has been growing to by a progressive increase of improvement, brought in by varieties of people, by succession of civilizing conquest and civilizing settlements in a series of Seventeen Hundred years, you shall see as much added to her by America in the course of a single life!" If this state of his country had been foretold to him, would it not require all the sanguine credulity of youth, and all the fervid glow of enthusiasm, to make him believe it? Fortunate man, he has lived to see it! Fortunate indeed, if he lives to see nothing that shall vary the prospect, and cloud the setting of his day! (3:114–16)

Burke's parliamentary audiences by this time must have learned to beware the approach of his complimentary mode. This set piece was designed to set up the Bathursts, father and son, Allen and Henry, as examples of the kinds of men, avid Tories, friends of Lord North, who, in the words of Burke's modern editors, "had done very well by the Brunswick line which of course they were known originally to have opposed" (3:115 n. 4). Of the younger Bathurst, created lord chancellor in 1771 more or less by default, the old *Dictionary of National Biography* reported that "by a universal consensus of opinion . . . Bathurst is pronounced to have been the least efficient lord chancellor of the century." In the same year, and surely not by coincidence, the elder Bathurst received the earldom which in due course (very due, as it turned out) the son would inherit. In fact, the elder Bathurst died in December at the age of ninety-one, probably unaware of the trick that had been played on him.

Burke's primary weapon was irony, some of it merely verbal. The process of getting an earldom into the family is described as "turning back the current of hereditary dignity to its fountain" and gaining "these bright and happy scenes of domestic honour and prosperity." The vision of America he is granted in this imaginary geography lesson, a "small seminal principle" in "the mass of the national interest," is the view of the colonies, Burke suggested, that Tories would naturally hold—a view of the New World as existing entirely for the economic interests of the English. And there are literary allusions, before the vision really opens, that deserve to be more than merely identified. Burke suggested that all the members of the House of Commons have for a moment been granted epistemological eminence. Will they be able to use it well? "It is good for us to be here," cites St. Mark's account of the transfiguration of Christ on "an high mountain" (9:2-6), a vision which Peter characteristically fails to understand in other than conventional, institutional terms. "Clouds indeed, and darkness, rest upon the future" may be a quotation from the most famous Whig play of the century, Addison's *Cato,* at the point where Cato, having decided that the world belongs to Caesar, prepares for suicide.[19]

But the major allusion—the vision of the future delivered to a young man by an angel—is still more ironic, more literary, and more provocative. It derives from the end of *Paradise Lost,* where the archangel Michael reveals to Adam the future history of the world; but it also, inevitably, would remind good readers of Milton of the parallel scene in *Paradise Regained,* where Satan carries the young Jesus to the top of a mountain to show him all the empires of the earth in order to tempt him with material dominion. Burke's version is, ethically, a blending of the Satanic vision, which the young hero must categorically reject, with the Angelic vision, whose message, though depressing, must be accepted by Adam if he is to live with any integrity in a fallen world. Burke's exhortation "Let us . . . before we descend from this noble eminence, reflect . . ." recalls how Michael closed down his lecture to Adam, "Let us descend now therefore from this top of Speculation; for the hour precise exacts our parting hence" (12:587-90). But it is the imperialism of Satan's temptation that really fits the context of Burke's adaptation, its focus on material wealth and nationalism conceived as expansionism.

The "purple" aspect of this passage about the angel was drawn to the attention of Dr. Johnson by Hester Thrale, who, as she tells us in her memoirs, was in 1775 "venturing to praise" Burke's speech as a whole and this piece of virtuosity in particular.[20] Johnson's anonymous anti-American pamphlet, *Taxation No Tyranny*, had just appeared.[21] On March 16, Charles Pratt, now Lord Camden (who as chief justice had ordered the release of John Wilkes in 1763 in the case of the *North Briton*), delivered a speech in the Lords against the bill for restraining American trade. In it he mentioned "a pamphlet published a few days ago, called 'Taxation no Tyranny,'" as one of the provocations in the press which required a response.[22] This places Johnson's pamphlet at the end, perhaps, of the first week of March. By the end of the month, Johnson could have read Burke's speech, which (perhaps to Johnson's irritation) makes no mention of his pamphlet and proceeds to make several of the arguments on which Johnson had poured scorn. Johnson was predictably indignant. Unlike Thrale, he was undeceived by Burke's irony and proceeded to offer his own rebuttal, choosing definitively between Angelic and Satanic prospects and turning the trick against the Whigs in an imaginary parliamentary riposte:

> Suppose Mr. Speaker, that to Wharton or Marlborough, or some of the most eminent Whigs in the last Age—the Devil had—not with any great Impropriety consented to appear, he would perhaps in these words have commenced the Conversation. "You seem my Lord to be concerned at the judicious Apprehension, that while you are sapping the Foundations of Royalty, and Propagating the Doctrines of Resistance here at home, the distance of America may secure its Inhabitants from your Arts though active; but I will unfold to you the gay Prospects of Futurity: the People now so innocent, so harmless, shall draw their Sword upon their Mother Country and break its Point in the blood of their Benefac-

tors: their people now contented with a little; shall then refuse to spare what they themselves could not miss; and these Men, now so honest and so grateful, shall in return for Peace and for Protection see their vile Agents in the house of Parliament, there to sow the seeds of Sedition, and propagate Confusion Perplexity and Pain. Be not dispirited then at the Contemplation of their present happy state; I promise you that Anarchy Poverty and Death shall carry even across the spacious Atlantick—and settle even in America the consequence of Whiggism."[23]

Thus Johnson rewrote the Miltonic script once more, unveiling the ironies of Burke's version and reappropriating the Pisgah prospect to demonic use.

I take Johnson's understanding of this famous passage as confirmation that Tory members of the House would not have been deceived, as was the modern critic Frans de Bruyn, into reading this "tribute" to Bathurst's "heroic gaze" as an appeal to a broad consensus of gentlemanly opinion. Can we really suppose that Burke selected Bathurst *because* "his association with the Tories, rather than Burke's Whig associates, guarantees the comprehensiveness and impartiality of the vision ascribed to him by placing it beyond narrow party interests?"[24] That Pope should have "mythologized" the elder Bathurst in his *Epistle to Burlington* (ll. 177–18) in 1731 (de Bruyn's main argument rests on this, though the *Epistle to Bathurst,* which had attacked avarice, would have been more pertinent) would scarcely in itself be a reason for Burke's idealizing him in 1775; and we have already seen, from his attack on Chatham's unstable "Mosaic" constructions, what Burke thought of the merits of supposedly nonparty government.

In his reference to "their vile Agents in the house of Parliament" Johnson may also have included a personal jab at Burke, whose official paid position as agent for the New York Assembly had begun in 1770. By 1774 it had become something of a political liability to him, casting a shadow over his vaunted independence. In June 1775, Burke wrote to the New York Assembly a long letter explaining how the petition they had sent him had been refused acceptance in the Commons but had been successfully presented in the Lords owing to the good offices of the dukes of Manchester and Richmond, Rockingham, Lord Camden, and the earl of Effingham. It is not without significance that this letter was intercepted and copied by the government.[25]

Introduced by this grand-style Miltonic premise, it would seem fair to suggest that other references to Milton in *On Conciliation* would bear rather more weight than the several Shakespearean allusions (though all are from the tragedies) and the several classical quotations (though five references to Juvenal's satires may also subliminally set the tone). Two of the quotations from *Paradise Lost* suggest that the Commons, and England in general, are in danger of adopting the subject-position (to use a current cant phrase) of the fallen angels in Milton's Hell. Refusing once again to encounter the argument for or against taxation of the colonies from a legal or theoretical position, Burke remarked: "These are deep questions, where great names militate against each other; where reason is perplexed; and an appeal to authorities only thickens the confusion. For high and reverend authorities lift up their heads on both sides; and there is no sure footing in the middle. The point is the *great Serbonian bog, betwixt Damatia and Mount Casius old, where armies whole have sunk*. I do not intend to be overwhelmed in that bog, though in such respectable company" (3:135).

Although he had used it years before, in a draft of a response in the *Public Advertiser* (March 1768) to the debates on *Nullum Tempus* (2:86), and there too as an analogy to the swamps of public policy, here in *On Conciliation* it gathers to it, by way of more extensive quotation, the whole threatening landscape of Hell as Milton understands it:

> Beyond this flood a frozen Continent
> Lies dark and wild, beat with perpetual storms
> Of Whirlwind and dire Hail, which on firm land
> Thaws not, but gathers heap, and ruin seems
> Of ancient pile; all else deep snow and ice,
> A gulf profound as that Serbonian Bog
> Betwixt Damatia and Mount Casius old,
> Where Armies whole have sunk.
>
> (2:587–94)

If we know the context, we know that the "such respectable company" eschewed by Burke at this moment are the fallen angels, on a voyage of exploration to see what *their* new world in the underworld can offer.

But Burke also acknowledges that, from another perspective, it is the colonists, the rebels, who occupy the Satanic position. Arguing against the latest version of the North plan for taxation, and in favor of returning to the era where the colonies made voluntary contributions, Burke wrote: "[W]hatever is got by acts of absolute power ill obeyed, because odious, or by contracts ill kept, because constrained; will be narrow, feeble, uncertain and precarious. '*Ease would retract vows made in pain, as violent and void*'" (3:163). The speaker here is Satan, at the beginning of book 4 of *Paradise Lost* (that book, we remember, which opened with the appeal for "that warning voice"), which contains his soliloquy on the motives for his initial rebellion and its continuance. Here we have a still more subtle test case of how the context of a quotation affects and rounds out the new usage. Satan himself admits that his response should have been one of gratefulness to his sovereign (the frequently reiterated position

of those who spoke in Parliament against the colonists as in-
grates), but speaks of that fealty as "a debt immense of endless
gratitude, / So burdensome, still paying, still to owe" (4:52–53),
a deep psychological truth that can readily be converted into the
taxation issue. And the lines about vows made in pain belonged
originally in a framework of demonic self-analysis that suggests
(once translated into the new context of Burke's speech) that
conciliation of the rebels would only lead to new kinds of resistance—precisely the position asserted by those who favored
penal laws against the colonists:

> But say I could repent and could obtain
> By Act of Grace my former state; how soon
> Would highth recall high thoughts, how soon unsay
> What feign'd submission swore: *ease would recant*
> *Vows made in pain, as violent and void,*
> For never can true reconcilement grow
> Where wounds of deadly hate have pierc'd so deep:
> This knows my punisher.
>
> (4:93–100, 103)

Does this mean that Burke, at the deeper level of his myth, was
admitting the very arguments against which his speech was marshalled? Or does it mean only that *punishment,* as distinct from
true conciliation, would be rebarbative? For any reader of *On
Conciliation* who was sufficiently puzzled by Burke's Miltonic
quotation to track it to its source, this quandary would be politically and psychologically enlightening.

   If the previous two instances have placed the House of Commons (and behind them, all England) in the position of fallen
(but possibly redeemable) Adam and the Americans in the position of the fallen angels, we are teetering on the edge of a moder-
ately trite political allegory. There is, however, one further twist
to Burke's redeployment of Milton, which unsettles such con-

ventional parallelism. This occurs in the famous central section of the speech where Burke explains why force will *not* work on the Americans, because of their national character. As a transition to this claim, Burke inserted an epic description of the American fishing industry:

> And pray, Sir, what in the world is equal to it? Pass by the other parts, and look at the manner in which the people of New England have of late carried on the Whale Fishery. Whilst we follow them among the tumbling mountains of ice, and behold them penetrating into the deepest frozen recesses of Hudson's Bay, and Davis's Streights, whilst we are looking for them beneath the Arctic circle, we hear that they have pierced into the opposite region of polar cold, that they are at the Antipodes, and engaged under the frozen serpent of the south. . . . Nor is the equinoctial heat more discouraging to them, than the accumulated winter of both the poles. We know that whilst some of them draw the line and strike the harpoon on the coast of Africa, others run the longtitude, and pursue their gigantic game along the coast of Brazil. No sea, but what is vexed by their fisheries. No climate that is not witness to their toils. . . . When I contemplate these things, when I know that the Colonies in general owe little or nothing to any care of ours, and that they are not squeezed into this happy form by the constraints of a watchful and suspicious government, but that through a wise and salutary neglect, a generous nature has been suffered to take her way to perfection: when I reflect upon these effects, when I see how profitable they have been to us, I feel all the pride of power sink,

and all presumption in the wisdom of human con-
trivances melt, and die away within me. My rigour
relents. I pardon something to the spirit of Liberty.
(3:117–18)

This writing raises the American fishing industry to the level
of a sublime victory over nature. The point was acknowledged
by Herman Melville in *Moby-Dick* (chapter 24, "The Advocate") when his defence of the grandeur of the whaling industry includes the rhetorical question and answer: "And who pronounced our glowing eulogy in Parliament? Who but Edmund
Burke!"—a move immediately followed by the claim that the
whalers have better than royal blood in their veins, being all descended from Benjamin Franklin's grandmother![26]

This heroic transition prepares audience and reader for an account of American national character that is itself heroic and,
moreover, heroically Whig. The colonists have been bred in the
spirit of liberty, and specifically that strain of English liberty
that has always defined itself around the question of taxation,
rather than, as in classical commonwealths, on the "right of election of magistrates; or on the balance among the several orders
of the state" (3:120). They are also Protestants, of a particularly oppositional kind. (Burke would deal, rather uncomfortably, with the obvious counterargument, that the Southern colonies had a very different religious constituency, by arguing that
as slaveholders the Southerners were equally committed to their
own liberty as their Northern colleagues). But in his zesty account of it, New England Protestantism became itself a version of Whiggism: "The Church of England . . . was formed
from her cradle under the nursing care of regular government.
But the dissenting interests have sprung up in direct opposition
to all the ordinary powers of the world; and could justify that
opposition only on a strong claim to natural liberty. Their very

existence depended on the powerful and unremitted assertion of that claim. All protestantism, even the most cold and passive, is a sort of dissent. But the religion most prevalent in our Northern Colonies is a refinement on the principle of resistance; it is the dissidence of dissent" (3:121–22). Finally, the importance to the colonists of education, especially their self-education in law, had made them especially well equipped to survive this conflict. "The profession itself is numerous and powerful. . . . The greater number of the Deputies sent to the Congress were Lawyers. But all who read, and most do read, endeavour to obtain some smattering in that science" (3:123). Copies of Blackstone's *Commentaries* were in hot demand. This study made the Americans *anticipate* problems with their rulers. "They augur misgovernment at a distance; and snuff the approach of tyranny in every tainted breeze" (3:124).

This essay in anthropology, brilliantly overstated, had a single purpose: to persuade the members of the House of Commons that none of their proposed solutions to the rebellion *except* conciliation could have the slightest effect on the colonists' determination. But there were two other irreversible factors, more basic, more fundamental still, than these cultural conditions. Both involve problems of scale. One was the sheer width of the Atlantic, which renders government at a distance unwieldy and desperately slow; the other was the colonists' extreme reproductive ability. There were so very many of them. "While we spend our time in deliberating on the mode of governing Two Millions, we shall find we have Millions more to manage" (3:111).

Most of these points, remarkably, had been anticipated and discredited in Johnson's *Taxation No Tyranny* a fortnight or so earlier. Johnson had complained: "[W]e are then told that the Americans, however wealthy, cannot be taxed; that they are the descendants of men who left all for liberty, and they have constantly preserved the principles and stubbornness of their progenitors; that they are too obstinate for persuasion, and too powerful for constraint; that they will laugh at argument, and defeat violence; that the continent of North America contains three millions, not of men merely, but of Whigs, of Whigs fierce for liberty, and disdainful of dominion; that they multiply with the fecundity of their own rattle-snakes, so that every quarter of a century doubles their numbers" (p. 4).

Did Burke read this pamphlet? If so, he never deigned to address it directly, but rather steered straight ahead down the path that Johnson excoriated. And on the subject of American fertility, he had one last great Miltonic (and biblical) move to make. To counter the argument that in order to curtail the population growth, the Crown should make no further grants of land in America, Burke declared simply that "the people would occupy without grants":

> If you drive the people from one place, they will carry on their annual Tillage, and remove with their flocks and herds to another. Many of the people in the back settlements are already little attached to particular situations. Already they have topped the Appalachian mountains. From thence they behold before them an immense plain, one vast, rich, level meadow; a square of five hundred miles. Over this they would wander, without a possibility of restraint; they would change their manners with the habits of their life; would soon forget a government, by which they were disowned; would become Hordes of English Tartars; . . . Such would, and in no long time, must be, the effect of attempting to forbid as a crime, and to suppress as an evil, the Command and Blessing of Providence, "Encrease and Multiply." Such would be the happy result of an

endeavour to keep as a lair of wild beasts, that earth,
which God, by an express Charter, has given to the
children of men. (3:128–29)

Thus Burke created a new, as yet innocent, subject-position for
the colonists, as a series of Adams and Eves at the beginning of
the story, before the Fall has taken place. Burke knew that moment had passed and that "Tillage" was not only Miltonic but
postlapsarian. Perhaps he glanced in his scenario of landlessness
at the story of Abraham, the first nomad, who, however, had a
divine mandate for his behaviour:

> I see him, but thou canst not, with what Faith
> He leaves his Gods, his Friends, and native Soil
> Ur of Chaldaea, passing now the Ford
> To Haran, after him a cumbrous Train
> Of Herds and Flocks, and numerous servitude;
> Not wand'ring poor, but trusting all his wealth
> With God, who call'd him, in a land unknown.
>
> (12:128–34)

But the conclusion of Burke's advice to the Parliament is benign. It echoes the song of the angels that sums up book 7 of
Paradise Lost, the book of the creation of the world, which ends
with God's *other* mandate:

> [God] blessed Mankind, and said
> Be fruitful, multiply, and fill the Earth,
> Subdue it, and throughout Dominion hold
> Over Fish of the Sea, and Fowl of the Air,
> And every living thing that moves on the Earth,
> Wherever thus created, *for no place*
> *Is yet distinct by name.*
>
> (7:530–36; italics added)

This sense of a world without borders and boundaries is what Burke, with deliberate unrealism, opposes to the complex proposals of the North government with respect to the treatment of individual American states.

BURKE AND JAMES BARRY: POLITICS FOR THE EYE

The polarization of England over the American war and the fate of the colonies has been increasingly well understood by historians, especially when they turn to analysing the activities of the popular press. As Kathleen Wilson has collated the evidence, the North government hired "authors with such considerable polemical talents as Samuel Johnson, John Shebbeare, James Macpherson, Sir John Dalrymple, William Knox and Israel Mauduit" to support the government's policies in print, and the radical and antiwar press replied in kind: "Copies of anti-war broadsides and tracts were priced to aid mass distribution, . . . and the tracts and essays of Arthur Lee, Burke, Richard Brinsley Sheridan, Charles James Fox, John Almon and Catharine Macaulay (not to mention Benjamin Franklin and Tom Paine) were excerpted in the newspaper press and monthly magazines."[27] But although Burke himself was active in penning antiwar petitions, his party in Parliament was hopelessly divided, hamstrung by their earlier support of the Declaratory Act and the overwhelming tendency of "country" Whigs to see the Americans as intransigent tenants on royal property.[28] Support for the colonists came largely from the provincial towns in the north and the west, with Bristol, Burke's own constituency, featured prominently as a source of pro-American petitions. And by April 1777, Burke would be writing his *Letter to the Sheriffs of Bristol,* apologising to his constituents for his party's decision, on his own advice, to secede from Parliament whenever American affairs were

Figure 8. *The Phoenix; or, The Resurrection of Freedom*. By James Barry. 1776–77. Courtesy of the Yale Center for British Art, Paul Mellon Collection.

to the Memory of | This | Monument
a Corrupt degen— | — | ish | Freed—
— Gentry, dissipa— | —poor | Nob—
dependent upon the | Court | rapacious

—by an Artist | —is thy more favor'd England when thy great Curru——— is Worthless, thou hast given them over to chains & despondency & taken
of Greece, Italy— | with honours. | Publish'd by I. Almon according to Act of Parliament Dec. 1776

discussed. This unfortunate secession allowed for the passage of legislation suppressing the rights of the colonists by partially suspending habeas corpus.

In the year following Burke's speech *On Conciliation* the American Declaration of Independence would, of course, be signed. Its signing would be celebrated by the publication of James Barry's grand-scale print *The Phoenix; or, The Resurrection of Freedom*, published (so the print itself declares) in December 1776, by (who else?) our friend John Almon (Figure 8).[29] Barry was a friend of Burke's, or rather a man whom Burke had befriended when he first arrived from Ireland, but with whom he had recently quarreled. The reason for the quarrel was Burke's request for a portrait of himself at very short notice, a request that Barry had declined to honour. Two versions of self-esteem butted each other on the head. Barry at this time was an aspiring artist dedicated to the grand genre of history painting, with his eyes on the Royal Academy, where he not only exhibited but obtained a position as teacher of painting. As Burke moved towards conservativism, however, Barry was to declare himself more and more firmly as a republican. From 1791 onwards he was closely involved with William Godwin, and he flaunted his friendship with John Horne Tooke and Mary Wollstonecraft in his anti-Academy *Letter to the Dilettanti Society* of 1798.[30] And in a letter to Charles James Fox written in 1800, Barry looked back not only on his friendship with Burke as the occasion of their first meeting, but on his own meetings with "ye principal Dissenters in London, who made me a member of their Clubb at S. Pauls Coffee house, where Dr. Price occasionally came & where I had frequently ye opportunity of hearing interesting Constitutional Questions honestly & ably discussed."[31] This was the same Dr. Richard Price whose sermon "Discourse on the Love of Our Country," preached at the Old

Jewry in November 1789 and published the following January, was to provoke Burke to write his *Reflections on the French Revolution*, in which he called Price the Hugh Peters of the moment.

The moment at which we are looking, however, is still only 1776, and the relation between the principles of Burke and Barry is not nearly so clear. The *Phoenix* tells us part of the story. For this complex allegorical image, said to be his first venture into political image-making, Barry provided an extensive set of textual glosses; but in partial defiance of the very function of the gloss these are abbreviated, fragmented, and decidedly difficult to read. These messages were first deciphered by William Pressly in his two studies of Barry, one the catalogue of the 1983 exhibition of Barry's works at the Tate Gallery and the other the already cited biographical and critical monograph.[32] Underneath the print is the explanation for its appearance, its intended audience, its tenor, and its timing: "The Phoenix or the Resurrection of Freedom/Respectfully dedicated to the Present Minority in both Houses of Parliament, by an Artist/O Liberty thou Parent of whatever is truly Amiable & Illustrious, . . . thou . . . hast successively abandon'd thy lov'd residence of Greece, Italy & thy more favor'd England when they grew Currupt & Worthless, thou hast given them over to chains & despondency & taken/thy flight to a new people of manners simple & untainted. . . . Publish'd by J. Almon according to Act of Parliament Decr. 1776."[33] The old civilizations whom Liberty has deserted are represented on the left of the composition by pieces of broken statuary upon which Time trickles funereal flowers. The "new people of manners simple & untainted" are represented in the background in pastoral repose or georgic activity, their geographical location explained by the classical temple on whose architrave is engraved "Libert. Americ."; and the dedication to the Whig minority indicates that the print is to be read in the light of recent debates in Parliament on the American issue. The monument, with its reflection in the water, is glossed by Barry as "the temple of Liberty whose door is open to all." Its shape, however, bears an uncanny, prophetic relation to the Jefferson Memorial in Washington, D.C., raising the extraordinary thought that that building echoes not only a classical temple but also Barry's updating of the premise that civilization, as freedom, is always on the move; now it has moved from the Old World to the New. And from the fragmented legend on the tombstone in the bottom left-hand corner, Pressly also reconstructed a message supposedly emanating from George III: "Upon pain of my displeasure death and Torture I prohibit my Subjects holding any Intercourse with those Audacious Assertors of human Rights on the other side of the Atlantic Given at our Palace."[34] This threat would also be seen as applying to figures like Almon himself, who was publishing the colonists' manifestoes, or to Burke, who at the end of 1776 was considering visiting France to negotiate with Benjamin Franklin.

So much for the moment of December 1776, with the signing of the Declaration of Independence as the print's most obvious topical reference. But on the right-hand side of the composition is a weightier group of human figures who belong not to the world of pure allegory but to seventeenth-century history, thus melding Barry's commitment to history painting — the highest of the visual genres — to political caricature, which was undoubtedly even lower than *nature morte*. True, they stand as mourners at the bier of Britannia; but their real identities are secured by tiny textual clues and by echoes of their portraits: John Locke, Andrew Marvell, John Milton, and Algernon Sidney. Locke, who looks almost dead himself, following a version of the famous Kneller portrait as engraved by George Vertue for the 1714 edition of Locke's works, clasps a volume identified as "Locke on Govt." Marvell, in left profile, would have been recognizable from the engraved portrait that introduces Captain Edward Thompson's 1776 edition of Marvell's *Works*, just published in July, but just in case he wasn't, "Andr Marvel" is embroidered on the two triangular flaps of his collar. Marvell points down at the corpse but looks towards Milton, whose olive wreath identifies him as the greater poet. In Milton's pocket is a volume whose title reads (of course) *Paradise Lost*. But with *his* right hand Milton is pointing (as is Sidney behind him) to the rising phoenix of American liberty in the background—that is to say, *Paradise Regained*. We know that it must be Algernon Sidney, because he bears a sword with Sidney's own motto inscribed on its blade, *"Manus haec inimica tyrannis ense petit placidam sub libertate quietem,"* a motto which Barry could have found on the frontispiece to Thomas Hollis's 1763 edition of Sidney's *Discourses Concerning Government*. The last part of his motto, "Ense petit placidam sub libertate quietem," had, moreover, in the summer of 1775 been officially adopted by the Commonwealth of Massachusetts as *its* motto.[35] Thus the seventeenth-century figures of dissenting political opinion whom, we know, were read and venerated by Thomas Jefferson, John Adams, Samuel Adams, and Benjamin Franklin are here represented as those who celebrate the transmission of their ideas across the Atlantic and their enactment in a soil more hospitable to them.[36]

But who is the figure who takes pride of place in the composition, standing with his back towards us but in left profile, his ankles chained together and a paper protruding from his back pocket that reads "Hab. Corp."? The gloss is a reference to the various assaults of George III's government on the venerable liberal right of habeas corpus. This last mourner, therefore, could be merely an abstract allegorical figure like Father Time—

that is to say, a figure of the "revolutionary principles" enunciated, if not exactly secured, in 1688 and 1689. But Pressly, who makes much of the friendship between Barry and Burke, suggests a more interesting identification, and one more in keeping with the human, historical, author-based premise that unites the other mourners. Earlier in 1776, Barry had exhibited at the Royal Academy his painting *Portraits of Barry and Burke in the Characters of Ulysses and a Companion Fleeing from the Cave of Polyphemus.* By the standards of the subsequent *Phoenix,* one could see this, too, as a political statement, with Burke and Barry publicly linked as figures in danger from a dreadful giant (George III), whose cannibalistic revenge upon them for their intrusion into his territory can be evaded only by silence and cunning. Burke, seen in left profile, and with surprisingly flowing locks, holds one finger to his lips—as a warning to Barry to keep quiet, or at least quieter than he might be tempted to be. According to Pressly, Burke had already once advised Barry to remove explanatory labels from a satirical drawing to avoid direct provocation of the authorities; and although Barry did the very opposite in the *Phoenix,* he had at least the discretion not to sign the print with his *own* name.[37] He did, however, inscribe at the base of the tombstone carrying the king's threats the cryptic message *"U & C fecit,"* which Pressly takes to be shorthand for "Ulysses and a Companion made this." Given the slight similarity between the long-haired, fleeing Ulysses and the chained figure, who also holds his left hand to his lips, we may reasonably suppose, with Pressly, that the most imposing of the mourners for liberty was intended as a portrait of Burke—the Burke of the famous speech *On Conciliation,* whose message, by December 1776, could be seen to have been tragically ignored.[38]

One could stop there, in high-minded liberal confidence that the print has been interpreted in Burke's favor and that the quarrel between Burke and Barry had been set aside in deference to their shared support for the American Revolution; but perhaps the task of interpretation is not yet complete. If the chained figure is Burke, why is he chained? Why do these two symbolic portraits of him show him as counselling silence, if the point of his presence in the print is to celebrate the importance of *On Conciliation?* What, if anything, was Burke's special relationship to the cause of defending habeas corpus? Unfortunately, that of *failing* to defend it. As Lock explains, when the government introduced the Habeas Corpus Suspension Bill on February 7, 1777, Burke was hamstrung by Rockingham's recent decision that his Opposition group, in protest against their defeat on the American issue, should secede from parliamentary business. But the secession did not hold back either Sir George Savile or Charles James Fox, who both attended Parliament in order to fight the bill. By February 21, 1777, Burke was writing to a friend that "many ask why I did not attend the [debate on] Habeas Corpus," and was planning a public apology.[39] The details of Barry's portrait of Burke in the *Phoenix*, therefore (if portrait of Burke it is), become considerably more enigmatic. Two possibilities suggest themselves: the first is that Barry's placement of Burke among these celebrated defenders of liberty might be as much a reproach as a compliment, a reproach for Burke's silencing of himself; just as Barry's boldness in explaining the political message of the *Phoenix* is implicitly a rejection of Burke's cautionary advice to him.[40] The second, which works better with the notion that *U* and *C* collaborated on the design, is that Burke's appearance constitutes something more like a self-reproach or apology.

This is where chronology—what may seem at times like an excessively detailed emphasis on dates—becomes itself an interpretive problem and a solution. The alert reader will have noticed that if Barry's aquatint was really published in December 1776, it *preceded* the bill for the suspension of habeas corpus. Pressly points out that the publication date for other prints by Barry did not always represent the date of their actual appearance;[41] thus "December 1776" was more important as fixing the political moment of the print than as indicating its availability, and the detail of "Hab. Corp." sticking out of a back pocket could well have been added after the next session of Parliament had begun. Further, the print was reissued as an etching at a moment identified by Pressly as circa 1790. It may have been premonitory of, or even a protest against, the suspension of habeas corpus in 1794 by William Pitt the Younger, as part of the anti-Jacobin panic. By then Barry and Burke were on opposite sides of the political spectrum, and the interpretive choice between reproach of Burke by Barry or partial apology by Burke himself was no longer necessary.

But we ought not ourselves be too much influenced by what happened in 1790. We ought to be fair, not only to Burke, but to the moment of the winter of 1776, when Burke was debating with himself and his friends in the Rockingham group the effect of the Whig secession (which could itself be interpreted as Achilles sulking in his tent) on the future of the Whig party. On January 6, 1777, Burke wrote to Rockingham a long and revealing letter expressing both his support of and his doubts about the secession and urging that the Rockingham group, rather than seceding in misinterpretable silence, should send an address to George III explaining their actions. In this letter Burke mentioned Benjamin Franklin's arrival in Paris, his assumption that Franklin had been sent to negotiate with Lord Stormont, the British ambassador in Paris, and his hope that it was "not wholly impossible that the Whigg party might be made a sort of Mediatours of the Peace." As to the secession, he wrote:

[A]fter rolling the matter in my head a good deal, and turning it a hundred ways, I confess I still think it the most advisable; notwithstanding the serious Objections which lie against it; and indeed the extreme uncertainty of the Effect of all political Maneuvres; especially at this time. It provides for your honour. I know of nothing else which can do this. It is something; and perhaps all that can be done under our present Circumstances. . . . However such as it is, (and for one I do not think I am inclined to overvalue it) both our Interest and our Duty make it necessary for us to attend to it very carefully as long as we act a part in publick. The Measure you take for this purpose may produce no *immediate* Effect; but with regard to the *party,* and the *principles,* for whose sake the party exists, all hope of their preservation, or recovery, depends upon your preserving your Reputation.

The "Measure" Burke had in mind was sending to the king the address he himself had written; and the latter part of the letter is devoted to imagining the consequences, none of which Burke seemed to have thought would fall directly on himself. He wondered aloud what either the Parliament or the court would do in revenge. "Though they have made some successful Experiments in Juries, they will hardly trust enough to them, to order a prosecution for a supposed Libel." Parliament might attempt an impeachment, as in the case of Henry Sacheverell, or a Bill of Pains and Penalties, as in the case of Francis Atterbury, bishop of Rochester. The court, on the other hand "may select three or four of the most distinguished among you for the Victims; and therefore nothing is more remote from the Tendency of the proposed act, than any Idea of retirement or repose. On the contrary, you have all of you, as principals or auxiliaries, a much hotter and more dangerous conflict in all probability to undergo than any you have yet been engaged in. The only question is, whether the risque ought to be run for the chance (and it is no more) of recalling the people of England to their antient principles, and to that personal Interest which formerly they took in all publick affairs?" Given this dark prognosis, it is hardly surprising that Rockingham decided against their doing anything of the sort!

Thus began, I suggest, the Burke problem; prevented by his patron and employer from writing the script for a rebellious gesture of epic proportions, Burke began the slide into more and more cautious (if compassionate) conservativism. In April 1777 he wrote to his Bristol constituents, sending them the obnoxious habeas corpus suspension act, along with the following self-indictment: "I have not debated against this bill in its progress through the house, because it would have been vain to oppose, and impossible to correct it. It is some time since I have been clearly convinced, that in the present state of things all opposition to any measures proposed by ministers, where the name of America appears, is vain and frivolous. . . . *Preserving my principles unshaken, I reserve my activity for rational endeavours.*"[42] In 1780 he lost his seat in the House for his Bristol constituency and had to make do with the far less important borough of Malton, which was within Rockingham's gift. When Rockingham took office in 1782, Burke was not offered the cabinet post he had hoped for. Although technically a member of the Privy Council as paymaster general of the forces, he seldom attended meetings and felt himself excluded from the inner circle. When Rockingham died, the hopes of the Whig party, as Burke had understood it, died with him. This was the moment of the other visual allusion to *Paradise Lost* as a paradigm of Burke's career, since it was shortly after Rockingham's death that James Sayers published his cruel cartoon. In July of that year Burke joined Fox, Lord John Cavendish, and a few others in an ill-judged resignation from Parliament. In the 1784 elections the party of Fox was decimated—and Burke, who *was* reelected, became daily more intemperate and more isolated. F. P. Lock, to whose biography this summary of a decline is indebted, happens to have closed the first volume with the following pertinent allusion of his own: "These incidents illustrate one of Burke's more heroic qualities, in the words of Milton's Satan, 'the unconquerable will . . . and courage never to submit or yield.' Still possessed of vast energies of mind and capable of intense application, once recovered from the shock of the 1784 election, he would find new causes to champion" (1:544). One of those new causes was his animus against Warren Hastings; the other was his crusade against the French Revolution.

But it will be evident from this chapter, and the book around it, that I take a somewhat less heroic (or even heroically demonic) view of the later Burke than do his apologists. Of the three explanations for his change of direction mentioned at the outset, the most persuasive seems to be Thomas Copeland's hypothesis that after the series of disappointments and diminishments that preceded and followed Rockingham's death, Burke needed to find a cause that would move him from the impotent left to the respectable center right, a stance that would bring him, in place of the friendship of Charles James Fox, the gratitude of George III. To those who argue (as Burke himself did) that the principles declared in the *Reflections* were those of the Revolution of 1688, I am inclined to reply, as did the *Gazetteer and New Daily Advertiser,* for November 4, 1790: "[I]n his argument on the *right of choice* in the people, which he refines upon so as totally to extinguish, he establishes a doctrine that would have kept England, and would keep the whole world in a state of villainage. If his principles had had weight on the public mind, at the time of the Reformation, they would have prevented the Reformation, . . . They would equally in 1688, have prevented the glorious Revolution."

4

The Meaning of Names

Sometime around July 1, 1776, Edmund Burke wrote a letter to Captain Edward Thompson, thanking him for a special gift. Regrettably, Burke does not seem to have fully appreciated it: "Mr. Burke presents his best compliments and thanks to Captain Thompson for the obliging communication of Marvells Letters with which he has honourd Mr. Burke and which he has read. Every thing which concerns so eminent a person and so interesting a period of History must certainly be entertaining; but as these Letters were originally of a publick Nature, and wrote with extraordinary Caution, they are rather less agreeable than if they were private, and contained Marvells free opinion of the ————"[1] What Burke had presumably been sent was the first volume of the three-volume new edition of Marvell's *Works,* advertised in the *Public Advertiser* on July 1, 1776, and edited by Captain Edward Thompson.[2] The first volume contained Marvell's letters to the Corporation of Kingston upon Hull, which he had represented in Parliament from 1658 until his death in August 1678. Burke was being less grateful than he might have been for material so sumptuously printed, and somewhat disingenuous when he claimed to have read it, since it also contained several of Marvell's personal letters to his nephew, William Popple, letters which revealed plenty of Marvell's "free opinion" of the government of Charles II. There is a certain irony in the fact that Burke, who had hoped for entertainment from Marvell's candor, himself resorted to the tiresome eighteenth-century trick of leaving a self-protective gap in his letter at the crucial spot.

Even more disconcerting is the fact that Burke fails to mention the final item in this volume, the complete text of Marvell's famous Opposition tract *An Account of the Growth of Popery and Arbitrary Government in England,* which had been published anonymously in 1677 and immediately became a potent weapon in the hands of the newly formed Whig party. Since the pagination of Thompson's first volume is continuous from the first of the Hull letters to the last page of the *Account,* it seems barely possible that Burke received only Marvell's official correspondence. Perhaps he quickly noticed this embarrassing error. At any rate, when the three-volume set appeared, with a long list of subscribers at the front of volume 1, Edmund Burke's name was featured therein as someone who was prepared to support an expensive and ideologically challenging publishing project. The cost of the set was 3 guineas.

Thompson's Marvell edition, never much discussed by modern scholars, acquires an energetic new field of meanings in the context of this book. It was the first edition of Marvell to include the major prose tracts that he had written during the Restoration in defence of religious toleration or constitutional government. It preceded only by days the American Declaration of Independence. It was posthumously a tribute to the efforts of Thomas Hollis, who had planned himself to produce such an edition and had collected the tracts that distinguished it from the small, two-volume edition of Thomas "Hesiod" Cooke, produced in the Walpole era. And its list of subscribers spoke directly to the question of whether, and in what form, party politics and Whig principles could or would survive the antiparty tactics of George III and the disunity caused by the American crisis.

The edition was exquisitely printed by Henry Baldwin, who had quite a record. As publisher of the *St. James's Chronicle*, he had been one of the six printers tried (and acquitted) in 1770 for publishing Junius's letter to the king.[3] In 1774 he was fined £500 for a libel upon a naval officer;[4] and in December 1766 he would be fined £100 for printing John Horne Tooke's advertisement for subscriptions on behalf of "our beloved American fellow-subjects." And it is no surprise to find that John Almon was one of the booksellers offering it for sale.

Thompson himself explained that among his motives in compiling this impressive new edition was the need to counter the reactionary historiography of the time, a project that we have seen also engaged John Almon in his various attacks on Hume and Dalrymple. That this revisionism also happened to be Scottish computed with Whig anxieties, first about the influence of Lord Bute and later about that of Lord Chief Justice Mansfield. Sir John Dalrymple's *Memoirs of Great Britain and Ireland from the Dissolution of the Last Parliament of Charles II* had appeared in three volumes in 1771 and had deeply offended the Whigs by its attacks on the character of some of their most famous "martyrs." As Thompson wrote in his preface: "[I]t hath been of late a kind of wicked fashion to decry the purest compositions of our noblest authors, to vainly render patriotism ridiculous, by attempting to laugh all patriot virtue out of countenance; yet I trust in the character of Mr. Marvell there will be developed such proofs to the contrary, that the very Dalrymple, who hath attempted to traduce the glorious names of Sydney and Russel, will fail in any malignant efforts to blacken so fair a page of character; and that one man, even with him, shall be found to be a proof against all bribery and corruption; and that no place in the gift of a King, nor any money in the Treasury, could warp his mind to desert his religion when attacked by Papists, or seduce him to abandon the post of a faithful and watchful centinel in the hour of ruin and danger" (1:li). Returning to this theme a few pages later, Thompson explained his larger motives: "One of my first and strongest reasons for publishing the works of Marvell, was the pleasing hopes of adding a number of strenuous and sincere friends to our Constitution; but alas! what is to be expected in this degenerate age, when virtue does not even nominally exist amongst us, when arbitrary power, by her baneful engines of venality and corruption, is daily putting a check to every notion of rational and manly liberty! Dalrymple's papers I have ever regarded with horror and detestation" (1:lvi–lvii). And he added a slur on the motto of the Scots that tarnished Dalrymple along with his nation of origin.

Why should this belated edition of Marvell's works carry, for Thompson and the strenuous friends he hoped to engage, such an ethical and ideological charge in 1776? In attempting to answer this question, it would be helpful to give a reprise of Andrew Marvell's political career as it could have been reconstructed from reading his *Works*. In the 1650s, Marvell was a commonwealthman, increasingly identified with the foreign policy of Oliver Cromwell. In the 1660s, there were two phases of Restoration culture and politics which deeply affected him. The first, in the first half of the decade, when the Cavalier Parliament was steadily enacting the restrictive and intolerant legislation of what is now known as the Clarendon Code: the Corporation Act of December 1661, the Act of Uniformity of 1662 (resulting in the expulsion of the nonconforming ministers from their pulpits), the Conventicles Act of 1664, and the Five Mile Act of 1665. Charles II was already drawing closer to Louis XIV of France by virtue of the marriage in 1661 of his sister Henrietta to Louis's brother, the duke of Orleans, and his own marriage to the French candidate among eligible princesses, Catherine of Braganza.

In the second half of the 1660s, pro-French policies resulted in the Second Dutch War, which galvanised Marvell into becoming a satirist in verse, author of the *Second* and *Third Advices to the Painter* and the *Last Instructions to the Painter*, all of which held up to representational inspection and political scorn the government's conduct of the war. On July 31, 1667, in the Treaty of Breda, the Second Dutch War came to an end ignominious for the English after the naval disaster at Chatham, which is one of the subjects of Marvell's *Last Instructions*. English shame and parliamentary outrage resulted in Charles's dismissal of Clarendon from the chancellorship, and a new phase of foreign policy began. For both Charles and Louis XIV it was initiated by the secret Treaty of Dover of April 1670, whereby Charles agreed to become a pensioner of France in return for neutrality in Louis's new war against the Dutch Republic and his own promise to return his country to Roman Catholicism and to rule without parliamentary interference. As Marvell wrote in 1671 to William Popple, "We truckle to France in all Things, to the Prejudice of our Alliance and Honour."[5]

Domestically the 1670s could be said to have begun with the passing of the new Conventicles Act of that year, outlawing religious meetings outside the Established Church of five or more persons. This new piece of parliamentary bigotry led to five years of dispute in the Privy Council, in both houses of Parliament, and especially in the press over enforced religious conformity or its various alternatives. To this period belong Samuel Parker's provocative diatribes against the Nonconformists, the king's own Declaration of Indulgence of 1672, and the Test Act against Catholics of March 1673, which drove all sincere Catholics from office. Marvell now began an entirely new career as a prose polemicist, an activity enabled, ironically, by the alarmingly infrequent sessions of Parliament, which gave him long spells of free time. Entering the fray against the repressive forces represented by the archdeacon of Canterbury, Samuel Parker, Marvell quickly developed a reputation as the wittiest pen on the side of the tolerationists. The two parts of the *Rehearsal Transpros'd* (the second of which was published over his name) were instant best-sellers.

The 1670s also provoked from Marvell a new series of occasional verse satires, including the gloriously mocking *Kings Vowes* (or *Royal Resolutions*), in which he catalogued Charles II's goals as the group around Shaftesbury had come to perceive them. Because this poem was of particular interest to Edward Thompson and was also to have a new life as a satire on George III, it is useful to sample the original here. The king is made to speak in his own person prior to the Restoration as to what he would do if he ever saw England again:

> I will have a Religion then all of my owne,
> Where Papist from Protestant shall not be knowne;
> But if it grow troublesome, I will have none.
>
> I will have a fine Parliament allwayes to Friend,
> That shall furnish me Treasure as fast as I spend;
> But when they will not, they shall be att an end.
>
> I will have as fine Bishops as were ere made with hands,
> With Consciences flexible to my Commands;
> But if they displease me, I will have all their Lands.
>
> . . . .
>
> I will have a fine Court with ne'er an old face,
> And allwayes who beards me shall have the next Grace,
> And I either will vacate, or buy him a place.
>
> I will have a Privy-purse without a Controll,
> I will winke all the while my Revenue is stole,
> And if any be Question'd, I'lle answer the whole.

I will have a Privy Councell to sit allwayes still,
I will have a fine Junto to doe what I will,
I will have two fine Secretaryes pisse thro one Quill.[6]

In other words, as Marvell saw it, Charles's attitude to government was entirely cynical and subversive of the Constitution. The next stage in the king's foreign and domestic policy, however, was alarming enough to motivate Marvell's most serious efforts. This was the Long Prorogation of Parliament, from November 1675 to February 1677, a possible strategy for the king since he was still being paid a substantial allowance for neutrality in the Franco-Dutch war. The Long Prorogation would become one of the strongest signs, for Marvell, that there was actually a conspiracy at work to destroy the Constitution, this being the opening premise of his *Account of the Growth of Popery and Arbitrary Government* in England, which appeared late in 1677.

This decade-long campaign on behalf of the political opposition or the Protestant religious minorities was what Thompson had in mind when he cited, as the deeper motive of the edition, his "pleasing hopes of adding a number of strenuous and sincere friends to our Constitution." His point was that nothing had changed after the Revolution of 1688, or if so, only for the worse. Thompson had some reason to believe that the works of a century-old writer might still carry some authority. The basis for Marvell's reputation as uncorruptible patriot had already been laid down by Thomas "Hesiod" Cooke in the 1720s. It was Cooke who circulated in his small two-volume edition (1726, reprinted 1772) the legend of how Danby had tried to buy Marvell's acquiescence in his policies in person, actually coming to his unpretentious lodgings and making proposals which Marvell, despite signs of moderate indigence, politely spurned.

Since I am explaining the tone and purport of Thompson's

edition, Cooke's narrative deserves resurrection here, without necessarily giving it credit for factuality:

> [Marvell] having one Night been entertained by the King, who had often delighted in his Company, his Majesty the next Day sent the Lord Treasurer Danby to find out his Lodging. Mr. Marvell, who then lodged up two Pair of Stairs in a little Court in the Strand, was writing when the Lord Treasurer opened the Door abruptly upon him. Surprized at the Sight of so unexpected a Visiter, he told him he believed he had mistook his Way. The Lord Danby replyed, not now I have found Mr. Marvell, telling him that he came with a Message from his Majesty, which was to know what he could do to serve him. His Answer was, in his usual facetious manner, that it was not in his Majesty's Power to serve him. But coming to a serious explanation of his Meaning, he told the Lord Treasurer he knew the Nature of Courts full well, he had been in many; that whoever is distinguished by a Prince's Favours is certainly expected to vote in his Interest. The Lord Danby told him, His Majesty had only a just Sense of his Merits, in Regard to which alone he desired to know whether there was any Place at Court he could be pleased with. These Offers had no Effect on him, tho urged with the greatest Earnestness. He told the Lord Treasurer he could not accept them with Honour, for he must be either ingrateful to the King in voting against him, or false to his Country in giving into the Measures of the Court; . . . The Lord Danby, finding no Arguments could prevail, told him the King his Master had ordered a thou-

sand Pounds for him, which he hoped he would receive, till he could think what farther to ask of his
Majesty. This last Offer was rejected with the same
Stedfastness of Mind, as was the first; tho, as soon
as the Lord Treasurer was gone, he was forced to
send to a Friend to borrow a Guinea. (pp. 11-13)

Thompson included a more ornamental version of this story in
the second volume of his edition (2:461-63), showing how much
it had formed his conception of Marvell but changing some of
the details in compliance with eighteenth-century taste. Thus
Marvell's "two Pair of Stairs" becomes "the very *gradus ad Par-
nassum*" (2:461)!

Though including in his "Life" a number of tempting quotations from Marvell's prose, Cooke did not tackle the task of
editing the tracts. He had hoped to persuade others to do so,
both by these inclusions and by exhortation. A journalist and
littérateur who had come to London in 1722 and attached himself to the Whig writers Dennis, Tickell, Steele, and Philips,
Cooke notoriously attacked Alexander Pope. Later in life he
took over the *Craftsman,* succeeding Nicholas Amhurst, and
in 1742 he published, anonymously, a letter "concerning Persecution for Religion and Freedom of Debate," which he dedicated to the third earl of Shaftesbury. His small, octavo edition of 1726, however, he dedicated to the young son of William
Cavendish, first duke of Devonshire, remarking that his father's
virtues "recommended him and Mr. Marvell to each other."[7]
This friendship would have been based on Cavendish's strong
move, in 1676, into the parliamentary opposition, his argument
that the Long Prorogation was in fact a dissolution, and his
move to lay on the table in the opening debates of 1677 the relevant act of Edward III. After Marvell's death, Cavendish had
plotted to bring over William of Orange and was one of the sig-

natories of the letter of June 30, 1688. He became prominent again in the context of Tory attacks on occasional conformity, that specious compromise allowing Dissenters to avoid the penal laws by performing minimal church attendance. Cavendish had been chief manager for the group in the Lords in 1702 who protected that compromise and again in 1703. But Cavendish's six-year-old heir was hardly the sponsor Cooke required for a complete Marvell's *Works,* and he cast his appeal more vaguely: "Nor will it, I believe, be ever said, that his other Pieces, in Prose, were not revived, for Want of sufficient Encouragement. Ever far be such a Reproach from any English man!" (xi–xii).

The person who did take up this challenge, however, was wealthy and zealous Thomas Hollis. The story of Hollis's dream of a new Marvell edition containing all of the prose by then attributed to him would be told in more detail by Archdeacon Francis Blackburne, whose *Memoirs of Thomas Hollis* would appear in 1780. Hollis's plan had been for a handsome royal quarto edition, with Richard Baron as the editor for the prose and William Bowyer the bookseller for "the poetical and Latin parts." After long negotiations, however, Bowyer pulled out of the project. John Nichols, who included this episode in his biography of Bowyer, felt obliged to defend him from the imputation of political cowardice: "What were Mr. Bowyer's reasons for this refusal does not appear. We may venture to say, that party considerations had no share in his reluctance; for this worthy and learned printer made no scruple to print other works, published about this time, which were, in their contents, *no less obnoxious to the Ruling Powers than the revival of Marvell's principles and strictures would have been.*"[8] The very terms, however, in which Bowyer is here excused serve, if not to increase that suspicion, to explain Hollis's interest in such a new edition and why it was handed over to Captain Edward Thompson for fulfilment. Another generation, with different resources, would take over the precious Marvell archive.

Thompson had already written his own version of this transaction in the opening paragraphs of his preface: "The late Mr. Thomas Hollis, of honourable memory, had once a design of making a collection of his compositions, and advertisements were published for that purpose by the late Andrew Millar; and all the manuscripts and scarce tracts, collected for that purpose, were afterwards given me by his ingenious friend [Thomas Brand Hollis]. In this design the late Mr. Robert Nettleton assisted; and all his papers, since his death, have been politely allowed to me by his kinsman Mr. Thomas Raikes" (i–ii). And again, a few pages later: "Since the death of Thomas Hollis, I have been favoured by his successor with many anecdotes, manuscripts, and scarce compositions of our author, such as I was unable to procure any where else; and by the attention and friendship of a volume of Mr. Marvell's poems, some written by his own hand, and the rest copied by his order: this valuable acquisition was many years in the care of Mr. Nettleton, which serves now (in his own words) to detect the theft and ignorance of some writers" (vi). Thompson saw it as part of his mission to clarify problems of authorship in the Restoration satires by way of this manuscript, in which he discovered, and proudly printed in his preface, a version of *Royal Resolutions* with additional stanzas. Admittedly he was insufficiently skeptical in his own attributions, but his attitude to manuscript sources was exemplary, and his trust in those that descended from Marvell's family is something that modern editors should perhaps revalue upwards.

This eighteenth-century Robert Nettleton, guardian of a family manuscript which now seems to have disappeared, was Marvell's grandnephew, who also, according to Thompson, wrote the epitaph commissioned by the Hull Corporation and placed near Marvell's tomb in 1688—significantly, the year of the Revolution, when such statements were encouraged (2:481–82). But this was not the only Marvell manuscript that Thompson would receive from privileged sources. Other precious family materials were made available to him, in this case at an inconvenient moment. "I had been very happy if all Mr. Marvell's works had fallen readily into my hands; but though I was some years in collecting them, yet when the three volumes were finished in the press, I was politely complimented by Mr. Mathias with a manuscript volume of poems written by Mr. William Popple, being a collection of his uncle Andrew Marvell's compositions after his decease. . . . By this manuscript I also find, that those two excellent satires, entitled, *A Direction to a Painter concerning the Dutch War in 1667,* and published in the State Poems, Vol. I, p. 24. as Sir John Denham's, are both of them compositions of Mr. Marvell; but as the work is already so largely swelled out, I shall beg leave to omit them in this preface" (xxxviii–xxxix). This statement is loaded with canonical dynamite, whose fuse we cannot follow here;[9] but it is important to note that the list of subscribers to Thompson's edition includes both Thomas Raikes (and a William Raikes also) and Vincent Matthias. As Thompson explained in a footnote, the Matthias family were also connected to Marvell, since Popple was the son of Marvell's sister by Edmund Popple, "from whom the present Mrs. Mathias is lineally descended."

Thompson himself must have been related to the various Hull Thompsons with whom Marvell corresponded. He was the son of a Hull merchant, beginning life as a sailor and receiving some help up the officers' ladder from David Garrick. Between 1772 and 1778, however, he seems to have been stranded in London on half pay, a hiatus he filled with writing undistinguished poems and plays—and editing Marvell. He evidently communicated during these years with John Almon, who had published his poem *The Soldier*, a tribute to General Conway, in 1764 and who had included other small pieces of Thompson's in his various anthologies. By 1770, as we saw in the Introduction, he was listed in the *Political Register* as a "Republican." Since Thomas Hollis died in 1774, and Thompson mentions having been "some years" in collecting materials, the Marvell project must at least have been begun immediately after Hollis's death. Perhaps it was partly motivated by the reappearance of Cooke's edition in 1772, the same year, notably, as Dalrymple's *Memoirs*.[10]

If these were the local circumstances and chances that drove the edition, its larger causes surely included the national events and crises dealt with in my previous chapters. This was a period of intense Whig activity in the press—of the anti-Bute *Letters of Junius* (1769–72), of Burke's *Causes of the Present Discontents* (1770), of the 1771 furor, with Almon and John Wilkes leading it, over the right to print parliamentary debates, of Almon's reprinting of the *Letter Concerning Libels*, of Burke's 1775 speech on conciliation of the American colonies. In the summer of 1776 the Americans would sign the Declaration of Independence. Yet during these same years, and especially in the light of the Rockingham group's secession from any parliamentary business involving America, the Whigs were even more than usually incapable of unity.[11] Behind them the country was equally divided and blanketed with propaganda on both sides of the argument. James Barry's idealist print celebrating American independence, *The Phoenix*, was balanced by *The Burning of the "Crisis,"* in which magistrates are shown burning a copy of the radical republican weekly, and the watching crowd of citizens are rendered as Hogarthian freaks (Figure 9).

Frederick, Lord North, who had taken power in January 1770, had been able to get the Boston Port Bill and the Massachusetts Government Bill passed with huge majorities in 1774. In the autumn of that year Parliament was dissolved, and the Oppo-

Figure 9. *The Burning of the "Crisis."* 1776. Courtesy of the Library of Congress.

sition lost heavily in the election, being reduced to a remnant of seventy-three members. This helps to explain why, having dedicated the first volume to the Hull Corporation and Trinity House, Thompson dedicated the second (on March 29, 1776) to Sir George Savile, member of Parliament for York, as a "right Patriot" who followed in Marvell's footsteps, but one who should now apply his sense of the "general rights of mankind" to the American situation: "May you be the happy instrument to heal the wounds now bleeding in our distracted empire, and reconcile her to her brave, though distressed children." Savile had indeed voted for the repeal of the Stamp Act and supported Burke's and Hartley's motions for conciliation, but he was also interested in electoral reform and in alleviating the condition of Dissenters, including Roman Catholics. It hardly needs saying that Savile's name was high on the list of the edition's most notable subscribers.

But who else was on that list? It is one of the few flaws of Pierre Legouis's great biography of Marvell that he pours scorn on Thompson's edition by focusing on its list of subscribers. It "provided the occasion," wrote Legouis, "for a so-called democratic demonstration of the Whigs, excluded from power by George III's policy." And, he continued, "[a] noisy and not over-scrupulous Opposition did not hesitate to call up memories of the Civil War, . . . or even to glorify, rather against logic, the tyrant Cromwell. The list of the 146 subscribers thus presents an interest more political than literary."[12] Of these subscribers Legouis mentions only "the notorious Duke of Cumberland" and "the Burke of the *Thoughts on the Causes of the Present Discontents* and of the speeches in favour of the American Whigs." His final comment on Thompson's edition was as follows: "What had become, amidst all this dust of the Forum, of those delicate poems of Marvell's in praise of the countryside?" This comment is typical of Marvell criticism in much of the twentieth century, but it will not do for the twenty-first. What Legouis missed was not only the significance of the names in the subscriber list (and perhaps also the significance of those that were missing, such as Dr. Samuel Johnson), but the meaning of their appearance *together,* under the broad umbrella of Andrew Marvell's life and works.

Let us begin with the most startling presences: Samuel Adams, Esq., the Hon. John Hancock, and General Charles Lee. Samuel Adams had directed the opposition to the Townsend acts, drafted the Boston Declaration of Rights, spearheaded the Boston Tea Party, voted for and signed the Declaration of Independence in January 1776, and been explicitly excluded from the offer of amnesty made by the British. John

Hancock, "the richest New Englander on the patriot side," had been elected president of the Provincial Congress, and then of the Continental Congress, also signing the Declaration of Independence. He, too, had been proscribed by the British government; but by the time the subscription list was printed, he and Samuel Adams were having strenuous disagreements over what role Hancock should play in the new republic.

General Charles Lee had the most colorful background of all the subscribers. He had been born and educated in England but in 1755 had gone to America as a lieutenant in the Forty-fourth Regiment. In Mohawk Valley, New York, he was adopted into a Mohawk tribe and married the daughter of a Seneca chieftain. He also spent time in Poland, but for two spells, in 1767–68 and in 1771, he returned to England and spent his time writing virulently Whig pamphlets. In 1773 he returned to America and became a violent patriot, earning the role of second major-general of the Continental Army. In 1775 he served at the seige of Boston and in June 1776 participated in the defeat of the British at Charleston. Later that year he would be captured by the British, in most humiliating circumstances. But at the time that the subscription list appeared in London, General Lee's name was synonymous with successful and flamboyant betrayal of the mother country.

What were these names doing in the same company as that of Frederick Henry, the king's brother, duke of Cumberland? (What was probably his set of the edition, beautifully bound with the royal arms on all three covers and with "GR" beneath a crown on the spine, now resides in the British Library, where it arrived as part of the King's Library donated by George IV in 1823.) Even though Cumberland had made a scandalous marriage and had spoken against the war with the colonies on March 5, 1776, one might not have expected his name to be grouped with stronger Opposition figures, whether or not they were "noisy and not overscrupulous." His Royal Highness comes third in the list of subscribers, just after the Hull Corporation and Trinity House, and his wife, the former Anne Horton, had a separate subscription. She was, moreover, the sister of Temple Luttrell, whose name also appears on the list right under that of John Hancock. Temple Luttrell's reputation among the Whigs had forever been sullied by his willingness to replace John Wilkes in the abortive Middlesex election. Yet the name of John Wilkes, Esq., M.P., also appears on the list (just above that of Samuel Adams), and so does that of his daughter, Miss Wilkes. By similar token, Edmund Burke, Esq., M.P., shares the same column as Mrs. Catharine Macaulay, who by 1776 would be seen as sharing the same umbrella uncomfortably. In 1770, Macaulay had published a virulent attack on Burke's *Thoughts on the Causes of the Present Discontents,* accusing him of simply seeking to replace one aristocratic junto with another. Later she would respond with even greater hostility to his *Reflections on the Revolution in France.* Sir William Meredith had been Lord of the Admiralty in the Rockingham administration and had, with Sir George Savile, moved in the Commons to have general warrants declared illegal in 1764; but by 1776 he had been bought out by a court appointment and was condemned as a trimmer by both sides. Was Meredith completely out of place on the subscription list, or did his commitment to Marvell signify an act of political reparation?

Several of the recognizable names, however, can be easily traced in the *Parliamentary History* [13] as prominent members of the Rockingham Opposition: William Petty, earl of Shelburne; Thomas Howard, earl of Effingham; and David Hartley, who introduced himself in one of his speeches as "a Whig of Revolution principles" (18:1170–71). Hartley was the son of the philosopher David Hartley. Between 1764 and 1766, John Almon had published eleven editions of his Opposition pamphlet *The*

Budget. In his *Life* of Hartley, Almon would later explain that the tract was "a very sharp attack upon Mr. Grenville's plan of finance for the year 1764. Mr. Grenville was very much hurt by it."[14] The next year Hartley was elected one of the two M.P.s for Hull and became a prominent pro-American speaker and writer. On April 1, 1776, he delivered a speech in the Commons, "Upon the State of the Nation and the Present Civil War with America," which was promptly printed as a pamphlet by Almon. The names of Lord Richard Cavendish, Sir Robert Clayton, Crisp Molineux, and the Hon. James Luttrell (as opposed to Temple Luttrell) can be found repeatedly on the voting lists of the minority. Richard Oliver was the radical London alderman who with his colleague Brass Crosby had defied the Parliament's ban on the printing of debates. George Kearsley, the Whig bookseller, might seem socially out of place, but politically he was certainly among friends. He had been the original publisher of *North Briton,* no. 45, was involved with Wilkes in the prosecutions and counterprosecutions of 1765, and became further notorious in 1775, when he incurred the wrath of Lord Chatham by publishing his speech of January 20, on a motion to withdraw the troops from Boston (*Parliamentary History,* 18:149–55).[15] Thomas Brand Hollis, who had helped the edition come into being, is an expected presence, as is "Rev. Archdeacon Blackbourne," who would soon describe its genesis in Thomas Hollis's devotion to Marvell. David Garrick, supreme actor of the day, was, as already mentioned, a friend and patron of Edward Thompson's. But he shares the list with the slippery and pugnacious Samuel Foote, also a noted actor, and the quarrels between them were common knowledge.

The "Hon. Mr. Erskine" who appears in the additional list of subscribers (inserted as a separate leaf?) was surely the future great barrister Thomas Erskine, son of the earl of Buchan and subject of my next chapter, who by 1776 had already attracted attention in London social circles and from Lord Chief Justice Mansfield, even though he had only matriculated from Cambridge with an M.A. (on the way to the bar) on January 13 of that year. Charles Manners, marquis of Granby, who would succeed to the dukedom in 1779, was an ardent, young, pro-American member of the House of Commons, who spoke against taxations and trade restrictions in 1775 (*Parliamentary History* 18:601–3). He was only twenty-one at the time, and nobody knew, when he joined the list of subscribers, that this early liberal enthusiasm would not continue. Horace Walpole remarked in his *Journal* that his speech was "a great disappointment to the Court" and that Lord Mansfield "had flattered himself he should govern Lord Granby" by way of family connections.[16]

But another celebrated name brings us back to the theoretical problem of what this list was supposed to represent, other than the capacity of its members to purchase expensive books. There is even a formal sign of the enigmatic, since the "Duke of G[rafton]" was the only person to claim procedural anonymity in a document whose very point is naming. Augustus Henry Fitzroy, second duke of Grafton, had been an ardent supporter of the Opposition to Bute in the 1760s and an ally of Lord Temple, and had visited Wilkes in the Tower. He was Rockingham's secretary of state in 1765, but when he himself was nominally in charge of the next ministry, he was denounced as weak and dissolute in Junius's *Letters* and Almon's *Political Register.* In June 1771 he accepted the office of lord privy seal in North's administration, from which he resigned in November 1775. Resignation, or threats of it, had marked his public career from the start, and his notorious affair with Nancy Parsons had depleted his authority. Was his half-anonymous presence in this list part of the same syndrome? Or was it, like that of Sir William Meredith's, possibly a belated act of penance?

Finally (though I have included only those persons whose importance at the time makes them traceable now), there is one name that seems completely out of place: that of "The Right Hon. Richard Rigby." Rigby was a client of the earl of Bedford, an energetic opponent of Wilkes, a great drinker, and "an unblushing placeman during the worst period of parliamentary corruption," according to the old *Dictionary of National Biography*. Walpole loathed him, and Disraeli gave him a second life as a corrupt politician in his novel *Coningsby*. It seems barely conceivable that Rigby admired Marvell, but perhaps he had no idea what the volumes actually contained.

I believe I have already discredited the stigmatic view of Thompson's Marvell edition and its subscribers that entered our systems of value with the work of Pierre Legouis. There is much more significance here than Legouis was willing to grant or was interested in discovering. The subscription list, a silent rather than a noisy demonstration of the power of names, offers us an elegant slice through the political and cultural history of the later eighteenth century. It rearranges categories that no longer inform and piques jaded intellectual appetites with the reminder that biography is, after all, the sign of the human. The edition appeared at a moment when the Whig Opposition was in serious disarray and when the cause of conciliation of the colonies was evidently lost. Its function, described by Thompson as gathering together the "strenuous" friends of the Constitution, was surely remedial and reconciliatory. Its implied argument was that "Revolution principles" had existed prior to the Revolution and could always be disinterred, provided that the men who at heart shared them could learn to submerge their other differences and competing interests. Those who had put their names up front were symbolically making such a commitment at a time when, to use the words of J. G. Nichols, "the revival of Marvell's principles and strictures" were "no less obnoxious to the Ruling Powers" than they would have been a decade earlier.

But there was one more name to reckon with, historically speaking. On the frontispiece of all three volumes Thompson reprinted the same nine lines from James Thomson's epic poem of the Walpole era, *Liberty:*

> By these three Virtues be the frame sustain'd,
> Of British Freedom; Independent Life,
> Integrity in Office; and o'er all
> Supreme, a Passion for the Common-Weal.
> Hail! Independence, hail! Heav'ns next best Gift,
> To that of Life and an immortal Soul!
> The Life of Life! that to the Banquet high
> And sober Meal gives Taste; to the bow'd Roof
> Fair-dream'd Repose, and to the Cottage Charms.

This passage derives from the fifth section of Thomson's poem, which was published serially, the last section, "The Prospect," being entered in the Stationers' Register on February 10, 1736. The publisher was Thomas Hollis's faithful Andrew Millar, the printer Henry Woodfall, who in 1769 would publish Junius's fatal letter to the king (no. 35) in his *Public Advertiser,* thereby unintentionally setting Lord Mansfield's trap for Almon. Today we do not think much of *Liberty* as poetry,[17] and even then, when the press was inflamed with pro- and anti-Walpole propaganda, Millar and Woodfall grievously overestimated the likely demand, such a high-minded and abstract poem not being found, perhaps, equal to its title.

But Captain Edward Thompson knew what he was doing in citing those lines from that other Thomson. He was connecting the problems of liberals in the reign of George II with those in the reign of George III. And thereby he connected, as James

Thomson had done in the previous generation, the problems of liberals in the reign of George II with those in the reign of Charles II:

> This wild delusive Cant; the rash Cabal
> Of hungry Courtiers, ravenous for Prey;
> The Bigot, restless in a double Chain
> To bind anew the Land; the constant Need
> Of finding Faithless Means, of shifting Forms,
> And flattering Senates, to supply his Waste;
>
> . . . .
>
> Nor on the Bench avow'd Corruption plac'd,
> And murderous Rage itself, in Jefferies' Form;
> Nor endless Acts of Arbitrary Power.
> Cruel, and false, could raise the Public Arm.
> Distrustful, scatter'd, of combining Chiefs
> Devoid, and dreading blind rapacious War.[18]

These accounts of Charles II's reign, both before and after Marvell's death, were pure Whig doctrine; they were also fairly accurate descriptions of the policies of George III, the behaviour of Lord Mansfield, and the failure to combine effectively the various branches of the Whigs in the later eighteenth century. The first six lines of this diatribe match exactly the tone of Marvell's personal letters to William Popple and his *Account of the Growth of Popery and Arbitrary Government.* The following seven lines constitute Whig or liberal doctrine as it developed after Marvell's death, with the fortuitous martyrdom of Algernon Sidney on the basis of an "unpublished page" (for which read *both* Sidney's *Discourses on Government* and Wilkes's privately printed *Essay on Woman*).

But this is all pretty pompous and not very amusing. If we really want to understand what Marvell meant to the later eighteenth century, we must include an updated version of his satire on Charles II, *Royal Resolutions,* the one foregrounded by Captain Edward Thompson in the preface to his new edition. In 1769, John Almon's *Political Register* published the following politically apt (and metrically correct) Georgian adaptation:

My grandfather reign'd like a silly old fool;
On a different system, my kingdom I'll rule,
By maxims I've learn'd in a very good school.

No parties of men shall have influence here
That they all are alike I would make it appear;
So—I'll have a new Ministry every year.

The Tories shall triumph, the Whigs shall repine,
For tho they brought hither the H-n-v-r line.
Being friends to Country—they cannot be mine.

. . . .

A Treas'rer I'll have, who will blindly agree,
Whatever his real opinion might be,
To carry all measures adopted by me.

If I knew of a statesman, wise, honest, and good,
From his friends I'd detach him as soon as I cou'd,
And if he stick to them—why God d-n his blood.

If I knew of a man ignominious and base,
Which had brought on himself and his Country disgrace,
I'd exalt him at once into power and place.

And when I have got all these men to my mind,
To my absolute pleasure completely resign'd,
How well I can govern my people shall find.

Such an army I'll have as this isle never saw,
To keep all those troublesome puppies in awe,
Who prate about liberty, justice, and law.

And there followed, prophetically, nine more stanzas on the troubles with the American colonies (2:99–102). It was in this oppositional way of thinking, I believe, that Captain Edward Thompson quoted James Thomson on the centrality of "Independence" in the ten commandments of political virtue—an idea no longer, as in Thomson, representative of ancient frugality and freedom from financial corruption,[19] but now, in its new context of 1776, a sign of what American freedom (and republicanism) could mean to the rest of the world.

5

The Two Snuffboxes

RECOVERING THE WHIG IN REYNOLDS

This chapter returns to art history and the portrait, by way of the career and reputation of Sir Joshua Reynolds. Like Edmund Burke, who was one of his friends and subjects, Reynolds made a major contribution to art theory and aesthetics. Unlike Burke, however, whose *Philosophical Enquiry into the Origin of Our Ideas of the Sublime and the Beautiful* recorded early enthusiasms, Reynolds's *Discourses on Art* were written at the height of his success, in relation to his presidency of the Royal Academy, and not published as a full set until Edmond Malone edited it as such in 1797. By that time Burke had moved from the liberal positions he maintained while Rockingham was alive to the conservative reaction against the French Revolution that remains, for many readers, definitive of his career. By claiming in his introduction that Reynolds had read Burke's *Reflections on the Revolution in France* in manuscript and enthusiastically endorsed it, Malone paved the way for one school of thought concerning Reynolds — that he was himself, at least by the 1790s, conservative in politics and, before then, at best apolitical. The *Discourses* themselves contained nothing to shake that view, since they argued for a lofty neoclassical style that strove for the general and the ideal and rigorously excluded the particular and the historically specific. Consequently, and very oddly, they contain no theory of the portrait, precisely the genre by which Reynolds had made his fortune. "An History-Painter," wrote Reynolds in the Fourth Discourse, "paints man in general; a Portrait-Painter, a particular man, and consequently a defective model."[1]

Thanks to the *Discourses,* to Malone's presentation of them, and to William Blake's outraged comment that "This Whole Book was Written to Serve Political Purposes,"[2] there has developed a modern consensus about Reynolds's conservativism that takes different forms, approving or disapproving, according to the persuasions of the critic. There was, however, an alternative tradition proposed in the late nineteenth century—that Reynolds was, for most of his life, the premier painter of the Whigs. This chapter will not only recover that alternative tradition, but reflect on what the competition between these two stories about Reynolds tells us about the history of art history and why the conservative tradition might seem to have carried the day.

It is important to realize that it was Malone's commentary, rather than anything in the *Discourses* themselves, that provoked William Blake's hostile reaction. In Malone's introductory account of Reynolds's life and writings, Reynolds, we are told, "has one claim to praise" which Malone thinks it his "particular duty to mention, because otherwise his merit in this respect might perhaps be unknown to future ages." Indeed, it might have remained unknown because otherwise unrecorded. This merit is the "rectitude of his judgement concerning those pernicious doctrines" driving the French Revolution, a judgement that Malone proceeds to describe with such revealing ferocity that it is worth our studying it again in most of its unbalanced entirety:

> Before the publication of Mr. Burke's *Discourses* on that subject, he had been favoured with a perusal of that incomparable work, and was lavish in his encomiums upon it. He was indeed never weary of expressing his admiration of the profound sagacity which saw, in their embryo state, all the evils with

which this country was threatened by that tremendous conclusion; he well knew how eagerly all the wild and erroneous principles of government attempted to be established by the pretended philosophers of France, would be cherished and enforced by those turbulent and unruly spirits among us, whom "no King could govern, nor no God could please"; and long before that book was written, frequently avowed his contempt of those "Adam-wits," who set at nought the accumulated wisdom of ages, and on all occasions are desirous of beginning the world anew. He did not live to see the accomplishment of almost every one of the predictions of the prophetick and philosophical work alluded to; happily for himself he did not live to participate of the gloom which now saddens every virtuous bosom, in consequence of all the civilized States of Europe being shaken to their foundations by those "troublers of the poor world's peace," whom Divine Providence has been pleased to make the scourge of human kind. Gloomy as our prospect is . . . and great as is the danger with which we are threatened, (I mean *internally,* for as to external violence, we are fully equal to any force which our assailants can bring against us,) I still cherish a hope that the cloud which hangs over us will be dispersed, and that we have *stamina* sufficiently strong to resist the pestilential contagion suspended in our atmosphere: and my confidence is founded on the good sense and firmness of my countrymen [who] . . . rather than suffer the smallest part of their inestimable Constitution to be changed, or any one of those detestable principles to take root in this soil, which our domestick and foreign enemies with such mischievous industry have endeavoured to propagate, will, I trust, risk every thing that is most dear to man. To be fully apprised of our danger, and to shew that we are resolved firmly to meet it, may prove our best security. If, however, at last we must fall, let us fall beneath the ruins of that fabrick, which has been erected by the wisdom and treasure of our ancestors, and which they generously cemented by their blood.[3]

It is not difficult to see through this prose; what Malone is describing are his own opinions and his own anti-Jacobin campaign, in which Reynolds has been enrolled posthumously and by hearsay.

The reference to "Adam-wits" is not, as it first appears, a quotation from Reynolds himself, nor from Pope, as the conventions of scholarship have continued to repeat,[4] but rather from John Dryden's political satire *Absalom and Achitophel*, published in 1681 as a weapon against Shaftesbury and the Whigs at the time of the Exclusion Crisis — a literary choice that reveals much about Edmond Malone but nothing about Reynolds. Malone filled out the "following lines of the same great Poet" without identifying him but so as to raise Blake's political suspicions along with his artist's hackles:

> These Adam-wits, too fortunately free,
> Began to dream they wanted liberty;
> And when no rule, no precedent was found
> Of men, by laws less circumscribed and bound,
> They led their wild desires to woods and caves,
> And thought that all but savages were slaves.[5]

"How justly," noted Malone, "may we apply" these lines to "those demagogues among us, who since the era above mentioned, have not only on all occasions gratuitously pleaded the cause of the enemies of their country with the zeal of fee'd advocates, but by every other mode incessantly endeavoured to debase and assimilate this *free* and *happy* country to the model of the *ferocious* and *enslaved* Republick of France!" (ciii; italics original). Reynolds may in old age have been converted by the French Revolution to Burke's reactionary position, though there is only the slightest of evidence outside of Malone's assertion to support such a view;[6] he would never have used such incendiary language.

The long-term offspring of the Malone-Blake polarities became visible in 1986, the year in which the Royal Academy staged a Reynolds retrospective. The exhibition catalogue by Nicholas Penny opens with an essay entitled "An Ambitious Man: The Career and the Achievement of Sir Joshua Reynolds" representing the artist as someone whose economic and social ambitions had always governed his practice as a painter; that is to say, interest took the place of principle. While Penny does not explicitly approve of this scenario, he seems to suggest that financial success was its own validation, a very 1980s position.[7] In the same year, however, there appeared John Barrell's provocative study *The Political Theory of Painting from Reynolds to Hazlitt*.[8] Barrell, who has already established a reputation for introducing a left-wing socioeconomic perspective on English landscape painting, takes up the subject of Reynolds's *Discourses* in the spirit of William Blake. Barrell teases out of the *Discourses*, especially the seventh, which deals with the superiority of custom to innovation, a reactionary theory of art's relation to the state. The seventh discourse, delivered in the Royal Academy on December 10, 1776, constitutes, according to Barrell, a negative reaction to the American Declaration of Independence in July and to the three London editions of Thomas Paine's *Common Sense* published by John Almon in that year. The seventh discourse, Barrell suggests, *already* anticipated Burke's *Reflections on the Revolution in France.* Thus its ostensible subject, the cultivation of national aesthetic taste, was really the veil for political conservatism: "Whoever would reform a nation, supposing a bad taste to prevail in it, will not accomplish his purpose by going directly against the stream of their prejudices. Men's minds must be prepared to receive what is new to them. Reformation is a work of time. A national taste, however wrong it may be, cannot be totally changed at once; we must yield a little to the prepossession which has taken hold on the mind, and we may then bring people to adopt what would offend them, if endeavoured to be introduced by violence."[9]

Barrell applied the same interpretive system to Reynolds's *Ironical Discourse,* which, as written in 1791, did indeed follow his reading in manuscript of Burke's *Reflections:* "Destroy every trace that remains of ancient taste. Let us pull the whole fabric down at once, root it up even to its foundation. Let us begin the art again upon this solid ground of nature and of reason. The world will then see what naked art is, in its uneducated, unprejudiced, unadulterated state."[10] Certainly Reynolds here articulated a dislike of radical innovation within his own discipline. But however neat may be the semantic fit between these statements and Burke's appeal to national custom and prejudice, it is doubtful whether they were intended to be read as politics encoded.

Although he engages in a brief discussion of the possible meanings of "political" in late-eighteenth-century England, Barrell does not distinguish between the kind of historically specific politics involved in pro- and anti-Jacobin debate or legislation and the far more diffused politics implied by his own commitment to class analysis and economics. Only at the end of his study, and even then obliquely, are these commitments on display, when he refers to the scandal provoked by David

Solkin's catalogue of the exhibition of Richard Wilson at the Tate Gallery in 1982 — the fuss caused by Solkin's modest suggestion, immediately denounced in the Tory *Daily Telegraph*, that "it might help us to understand Wilson's classical landscapes if we place them in the context of the structure of social and economic relations" in the eighteenth century.[11] Thus, by the coincidences of exhibition and publishing history we can see, more clearly marked than usual by being focused on the same object, the ideological divide: between the Royal Academy and the then-dominant Thatcherian ideals, on the one hand, and, on the other, what were still recognisably Marxist aesthetics and sociology.

Solkin's own position, however, is subsequently revealed as quite different from Barrell's. In *Painting for Money: The Visual Arts and the Public Sphere in Eighteenth-Century England,* Solkin explains that he intends "to concentrate on those artists and writers about art who embraced the realities of a burgeoning market economy, instead of bemoaning its arrival as a sign of social and spiritual degeneration."[12] The result was an art-historical book that seemed to celebrate the new culture of politeness that he found, say, in Andrew Thornhill's group portrait *Andrew Quicke in Conversation with the 1st Earl of Godolphin, Joseph Addison, Sir Richard Steele, and the Artist,* circa 1711-12 (pp. 40-47). Solkin therefore contributes to one of the stories told about the eighteenth century, both during that century and today, that the old wars of belief and contesting principles were over. In our time, this story has declared that money and commercial interests generally replaced political ideology. Thus in the Thornhill portrait, the recognition that Quicke had just been elected to Parliament, that Godolphin was his patron, that the picture seems to represent "[a] quasi-official gathering, perhaps the signing of some sort of compact between the new MP and his sponsor," and even the uninterpreted letter that Addison is shown receiving and that marks an interruption, all are taken to show "what contemporary viewers would have taken for granted: that the ostensibly disinterested performance of civility served its primary purpose as a vehicle for the interplay of unmistakably interested motives" (p. 42). We are back with unmitigated Namierism.

But, Solkin continues, "it doesn't really matter" what the subjects are discussing. What counts is the levelling effect of the composition and the social practices it registers: "Whigs and Tories, landlords and literati, nobleman and commoners, all—like the members of Mr. Spectator's club—find themselves (literally) on the same level in an arena where established hierarchical and political divisions have been set aside to permit the creation of a horizontal unity based on cultural consensus. Here the bourgeois public sphere assumes the guise of an undifferentiated 'class of the polite'" (p. 43).

How far this new class and culture really pervaded England in the eighteenth century is, of course, itself a matter for ideological debate. This is not the world inhabited by John Wilkes or John Almon, and it can be posited only by deliberately excluding those very different visual representations of the period, in which placid and gentlemanly interiors are replaced by ugly and threatening street scenes, as in *The Burning of the "Crisis."* The deliberately harmonious arrangements of the Kit-Cat Club, which according to Solkin included "virtually every important Whig potentate of the period" (p. 28), seems itself out of harmony with the massively documented schisms in the Whig party, from Pulteney's defection to Bolingbroke's Patriot party to the war between Burke and Fox. In part the disparity is caused by chronology, since Solkin focuses on the era of George I, and I on that of George III. In part, however, it is and will always be a question of preference and perspective.

A New Whig Interpretation

How have these different views of the eighteenth century affected our understanding of the life and work of Sir Joshua Reynolds, the premier visual codifier of his age? This chapter will mediate between two interpretative traditions, one a strange blend of Malone, Penny, Solkin, and Barrell, which makes of Reynolds a conservative, not least because of his interest in maintaining a profitable business in social portraiture. The alternative tradition, which I am tempted to call "real" politics, is that Reynolds was a Whig, and that his friendships with the early Burke, with John Wilkes, with Charles James Fox, with Admiral Augustus Keppel, Lord Edgecumbe, the Molesworths, the Crewes, and with members of the Rockingham administration or various Whig Opposition groups did more than balance his friendship with the inveterate Tory Dr. Johnson. This tradition was established by Charles Leslie in his 1865 *Life and Times of Sir Joshua Reynolds,* a work completed by Tom Taylor. This two-volume biography was, unlike Malone's account of Reynolds, constructed on a documentary base: an exhaustive study of Reynolds's pocket and account books, from which could be extracted the lists of Reynolds's sitters, as well as his personal friends and dinner party companions. As a record it is well worth calling back into the center of discussion. It constitutes a remarkably detailed, year-by-year, political and cultural history of the late eighteenth century; and as a source of Reynolds's theory and practice of the *portrait* it is infinitely more valuable than the *Discourses.*

Both Leslie and Taylor agree that, although Reynolds "was from the first thrown among the Whigs" by his friendship with Keppel (1:125), his early success as a portraitist was marked by a remarkable catholicity of subjects. Taylor added to Leslie's account a vivid and comic sketch of Reynolds's clientage in 1764:

This was a period of vehement struggles in Parliament and strong excitement and unruliness out of doors. It was the year of the great Wilkes agitation and of the famous debate on the legality of general warrants so graphically described by Walpole; when the House sat on successive nights, eleven hours, seventeen hours, thirteen hours; when "votes were brought down in flannels and blankets, till the floor of the House looked like the Pool of Bethesda"; when the "patriotesses" of the anti-Bute party and the great ladies of the Court faction sat out those protracted fights night after night. . . . We find the leaders of these Amazonian cohorts, both on the Opposition and the Court side, among Reynolds's sitters for this year, or the year immediately preceding—the Duchess of Richmond, Lady Sandes, Lady Rockingham, and Mrs. Fitzroy, on the side of the Opposition; Lady Mary Coke and Lady Pembroke, on that of the Court. The case is the same with the leading men of the time. *The Leicester Fields painting-room was neutral ground, where as yet all parties might meet.* If Reynolds had planned his list of sitters for 1764 to illustrate the catholicity of his own popularity, he could hardly have chosen them better. To his painting-room comes the Minister who granted the general warrant, and the Chief Justice who received the freedom of the City as a tribute of grateful respect for his judgement declaring general warrants illegal, unconstitutional, and altogether void; . . . Shelburne, still holding office, but chafing against the collar, may here take counsel about the policy of resigning with Lord Holland. . . . [Y]oung Charles James Fox, just entered at Oxford,

can find time to sit to Reynolds between play and
politics. . . . Here, too, classes and callings cross each
other as oddly as opinions. The Archbishops of York
and Canterbury take the chair just vacated by Kitty
Fisher or Nelly O'Brien; and Mrs. Abingdon makes
her saucy curtsy to the painter as the august Chief
Justice bows himself in. (1:225–26; italics added)

The "great Wilkes agitation" here referred to was the political uproar described in Chapter 1, initially caused by *North
Briton*, no. 45, and the various attempts to prosecute or crimi-
nalize Wilkes that followed. On April 25, the "Minister who
granted the general warrant" was Lord Halifax, secretary of
state, and the "Chief Justice who received the freedom of the
City" was Charles Pratt, who first issued a writ of habeas corpus for Wilkes and then, when he appeared before the Court of
Common Pleas on May 6, ruled that Wilkes's arrest had been an
infringement of parliamentary privilege. The issue of the legality
of general warrants thereby became a major constitutional issue,
to be debated in February 1764 in what Horace Walpole thought
the longest sitting ever of the Commons (the moment described
by Taylor).[13]

And, most important, it was Joshua Reynolds who was
promptly commissioned to paint Pratt, as the legal hero of the
hour, by the mayor and corporation of the city of London, and
the portrait was hung in the Guildhall on February 22, 1764
(Figure 10). This was clearly a moment when the portrait painter
and the history painter, despite the breach between them that
Reynolds raised in the *Discourses,* necessarily converged. Pratt
would thereafter be raised to the peerage as Baron Camden by
Rockingham and become a staunch constitutionalist in Parliament.

As the ironies of Taylor's sketch play themselves out, one

Figure 10. *Chief Justice Pratt*. By Sir Joshua Reynolds. February 1764. Courtesy of the London Guildhall.

begins to see the sticky webs of interest and negotiation, if not double-dealing, that encumbered the world through which Reynolds was trying to manoeuvre. It was particularly sardonic to cast Henry Fox, Lord Holland, as an expert on resignation. Beginning as a Whig under Walpole, he had sold out to the

Court party in 1755, and in 1762 was admitted to Bute's cabinet, in return for taking on the leadership of the Commons, where he committed himself to getting the Peace of Paris approved, a feat he accomplished by a mixture of bribery and intimidation. When Fox sat to Reynolds in January 1764, he had recently turned on his Whig friends, claimed his reward—his title as Baron Holland—and retired from active parliamentary duty. Shelburne, or William Petty (born Fitzmaurice), later first marquess of Lansdowne, was moving in the opposite direction. He had been used by Bute as a negotiator and in the Grenville ministry became a member of the Privy Council, in charge of the Board of Trade; but in September 1763 he attached himself to Pitt and joined the ranks of the Whig Opposition. When the Grenville ministry proposed a resolution in the Commons "That Privilege of Parliament does not extend to the case of writing, and publishing seditious Libels," Shelburne spoke *against* the resolution in the important debate in the Lords on November 29 and was promptly dismissed from his government position. Soon he would become secretary of state in Pitt's administration and an ardent opponent of the war with America.

Those great ladies of colorful reputation Kitty Fisher and Nelly O'Brien, presented here in salacious contact (a still warm seat) with the leaders of the Established Church (Thomas Secker, archbishop of Canterbury, and Robert Drummond, archbishop of York) are another story.[14] Reynolds's remarkable portraits of these famous courtesans are also in conflict with the high moral tone of the *Discourses* and suggest that the sexual hypocrisy of Reynolds's society was as visible to him as was the political chicanery. Everybody who was anybody had a mistress and kept her in plain view. When the decision to expel Wilkes from his Middlesex seat was being worked out behind closed doors on April 25, 1768, on the grounds that the *Essay on Woman* he had printed for private use was an obscene libel, with Grafton

Figure 11. *Lord Bute with His Secretary, Mr. Jenkinson.* By Sir Joshua Reynolds. 1763. Private collection.

following George III's instructions, both king and minister were fully aware that a few days earlier, on April 16, Grafton had publicly escorted his mistress Nancy Parsons to the Opera House, where his wife was also in the audience.[15] The point of Tom Taylor's sketch, however, was less to satirize Georgian values

than to establish an early plateau of wide social acceptance for Reynolds, the moment of his being at the center of the picture, which would be altered considerably by the events of the 1770s.

Reynolds's own relation to the Wilkes affair was, to put it mildly, complex. One could read it as casual or intense, bipartisan or double-dealing, merely professional or strangely prophetic. Reynolds had painted Bute with his undersecretary, Jenkinson, only weeks before his resignation on April 8, 1763. George III paid for the portrait (Figure 11). Beyond assimilating it to Reynolds's supposed ambition to become a court painter,[16] modern criticism of Reynolds has seen nothing odd about this portrait. Yet one of the papers Bute is shown receiving from his undersecretary in the treasury is ostentatiously dated 1763, a date famous in Whig history because of the Wilkes crisis. This historical marker would certainly have become ironic after the resignation, but even more so after 1765, when the friction between Grenville and Bute so irritated George III that it led to the Rockingham ministry. And whatever its intended meaning when the portrait was painted, that sign of the historically specific was inconsistent with Reynolds's theory, as later formalized in the *Discourses*. "Present time and future may be considered as rivals," Reynolds would write in December 1771, "and he who solicits the one must expect to be discountenanced by the other."[17]

As far as Wilkes himself was concerned, his appearance in the documentary record of Reynolds' pocket books is odd and rendered stranger by Taylor's reactions. From August 5, 1764, Wilkes was an outlaw, having refused to appear before the King's Bench on charges of sedition and obscenity. Nevertheless, Taylor found a record of a private dinner between Wilkes and Reynolds in September, "which it is impossible to account for, except by supposing that daring agitator to have paid a flying visit to London *sub rosa*" (1:237). This vaguely criminal subtext of private dinners with Wilkes, who was believed to be in exile in France, continues through 1765 (1:250) and 1766, when Taylor discovered "not fewer than seven engagements to Wilkes, either for dinner *or the evening*" (1:259; italics added), on January 13, February 2 and 22, March 11 and 21, August 28, and December 6.[18] While Taylor was in ideological approval of Reynolds's Whiggish allegiances, he was unhappy about having to present this evidence of what looked like conspiratorial behaviour in relation to such an embarrassingly radical and scofflaw figure as Wilkes. His language expresses psychic discomfort and confusion. Wilkes is "a conspicuous though sinister figure" in Reynolds's pocket book, "a frequent shifter of his addresses." In his discomfort, Taylor draws a word-portrait of Wilkes based, though he does not say so, on Hogarth's caricature of May 1763, and already discussed in Chapter 1. "The eyes have a portentous squint, the lips wear a Mephistophelic grin, and yet there is a charm in the acuteness and humour of the physiognomy, in spite of the uneasy, sidelong glancing look, as of one who fears pursuers" (1:258). Taylor's conclusion was that Reynolds's attraction to Wilkes "must have been personal, not political" (1:259); a face-saver that rather flies in the face of the evidence Taylor himself reluctantly reviewed. And since Rockingham himself had conveyed to Wilkes, through Burke, his aversion to "asking anything for him from the King at the same time that he is willing to do almost anything for him from his private pocket,"[19] Reynolds would surely have known that the last thing that Rockingham wanted was Wilkes's presence in London.

This same year, 1766, the Taylor *Life* noted the "impress of the Rockingham administration" on Reynolds's list of sitters: Lord Albemarle and Sir Charles Saunders, the dukes of Portland and Devonshire, General Conway, Edmund Burke, and Charles Wentworth, second marquess of Rockingham (1:253). Let us pause here and consider the reputation of that first Rockingham ministry, which has suffered from the same divided assessments as has Reynolds. As we saw in Chapter 1, the ministry was formed in July 1765 and returned in a single year to the status of a coalition Opposition; its one major achievement was the repeal of the Stamp Act in 1766. Consider first the unsympathetic assessment of the Rockingham group put forward by Paul Langford in 1973, *explicitly* with the intent of helping to dismantle "the Whig mythology of the nineteenth century."[20] For Langford, Rockingham was merely the nominal leader of a coalition (of the elderly "Old Whigs" and the young and inexperienced) that came into existence not through its own merits but as a result of court faction. He is described as a very poor speaker who owed much of his credibility to his Irish secretary (Burke) and his wife, and as "fundamentally an indolent, ineffectual, and only spasmodically interested politician" whose abilities were insufficient for his job (p. 246). Contrast this with the "Whig" view endorsed by Taylor's *Life*, where "the brilliant but brief administration of Lord Rockingham" (1:267) was only

Figure 12. *Lord Rockingham and His Secretary, Edmund Burke.* By Sir Joshua Reynolds. 1766. Courtesy of the Fitzwilliam Museum, University of Cambridge, U.K./Bridgeman Art Library.

the beginning of a long connection between Reynolds and the Rockingham Whigs, who though seldom in office constituted a principled Opposition during the long years when their "creed was both unpopular and unprofitable"; they were eventually to be rewarded by the equally brief administration of 1782, which in turn was cut short by the death of "its pure and disinterested chief" (2:353).

Reynolds painted Rockingham more than once, but the portrait that belongs to this early period, now in the Fitzwilliam Museum, Cambridge, is strikingly unfinished (Figure 12). What does it tell us of Reynolds's view of the matter? In the 1986 catalogue, David Manning appropriately places the double portrait in its genre (of administrators with their secretaries), especially with Titian's portrait of Georges d'Armagnac with his secretary

Figure 13. *Thomas Wentworth, 1st Earl of Strafford, with Sir Philip Mainwaring.* By Van Dyck. 1639–40. Courtesy of the National Portrait Gallery, London.

and Van Dyck's portrait (1639–40) of Thomas Wentworth, first earl of Strafford, with his secretary, Sir Philip Mainwaring, both of which Reynolds could have seen. Yet the effect of Reynolds's double portrait is very different from that of Van Dyck's, who at a crisis moment in Strafford's career chose to emphasize his iron man reputation (Figure 13). The unfolded document in Strafford's lap is presumably the cause of his grim expression, and Mainwaring leans forward in a posture of ready service, his eyes fixed expectantly on his master, pen awaiting instructions. In contrast, Reynolds's Rockingham sits at ease with a slight smile, one hand tucked into his coat, the other inviting the spectator to notice the slightly untidy pile of documents that constitutes the day's agenda. Burke, too, is holding a ghost of a pen, but his posture is far less deferential. Reynolds seems to be correcting the relationship, replacing master and servant with two men of equal intellectual stature and common goals. The composition has a subtle chiasmic structure, with Rockingham's folded left arm balanced by Burke's folded right one, and Rockingham's outstretched right hand directing our eye to Burke's pen. The chiasmic structure is repeated in the folds of the drapery round the column behind the figures. But Reynolds's new approach to the idea of the secretary must also have been shaped in deliberate contrast to the standing posture of Bute and *his* secretary, Jenkinson. A certain ease, a certain egalitarianism, seems aimed at. But why did Reynolds abandon this portrait, leaving Burke as little more than a sketch? Was he worried that the egalitarianism of the design would work to Rockingham's disadvantage?

Along with the orientalism of the drapery, the documents and the inkwell are the most finished elements of the *Rockingham*, suggesting that they were completed by an apprentice. Reynolds did finish other portraits of Rockingham, including a full-length one in Garter robes (*Reynolds*, p. 237). In May and June 1768, Rockingham sat to Reynolds again, but we do not know which picture was the product. On December 11, 1775 (a year for which Reynolds's list of sitters is missing), the duke of Richmond wrote to Rockingham: "I do not wonder at your not having sat for your Picture during this Bustling time. I know the ninety nine grains of Friendship are very strong. The one grain of Vanity will not do much, but if it arises from having one devoted Friend it is not ill founded."[21] Conceivably this refers to yet another aborted portrait; but Richmond's guess as to Rockingham's reasons for its incompletion are entirely creditable to him, suggesting that his first ministry may also have been too "bustling" a time to allow for personal vanity.

It would be excessive to follow Taylor's narrative of Whig

connections in all its detail from 1765 to 1782, the year which for him was its natural culmination. But certain points of emphasis need to be recorded. By 1767, Reynolds's reputation as "the Whig or Opposition painter" (1:274) must already "have been remarked at Court" and have become the principal cause of George III's dislike or distrust of Reynolds, emotions hidden for political reasons when the Royal Academy was founded and its president knighted, on April 21, 1769. In 1770 and 1771 there was a marked falling-off in the number of Reynolds's sitters, a decline attributed by Taylor partly to the growing success of Romney as a portraitist, partly to Reynolds's now clearly marked political affiliations. During this time a completed portrait of Burke was engraved for general distribution by James Watson on June 20, 1770, to capitalize on the publication of *Thoughts on the Causes of the Present Discontents* on April 23. Reynolds's portrait was thus distributed as support for Burke's great theoretical defence of the ideas of party, principle, and the Rockingham version of both. But Reynolds's sympathies by now evidently included radicals whom Burke deplored. In 1771 a new constitutional issue (already described in Chapter 1) had succeeded the challenges to the administration over general warrants—a struggle, led by John Almon the radical publisher and supported by the mayor, Brass Crosby, and by Alderman Oliver, for the right to publish parliamentary proceedings. Now it was Parliament restricting the press and the public's access to crucial information. When the printers of the London papers were ordered to the bar of the House of Commons for reporting the debates, Crosby and Oliver discharged the printers from arrest under the speaker's warrant and were accordingly themselves dispatched to the Tower. "It was the lawyers," Taylor reported, "whom Sir Joshua visited, entertained and painted—Glynne, and Lee, and Dunning—who moved for the Habeas Corpora of the imprisoned Aldermen. . . . It was Alderman Wilkes, his old friend, who took the leading place in the civic councils while the Lord Mayor was in the Tower, and helped to swear in the grand jury who found true bills against the messengers of the House of Commons for arresting the printers on the Speaker's warrant" (1:378–80). No wonder, Taylor concluded, that Reynolds had to *negotiate* permission to paint the portraits of George III and Queen Caroline as a condition of his accepting the presidency of the Academy.

John Dunning, in particular, sat to Reynolds both before and after he had become a major speaker for the Opposition in the Commons. He sat in January and May 1768, in February 1772 (right after the scandal of the printers' case), in July 1773, and, as Lord Ashburton in the second Rockingham administration, in July 1783. In January 1770 he had spoken for the amendment to the address urging an inquiry "into the causes of the unhappy discontents," Burke's issue, and resigned his solicitor generalship; in October he was voted the freedom of the city of London for his support of their remonstrance and of constitutional safeguards. During the war with the American colonies he was a vehement opponent of ministerial policy. In September 1780, Reynolds was a guest of Dunning at his home in Dartmoor, just five months after Dunning had moved his famous resolution "that the influence of the crown . . . ought to be diminished." His portrait, now in the National Portrait Gallery, is a famous example of Reynolds's capacity (and willingness) to convey exceptional ugliness of feature when the sitter's reputation did not depend on appearances. But Reynolds's friendship with Dunning did not prevent him from *also* painting in 1781 the man who succeeded him as solicitor general, Lord Chancellor Edward Thurlow. Are we therefore forced to conclude, with Nicholas Penny, that the existence of this portrait (now at Longleat) "damages assumptions concerning the artist's close identification with Whig circles" (*Reynolds*, p. 298), on the grounds that Thurlow was "a consistently servile supporter of the crown, a steady advocate of war with the American colonies and an opponent of Burke and Fox"? This seems to me an unnecessarily defensive argument—defensive against the Whig interpretation, and out of touch with the painter's need to play out his span as the national portraitist, not to mention the 100 guineas Reynolds received as his fee. Legal subjects, too, seem to have interested him. He painted Lord Mansfield, supposedly, according to Mansfield, having long requested that the law lord should sit for him. The formidable confidence of the Thurlow portrait, finally, is itself a tribute to a great subject, to negative charisma; for if Thurlow was a blackguard, he was at least an interesting one. "Dark and daring," wrote Walpole, "he was fitted to serve a bold and arbitrary Court, rather than to please a designing but irresolute one; and as ready to betray it, when it tottered from its own misconducts."[22] Reynolds's painting and Walpole's word-portrait reciprocally confirm each other's assessment.

In the late 1770s and 1780s, Reynolds's commissions, like his dinner parties, were again politically polyglot. But the catholicity of his subjects should not mislead us. Several of the "whig" portraits of this period carried more ideological freight than ever. There was the portrait of Richard Grenville, Earl Temple, John Almon's patron and the man who had paid for all John Wilkes's legal fees; the portrait (no. 765 in the *Complete Catalogue*) is dated 1775–76 by Manning. There is the 1786 portrait of Thomas Erskine (*Complete Catalogue*, no. 586), the protagonist of our next chapter, painted to celebrate his epic battle with Lord Mansfield in the trial of the dean of St. Asaph, a portrait which balances that of Mansfield himself painted the previous year. In 1788, shortly before his death, Reynolds painted a highly celebrated portrait of Richard Brinsley Sheridan (*Complete Catalogue*, no. 1612), a representation designed to commemorate Sheridan's prowess as speaker in the House of Commons, not only on the Regency Bill of that year, but also, surely, on his two speeches in favour of the impeachment of Warren Hastings, the first of which was published in the *London Chronicle* for February 8, 1787, and the second of which was so eagerly expected that admission tickets were being sold at £50 apiece. Sheridan is supposed to be standing at a table in the Commons, gazing at his audience. Sheridan, like Temple, was vehemently pro-American and, though Reynolds would not live to witness it, a powerful defender of whig principles during the reactionary 1790s.

Another essential moment in the Whig account of Reynolds's career—essential in that it helps to establish Reynolds's deliberate involvement in political life and self-consciousness about its representation—was his response to the second court-martial, in February 1779, of his old friend Admiral Keppel. The court-martial was clearly seen as a trial of strength for the North administration and its policy towards the American colonies, especially since the Franco-American treaty of alliance of March of that year had given that policy wider international dimensions. The charges were that in July 1778, Keppel, after an indecisive engagement with a French fleet of Ushant, had allowed it to escape under cover of darkness; whereas in fact the blame lay with one of his subordinates, Sir Hugh Palliser. Keppel's initial attempt to shield Palliser led to a quarrel between them, and Palliser's charges led to Keppel's court-martial. The earl of Sandwich, the same man who had betrayed Wilkes in the matter of the *Essay on Woman* and who now as First Lord of the Admiralty had responsibility for the naval war with France, was intricately involved in the case, and the more paranoid suspected him of having used Palliser as an instrument to ruin Keppel's career. It is amusing to compare Horace Walpole's respectful tributes to Keppel with the surlier view of a modern biographer of Sandwich;[23] both are salient instances of how ideological bias smears the lenses through which we peer at the past.

"But what must the trial and its event have been to Reynolds?" asked Charles Leslie, in his part of the Whig *Life:* "The friends who surrounded Keppel, . . . the Dukes of Portland, Richmond and Bolton, the Marquises of Rockingham and Granby, the Earl of Effingham, Fox, Burke, and Sheridan— the Counsel who aided the Admiral with their advice, Dunning, Lee and Erskine—were, almost to a man, members of Sir Joshua's intimate circle" (1:230). We have met several of these men before—in the list of subscribers to Thompson's edition of Marvell. When Keppel was acquitted, there were huge demonstrations in London, showing that he, too, like Wilkes a decade earlier, had become a popular hero; and the next day, February 12, 1779, Reynolds wrote to Keppel a letter of intense congratulation, noting with apparent satisfaction that Lord North and Lord Bute both had their windows broken in the celebrations, and ending, "I have taken the liberty, without waiting for leave, to lend your picture to an engraver, to make a large print" (1:232–33). The portrait he referred to, significantly, was the heroic full-length portrait of 1752–53, painted on the occasion of Keppel's acquittal in his *first* court-martial, a painting which had been hanging in Reynolds's own house ever since.

Augustus Keppel was the grandson of one of the young Dutch courtiers who had accompanied William III to England in 1688. He and Reynolds had been friends since their introduction by Lord Edgecumbe in 1749, and Reynolds had sailed with him on a diplomatic mission to Algiers. When he returned to England, Reynolds completed this splendid portrait, now in the National Maritime Museum, which brought him immediate fame (Figure 14). Rather than being given to Keppel, however, the portrait apparently remained on display in Reynolds's house,

Figure 14. *Commodore Augustus Keppel*. By Sir Joshua Reynolds. 1752–53. Courtesy of the National Maritime Museum, Greenwich.

presumably as an advertisement for his bold new style. It shows Keppel striding forward on a rocky shore with a storm-tossed sea behind him and traces of wreckage in the water. According to James Northcote, Reynolds's student and first memoirist, the painting was intended to celebrate Keppel's legal triumph in the affair of the wreck of the Maidstone in 1747—the occasion when Keppel miscalculated the depth while chasing a French privateer and managed to wreck his own vessel. The heroism of his stance alluded, according to Northcote, to Keppel's fortitude and skill in saving the lives of his crew.

The *Keppel* had been previously engraved by Edward Fisher in November 1759, apparently on Reynolds's instructions.[24] But the second engraving, unmentioned in the 1986 catalogue, was inarguably made on Reynolds's instructions, as his letter to Keppel indicates. After his second acquittal, moreover, Keppel sat to Reynolds for a half-length portrait, of which several copies were made and given to his rescuers, Lee, Dunning, and Burke. Later, another copy was presented to Erskine, the barrister who had helped Keppel with his defence and whose own story will be told in the penultimate chapter of this book.[25] There could scarcely be stronger evidence that both Reynolds and Keppel understood the political function of portraiture—or, rather, that one of the functions of the portrait was to encapsulate ideological goals and values and to commemorate, in the struggle towards them, the merely temporary victories.

The last political portrait we need to consider in order to round out (and slightly modify) the Whig (or whig) interpretation is that of Charles James Fox, a painting exhibited in 1784 and now at Holkham Hall (Figures 15 and 16). As a representation of Fox, the man, there is at first sight nothing remarkable about it except, perhaps, its acknowledgement of his corpulence (only one of his coat buttons has any chance of closing). The meaning of the portrait, however, resides in the documents

Figure 15. *The Right Honourable Charles James Fox*. Engraved by John Jones after a portrait by Sir Joshua Reynolds. November 1784. Courtesy of the Yale Center for British Art, Paul Mellon Fund.

to which his right hand directs our attention. As Taylor tells it, Fox had been sitting to Reynolds just before the demise of the Coalition, an ill-judged mésalliance between himself and Lord North, who was previously, of course, his antagonist on the issue of the American Revolution. When Rockingham died,

Figure 16. *The Right Honourable Charles James Fox* (detail). Engraved by John Jones after a portrait by Sir Joshua Reynolds. November 1784. Courtesy of the Yale Center for British Art, Paul Mellon Collection.

the king's selection of Shelburne as prime minister had led, designedly, to Fox's resignation on the grounds that he could not serve in a ministry of which Shelburne was the head. When the Coalition defeated Shelburne's ministry in April 1783, Fox became foreign secretary, and he inadvisedly put the strength of the new ministry to the test by presenting in November a bill for the reform of the government of India. The East India Bill was interpreted as an attack on the royal prerogative and as tending to place control over Indian affairs in the hands of the Whig leadership. A magnificently effective cartoon by James Sayer displayed Fox as "Carlo Khan" riding an elephant with the features of Lord North, with Burke as the herald of the proposed new dispensation. On December 17 the bill was rejected, and the next day Fox and North were directed by George III to surrender their seals of office.[26] Reynolds's pocket book for 1783, when Fox must have sat for the portrait, is missing; but there is a strong likelihood that it was conceived as publicity for Fox's Indian affairs initiative while its success was still unknown and also, no doubt, as an antidote to the many caricatures of him that had circulated since his resignation. After the bill's defeat, its valence would inevitably have shifted towards the ironical register.

Taylor states that Fox had requested Reynolds to reproduce the India Bill on the table beside him, with his finger pointing to the title, and that after his defeat, Reynolds had "omitted the title of the Bill in his picture, in submission to the altered state of things." This reads like a faulty inference from the document that Taylor then himself produced—a letter from Fox to Reynolds dated only "Monday-night, St. James's Street," as follows:

> If is not too late to have one of the papers upon the table in my picture docketed "A Bill for the better regulating the Affairs of the E. I. Company, &c.," I should be very much obliged to you if you would get it done immediately. If my object in this were only a little vanity, I should not be so anxious about it; but as I have told many persons that it would be so, and as I intend it shall be so whenever the picture goes home, the omission of the Docket at the Exhibition, at this particular time, might be misconstrued into a desire of avoiding the public discussion upon a measure which will always be the pride of my life. This is the point upon which I am most anxious; but if another paper could be docketed "Representation

of the Commons to the King, March 15, 1784," it would be so much the better. I beg your pardon for troubling you upon these things, which may appear trifles, but which are not so, from the misconstructions that may be made. (*Life*, 2:429-30)

This extraordinary piece of evidence is rich with intimations of what role Fox intended the portrait to play in his political life, as well as with the hermeneutical issues that plague us when we try to read from the life into the portrait and from thence into the territory of motives now lost to us. Note particularly Fox's repeated emphasis upon possible "misconstruction" of the portrait should the defiant titles *not* be represented. This is equivalent to saying that the absence of topical allusion would be misconstrued as cowardice in defeat — or, to use Taylor's term, submission.

This letter does not unequivocally support Taylor's inference that there existed a prior agreement between Reynolds and Fox as to the presence of the East India Bill in the portrait, an agreement that Reynolds, "in submission to the altered state of things," had unilaterally decided to break. It sounds, rather, as though Fox only now, a few days before the exhibition in April and perhaps before voting began in the new election on April 1, had grasped the importance of flying this flag of defiance in public view. Instead of laying low, as in Taylor's hypothesis of Reynolds's motives, Fox wished to be seen in April 1783 as the honorable promoter of reform legislation for England's greatest colony; furthermore, he wanted to remind his viewers of the series of rearguard actions he had attempted in the Commons since Pitt's promotion to prime minister. On March 1, 1784, Fox had moved "for an address to the king to remove his ministers," which narrowly passed in the Commons by a majority of twelve votes; and on March 8 he moved "for a Representation to the king on the state of public affairs," another barely veiled no-confidence motion which passed the Commons by a majority of one! The bravado of this performance was remarkable. "It was better," he said, "to be a courtier in France than in England, for there the king's favour was the sole object; but here the courtier must play a double part; for he must also delude or enslave the House of Commons into obedience to the crown and its secret advisors." "This representation," concluded the nineteenth-century editor of Fox's collected speeches, "was the last effort made by Opposition. . . . [O]n the 24th March the parliament was prorogued, and the day following dissolved by proclamation." The *Representation* must have been sent up to the palace on March 15 and would probably have been the last straw.[27] When Fox gave his own *Last Instructions to the Painter,* requesting the permanent inscription of the representation on his own image, he was engaged in an act of extreme pictorial resistance. By May 17, Fox had been reelected for Westminster, but about 160 seats had been lost by the Whigs as a result of the Fox-North Coalition. Their majority in the Commons had been sacrificed to Fox's personal agenda. Nevertheless (or perhaps consequently), the portrait was exhibited at the Royal Academy as only "A portrait of a Gentleman"—a form of nondescription that better became the author of the *Discourses* than the agent or instrument of Fox's manifesto.

How does Reynolds's portrait of Fox read now that these facts are upon the table? A little melancholy, perhaps, a little slovenly, certainly neither defiant nor triumphant. The salient words requested by Fox were transcribed in paint so clearly that they are still legible on the original portrait and most of the copies. As Nicholas Penny observes, they were also exceptionally faithfully transcribed in the mezzotint of the painting made by John Jones, the artist responsible for the political cartoons in John Almon's *Political Register.* The print was published on November 1, 1784.

"The plate," Penny reports, "was quickly exhausted and others had to be engraved to meet the demand of Fox's fervent admirers." Later still, new states of the print were released, in 1792 and 1796, the first to accompany the final passage of Fox's Libel Act, the second in the aftermath of Fox's resistance to the Treasonable Practices Act, which, with its denial of the defence of good intentions, significantly undermined a central provision of Fox's legal reform.

To return, then, to Reynolds's *Discourses:* one way of explaining their massive inconsistency, not so much internally as with his practice, is to consider them a formal screen for that practice. If Taylor's speculations as to the cause of the temporary decline in the sheer number of Reynolds's clients in 1770 and 1771 have any merit, it is plausible to consider the tenor of the *Discourses* (especially, of course, the first, with its lavish compliments to George III) as a form of damage control. If so, the strategy seems to have worked, both at the time and in ours. Reynolds's clientage seems to have recovered much of its earlier catholicity, which in turn supported and shielded what one might call the late manifesto portraits: the Keppels, the Dunnings, the Fox, the Sheridan. And perhaps most tellingly, since we began with David Solkin's focus on Andrew Thornhill's group portrait of Quicke, Godolphin, Addison, and Steele—the new community of interested politeness that Solkin saw emerging in the early eighteenth century—we can round off the "whig" canon of Reynolds's work with the group portrait of John Dunning, Colonel Barré, and William, first marquess of Lansdowne, dated by Manning 1787–88 (*Complete Catalogue,* no. 543). By this time Reynolds was in his (supposedly conservative) sixties. The portrait of Dunning is posthumous; until his death in 1783, he had been resolute as ever in the parliamentary opposition, but the portrait, which shows him in his judge's robes, celebrates his past as a liberal lawyer. Colonel Isaac Barré, whom Reynolds had first painted in 1766, had spent a quarter of a century in the Commons as a fearsome Opposition orator hated by George III and feared by the Tory ministers, a passionate defender of the American colonies whose name, significantly linked with that of John Wilkes, survives in the Pennsylvania city of Wilkes-Barre. A few days after his arrival in the Commons in 1761 he furiously attacked Pitt—not the behaviour of your ordinarily ambitious newcomer. He had refused to join the first Rockingham ministry but was treasurer of the navy for the second one. By the time of this portrait he was blind—as perhaps we can tell from the portrait—but still standing erect as if, like Sheridan, at a table in the House of Commons, in the orator's position. William, first marquess of Lansdowne, is our old friend William Petty, Earl Shelburne, who had, after Rockingham's death been briefly prime minister but had held no power since 1783. Barré had been his paymaster general. The portrait was commissioned, in memoriam, perhaps, by the great merchant banker Francis Baring, himself a Whig in the House of Commons. Unlike those in the Thornhill group portrait, these men look neither at each other nor at the viewer. They gaze, if anywhere, into the past. In *this* group, the bonds that join these veteran warriors are those of political principles shared as far as possible, rather than social ideals of harmony and gentlemanly consensus.

The *Life* of Reynolds, as Leslie and Taylor reconstructed it, was avowedly based on "the principle *noscitur a sociis* [you know a man by his colleagues]" (2:308). So, too, was the counterargument, the one that modern scholarship has accepted. Much was made by Malone of Johnson's influence on Reynolds, and later biographers drew the conclusion that the only way Reynolds could have mediated the polar oppositions among his friends was by a charming objectivity and tolerance. Possibly he was both objective and tolerant; but the evidence, and even the inferences, mustered by Leslie and Taylor should not be allowed to disappear either in warm and fuzzy thinking or in new definitions of "politics" that are class-centered and unmoored from historical events. Boswell reported that Johnson in 1778 was displeased by the influence on Reynolds of Fox and Burke: "Reynolds is too much under Fox and Burke at present. He is always under some planet" (2:210).

One of the obvious difficulties in mediating between such conflicting interpretations is that Reynolds's personal statements on matters outside of the fine arts are in extremely short supply. His surviving correspondence is small for a man with literary ambitions, a mere handful of 161 letters, the majority concerned, unsurprisingly, with transactions about paintings; given the small size of the sample, the letters to Keppel and from Fox cited here must bear considerable weight. We might see them as atypical, or, conversely, as the tip of an iceberg that time has melted.

One tantalizing exception to the reticence of Reynolds's correspondence is a letter to Lord Hardwicke, dated March 5, 1783. Hardwicke had been earlier a member of the Rockingham administration, and in the letter Reynolds describes to him two proposals he has received for historical paintings.[28] The first, proposed by Hardwicke himself, was "the interview between the Duke of Monmouth and James 2nd," presumably at the moment when the Monmouth rebellion has failed and the young man is about to be executed. The second, suggested by Charles Townsend, chancellor of the exchequer in 1767, was "the interview of the Duke of Bedford and K. James," when James II, whose subjects are about to expel him in favor of William III, appeals for help to Bedford. History tells us that Bedford's response was to remind him that his own son, Lord William Russell, had been executed in 1683 as a rebel. Of course one cannot tell from Reynolds's brief description of these subjects where his own sympathies would have lain, with James II or his antagonists, but there is a strong inference, based on the inherent irony of the second scene, which then infects the first, that Reynolds was himself committed to the principles of the Glorious Revolution. An even more interventionist interpretation notes that the two scenes share the same theme: of mercy besought by Monmouth and denied by James, of mercy besought by the same James and denied by Bedford. The two portraits together would have suggested that a king who shows no mercy shall receive none.

When drawing their own inferences of Reynolds's Whiggism, Leslie and Taylor both used the phrase "must have" a little too often for comfort. But there is one piece of evidence from which they oddly failed to extract the juice it surely contains. In 1784, when Reynolds was sixty-one, he discovered in an auction room a miniature of John Milton by Samuel Cooper, dated 1653, signed with Cooper's initials and with a written memorandum on the back describing it as having been owned by Milton's daughter Deborah (2:440–41), and left at her death to the family of Sir William Davenant. This miniature became one of his most treasured possessions. Northcote remembered him as saying that it was "admirably painted, and with such a character of nature that [he was] sure it was a striking likeness," a statement magnificently out of tune with the *Discourses* (*Life*, 2:441). He defended its authenticity in a letter of June 1791 to the *Gentleman's Magazine;* and he left it in his will to William Mason (whose Whiggishness Dr. Johnson had deplored), as he also willed his Cooper miniature of Oliver Cromwell to Richard Burke, Jr. (2:636). These bequests tell their own story, one that must modestly qualify the standard view of Reynolds as the painter committed to caste, beauty, and Italian art.

The image of Sir Joshua Reynolds as the Whig painter was first attacked (though not explicitly) when, in 1900, Walter Armstrong published a magnificent volume of Reynolds's portraits incorporated into a new biography. Without stating that this was his objective, Armstrong reacted against the story told by Leslie and Taylor, which he had obviously read with some care. Raising the question of Reynolds's politics by way of his friendship with John Wilkes, and implicitly by way of Taylor's discomfort about the Wilkes connection, Armstrong took refuge in what we would now recognize as the high road of indifference: "I must confess that I can see nothing strange about it. . . . In my view, Sir Joshua was a man without deep-seated convictions of any kind. . . . He was essentially a spectator. . . . A righteous indignation was not among his emotions. It would never occur to him to shut his door in the face of the editor of the *North Briton,* or even of the author of the *Essay on Woman.*"[29] Significantly, Armstrong reprinted at full length Taylor's graphic account of Reynolds's painting room in 1754, with its tribute to Reynolds's capacity to capture as one a divided society; Armstrong ignored all the later evidence of Whig affinities. He took issue with the way Leslie and Taylor had processed James Northcote's evidence of Reynolds' taking wagers with his friends on the outcome of the war with the American colonies. Northcote had reported that Reynolds, who believed that the colonies would win the war, "actually received five guineas each from several gentlemen under a promise to pay them in return one thousand pounds if ever he painted the portrait of General Washington in England, and which he was not to refuse to do in case the General should be brought to him to that intent."[30] Leslie and Taylor had speculated as to how dispirited Reynolds "must have" felt in 1777 when "the tide of success seemed to be running strong and steadily for the mother-country" (*Life,* 2:190). Armstrong strongly rejected any such inference. "He had an opinion, and he backed it, as to which side had the best prospects of military success, but that gives us no right to assume that he wished for the defeat of the mother-country" (p. 100). This was to drain from the wager all coloring of Opposition policy during the war years. Armstrong's final assessment of Reynolds's political character was as follows: "Politically he was an opportunist, with a leaning towards the side of Burke and Fox determined by nothing more profound than those social predilections which had brought him acquainted with more Whigs than Tories" (p. 100). This deep condescension is hardly modified by Armstrong's suspicion that Reynolds, for all his reputation as an equable and unquarrelsome host, managed the conflicts in his circle less by true objectivity than by emotional coldness, an incapacity to feel things strongly.

One can still see the traces of this argument in Nicholas Penny's 1986 summary of Reynolds's career as essentially that of "An Ambitious Man." No doubt he was; no doubt he coveted social and financial success. But he also seemed to have kept alive a desire to be serviceable to certain causes and loyal to certain figures that, now as then, the academy finds it easy to sneer at. Fanny Burney, who entered the Reynolds circle shortly after the publication of *Evelina* in 1782, reported a telling anecdote, retold by Taylor for the year 1782, when Reynolds was nearing sixty: "She examines Sir Joshua's two famous snuffboxes, the one of gold, the other of tin, and wonders why he should use the vile and shabby tin one. 'Why,' he tells her, laughing, 'because I naturally love a little of the blackguard. Ay, and so do you, too, little as you look as if you did'" (*Life*, 2:385). The gold snuffbox, I suggest, represents the Reynolds of the *Discourses;* the tin snuffbox stands for his more democratic principles and sympathies.

6

Thomas Erskine

THE GREAT DEFENDER

Alas! poor ——— *

This witty testimonial to a dog in the opening pages of *Armata,*
a utopian romance which is also a tract on eighteenth-century
English politics, is a prophylactic against too much high-
mindedness. By playing on the eighteenth-century habit of
"concealing" famous names in typographically marked ellipses,
and ironizing the narrator who cannot remember the name of
the animal who saved him from drowning, Thomas Erskine,
animal-rights activist, recommends himself to us from the start.
I hope, therefore, not to be thought sentimental in reintroducing
one of the greatest liberal barristers in English history, most famous, perhaps, for his successful defence of Thomas Hardy and
John Horne Tooke in the Treason Trials of 1794. We have already met him twice, briefly: as counsel for the defence of John
Almon against the charge of personal libel against William Pitt
the Younger, in 1786; and as one of the subscribers to Captain
Edward Thompson's edition of the works of Andrew Marvell.
In many ways he is a perfect instance of the role of principle in
political life and its forward leverage in history, not least because
he frequently articulated principle's necessity and its dilemmas.
Moreover, he seems to be in danger of vanishing from the record,
his own name succumbing to the fate of "poor ———" the famous dog.

*Footnote: The name of this famous dog I have forgotten. — Thomas
Erskine, *Armata*

In the memoir written by James L. High for the 1876 edition of Erskine's speeches (privately printed for the Legal Classics Library), Erskine was described as "the greatest advocate as well as the first forensic orator who ever appeared in any age."[1] Large claims indeed, but Erskine's reputation did not spread very far into the future. There are only two modern biographies. The first, by Lloyd Stryker, was published in 1947, and although it tells its stories well and was eminently suited to reach a broad reading public, it has the scholarly disadvantage of a complete absence of footnotes, making its sources unrecoverable.[2] It also scants Erskine's last decade, which yields to a disproportionately long and intense account of the misfortunes of Queen Caroline, whom Erskine had defended against George IV. It barely mentions Erskine's spirited defence in the House of Lords against the new wave of reactionary legislation designed to outlaw popular protest in the second decade of the nineteenth century. We would not know from this biography that in late life Erskine had written *Armata*, the utopian fiction mentioned above, which was published in four editions in 1817–18. A second biography, briefer and only marginally more scholarly, was written by a solicitor of the British Supreme Court, John Hostettler, and published in 1996.[3] It covers almost all the major events and contributions of Erskine's long career, but so briefly as to leach all the color (and almost all of Erskine's potent and literary language) from the story. Hostettler ends his book, however, with the sonnet written by Samuel Taylor Coleridge to honor Erskine in the immediate wake of his triumphs against the government in the 1794 Treason Trials.

For the generally educated public, and even for scholars of the British eighteenth century, Erskine's name today has none of the conjuring value retained by that of Edmund Burke or Thomas Paine (whom Erskine also defended, unsuccessfully, at considerable risk to himself). This default illustrates a disciplinary chasm. Legal history today, in absolute contrast to the situation in the early modern period, is largely cut off from political history, and both are estranged from the so-called humanities. The subject of oratory was relegated to humanists as early as the sixteenth century and had a brief revival in the early twentieth century; it has now virtually disappeared from view. And insofar as the present academy occasionally recuperates the legal history of the past in the service of a particular cause, it is not usually the lawyers who are the focus, unless, like the notorious Judge Jeffreys, they are the villains in the case. Possibly legal arguments and case histories seem themselves too specialized a knowledge and hence intimidating for those outside law schools, though there are, as always, impressive exceptions.[4]

When writing or reading about Erskine, comparisons with Burke are inevitable. Erskine's genius, especially with language, resembled Burke's, but his career did not take an ideological about-turn in the English traumas caused by the French Revolution. Perhaps Erskine was luckier than Burke, in that he was a younger man when he came to confront the wave of national anti-Jacobinism of the 1790s. Perhaps he was simply braver, since he refused to accede to pressure from the Prince of Wales that he *not* accept the brief to defend Paine, and consequently he lost his position as the Prince's attorney general. Like Burke, because of his Opposition stance (which caused the government more humiliation and certainly more actual defeats in Westminster Hall than Burke's speeches in Parliament) he had to watch men of inferior talents being promoted in the legal hierarchy over his head. His elevation to Chancellor did not occur and his title was not granted until after Pitt's death in 1806, and the chancellorship lasted only a year. He certainly did not grow more conservative with age. As late as 1817, at the age of sixty-seven, he was fighting in the House of Lords against a new wave of reactionary legislation designed to counter labour riots, the so-called Gag Acts, which re-suspended habeas corpus and legislated against public meetings and lectures (57 Geo. III, c.3,7), and he also opposed the notorious Six Acts that followed the Peterloo Massacre in 1819–20. Not that Erskine, as we shall see, was perfect; but there is no "Erskine problem" in liberal historiography.

Moreover, Erskine understood the place of imperfection in an idealistic view of the world. In one of his many defences of the freedom of the press, in the case of *Rex v. John Stockdale,* Erskine declaimed: "It is the nature of everything that is great and useful, both in the animate and inanimate world, to be wild and irregular; and we must be contented to take them with the alloys which belong to them, or live without them. . . . Mighty rivers break down their banks in the winter, sweeping away to death the flocks which are fattened on the soil that they fertilize in the summer; the few may be saved by embankments from drowning; but the flocks must perish from hunger. . . . In like manner, liberty herself, the last and best gift of God to His creatures, must be taken just as she is; you might pare her down into bashful regularity, and shape her into a perfect model of severe, scrupulous law, but she would then be liberty no longer."[5] Where did Erskine learn oratory like this? In part, as we shall see, from Milton.

Born in Edinburgh at the exact midpoint of the century, in January 1750, the third son of the impoverished duke of Buchan, Erskine had some rank but no family money to climb with or to acquire a professional education. So with the financial assistance of Lord Mansfield, another Scot, he joined the navy as a midshipman at the age of fourteen and then transferred at eighteen to the army. He married at twenty and stayed happily married until his wife died late in life. While his regiment was in Minorca for two years, he apparently became an autodidact in literature, reading Shakespeare, Milton, Dryden, and Pope until they became part of his natural vocabulary. The old *Dictionary of National Biography* claimed that he knew both *Paradise Lost* and *Paradise Regained* by heart. And when his regiment returned to London, he used his knowledge of literature, his natural wit and charm, and no doubt his family connections to make his way into society. He became acquainted with Sir Joshua Reynolds and managed to impress even Dr. Johnson. But without money to purchase promotions, a career in the army would be slow and painful. Accident met talent and produced something better than fiction: "During the summer of 1774, while stationed at a country town where the assizes were being held, the 'lounging Lieutenant' chanced to stroll into court in the full uniform of the [Scots Royal]. Lord Mansfield, who was holding the assizes, noticing his uniform, was led to inquire who the young officer was. Upon learning that it was he whom he had aided in sending to sea ten years before, he invited him to a seat on the bench, explained the salient features of the case on trial, and showed him other gratifying marks of attention" (*Speeches*, 1:5–6). Erskine's intelligence impressed Mansfield, who invited him to dinner and encouraged him to think of entering the law. Their relationship would subsequently be complex. Unlike John Almon, who hated and feared Mansfield, and Horace Walpole, who hated and despised him for cowardice, Erskine, though he shared their whig values in general, saw Mansfield as a generous patron, a man of high intelligence, and a worthy antagonist. For in the arena of the theory of trial by jury, especially in cases of libel, antagonist he certainly was.

What followed being noticed by Mansfield and encouraged to enter the law was typical of Erskine's shrewdness and determination. In the spring of 1775, he entered Lincoln's Inn, and the next year matriculated at Cambridge, where his rank entitled him to an M.A. degree without examination. He managed to pay for his fees by the sale of his military commission. This cut his required term of legal study from five years to three, and in 1778 he was called to the bar, at the age of twenty-eight. Here, too, he would have had a slow and laborious rise had not Chance again conspired with brains and nerve to bring him sudden glorious publicity. Having been driven by rain into a friend's house, he happened to meet Captain Thomas Baillie, currently facing charges of libel against Lord Sandwich (the "Jemmy Twitcher" of the affair of John Wilkes and the *Essay on Woman* who at the time was First Lord of the Admiralty) for his management of Greenwich Hospital, the royal hospital for naval veterans. Baillie's supposed libel had consisted in his distributing a printed appeal, as lieutenant governor of the hospital, to its board of governors, complaining that the pensioners were being defrauded of their food, clothing, and other comforts by the management. The facts were not disputed. They had been complained of before. Strictly speaking, then, this was an instance of a whistle-blower who was being persecuted for his attempts to reform an institution.

Without at the time knowing Baillie's identity, Erskine attacked Sandwich's chicanery over the dinner table, and Baillie saw an opportunity to add a man with some naval experience to his band of defence lawyers. This was Erskine's first retainer, his debut in court, and another opportunity, as it turned out, to demonstrate his skills to Lord Mansfield. When the other four defence lawyers had spoken (the last, Hargrave, being a particularly slow speaker because of a urinary problem[6]), Mansfield declared that the rest of the defence should be postponed to the next day; thus Erskine, the junior counsel, had, as he subsequently remembered, the whole night to prepare his maiden speech, which was an intrepid attack on Sandwich. At one point Mansfield checked him by reminding him that Sandwich was not before the court. Erskine replied, "I know that he is not before the court, but for that very reason I will bring him before the court" (*Speeches,* 1:10). The charge of libel against Baillie was dismissed with costs. As Erskine tells us himself, with the egoism that became one of his signatures: "[I] succeeded quite to my own satisfaction, (sometimes the surest proof that you have satisfied others), and, as I marched along the hall, . . . the attorneys flocked around me with their retainers. I have since flourished, but I have always blessed God for the providential strangury of poor Hargrave" (*Speeches,* 1:9).

This debut greatly accelerated Erskine's rise to prominence. In the very next year he was retained by Admiral Augustus Keppel to assist him in his court-martial, the event that so concerned Sir Joshua Reynolds. The case was another struggle against Sandwich, who was suspected not only of putting Sir Hugh Palliser up to his false charge that Keppel had failed to issue the orders that might have brought about an English victory at the Battle of Ushant, but also of arranging for the logbooks of two of the ships to be doctored. This was, therefore, a test of Whig solidarity, and, as Stryker remarked, "all Whig London seemed to have coached down . . . to Portsmouth to jostle for seats" in the courtroom.[7] Watching the proceedings were the dukes of Richmond and Gloucester, Sir George Savile, Charles James Fox, and Edmund Burke. As the rules of a court-martial forbade a defendant's legal counsel from speaking, Erskine had in effect to ventriloquize the defence of Keppel by writing his speeches for him and advising him closely throughout. When Keppel was acquitted, riotous celebration took place in London, and a mob stormed Sandwich's official residence. Keppel rewarded Erskine with £1,000 in cash.

These were heady victories for a young barrister. They were both, moreover, popular, uncomplicated victories. Not so with his defence of Lord George Gordon in 1780 against a charge of high treason for having incited the riots that still, unfairly, bear his name. What rendered the Gordon trial more troublesome was that Lord George had become the leader of popular opposition to Sir George Savile's bill, passed in 1778, for withdrawing some of the penal laws against Roman Catholics. Gordon spearheaded a huge petitioning movement to repeal the new law. Petitioning had always been a strategy defended by popular reformers such as John Lilburne. In 1791 the American Bill of Rights would establish the right of the American people "peaceably to assemble, and to petition the Government for a redress of grievances." Thus one liberal principle, the extension of religious toleration, was pitted against another; and worse still, the man leading the petition of twenty thousand citizens was now charged with inciting a vicious rebellion.

The parliamentarians had panicked at the sight of the crowds milling around their doors and postponed acting upon the petition. The crowds, who had assembled originally in St. George's Fields, got out of Gordon's control; overnight they attacked Catholic churches and burned the house of Lord Mansfield. Mansfield did not recuse himself from the trial, a decision that *could* be interpreted as proof of his reputation for objectivity. He would be one of the four judges. John Dunning, who had received one of the celebratory portraits of Keppel after *that* trial, would here be one of the prosecution lawyers. Thus Erskine found himself with no clear body of supporters. He had to tread the delicate line between Catholic and Protestant sympathies and avoid dishonoring either the "wise regulations of our patriot ancestors" (*Speeches*, 1:105) who maintained the penal laws at the Revolution, or Sir George Savile and other sponsors of the bill for their repeal. He prudently refused to take a position on the merits of either, except to say that Savile's bill "passed with uncommon precipitation, . . . underwent no discussion, and . . . the heads of the church . . . were never consulted upon it" (1:107). But Erskine could properly claim that Gordon was being blamed for events that he did not intend or encourage. He deplored the practice of "judging from consequences instead of from causes and designs," and "the artful manner in which the Crown has endeavored to blend the petitioning in a body . . . with the melancholy crimes that followed" (1:152). These distinctions, as well as his opening attack on constructive treason (when, as he put it with elegant simplicity, the definition of treason "could be made at pleasure by the state to fit the fact that was to be tried"), saved Lord George's life.

This was Erskine's first jury trial; and though his respectful treatment of the jurors was undoubtedly one of the reasons for his success, he apparently had not yet formulated his (almost) absolute commitment to trial by common jury and his concern for the freedoms of speech and the press that made most of his subsequent cases into classic statements of these principles. The next of these landmark trials, Erskine's 1784 defence of William Shipley, the dean of St. Asaph, against the charge of publishing a seditious libel, enunciates these principles clearly. Because this was the trial designed by Erskine to build support for Fox's Libel Bill, which was first introduced in that same year (and hence directly connected to the concerns and campaigns of John Almon, whom Erskine would defend two years later), it deserves some detailed exposition, even though, in terms of political history, it was not nearly so significant as Erskine's handling of the Treason Trials of the 1790s.

The circumstances that led to this trial were intricate to a degree. Sir William Jones, Shipley's brother-in-law, had written and published a dialogue, *The Principles of Government*, intended to educate the public on the issue of parliamentary reform—that is, of the structures of parliamentary representation. The dialogue is between G. (a Gentleman) and F. (a Farmer), and it begins as a negative response by the Farmer to a request that he sign a petition for broader representation, negative only because "it is better for us farmers to mind our husbandry, and leave what we cannot comprehend to the King and Parliament" (*Speeches*, 1:159). The Gentleman explains the English Constitution on the analogy of the village club, as a voluntary association whose members have all agreed to a set of equal rules. Later he explains that the state is one great club, in which, however, citizens by no means have equal membership since "six men in seven have, like you, no votes." By the end of the dialogue Farmer has been converted to petitioner, saying, "Give me your pen. I never wrote my name, ill as it may be written, with greater eagerness" (1:163). But after the signature has been obtained, the Gentleman continues his political catechism, asking the Farmer, "[W]hat ought to be the consequence if the King alone were to insist on making laws, or on altering them at his will and pleasure?" The Farmer replies, "He, too, must be expelled." It was this excerpt from the exchange, and the reference to firelocks that eventually follows, that rendered this otherwise innocuous piece of public education an object of suspicion.

Not that the government as such took any notice of it. The objections were all at the level of local malice. Shipley had drawn the tract to the attention of the Flint branch of the Society for Constitutional Information with the hope of getting it translated into Welsh, but the plan was dropped. In January 1783, however, the local sheriff, a Tory, attacked Shipley for promoting the pamphlet. Shipley responded by having a few copies reprinted with a preface defending it, as follows: "If the doctrines which it slightly touches . . . be 'seditious, treasonable, and diabolical,' Lord Somers was an incendiary, Locke a traitor, and the Convention Parliament a Pandemonium" (*Speeches*, 1:157). The sheriff, Thomas Fitzmaurice, persuaded the grand jury of the county to hand down an indictment against Shipley for publishing a seditious libel. There were a series of delays and relocations of the case, involving Erskine in long and useless travel; it was finally heard in Shrewsbury in August 1784. It was perhaps Erskine's anger at the prosecutor for these tricks which caused him to make an unusual opening declaration, echoing and supporting in his own person the words of Shipley's defensive preface to the dialogue:

> Every sentiment contained in it, if the interpretations of words are to be settled, not according to fancy, but by the common rules of language, is to be found in the brightest pages of English literature, and in the most sacred volumes of English laws: if any one sentence from the beginning to the end of it be seditious or libellous, the Bill of Rights [of 1689] . . . was a seditious libel; the Revolution was a wicked rebellion; the existing government is a traitorous conspiracy against the hereditary monarchy of England; and our gracious Sovereign . . . is an usurper of the crowns of these kingdoms. . . . I desire to be considered the fellow criminal of the defendant, if by your verdict he should be found one, by publishing in advised speaking, which is substantially equal in guilt to the publication that he is accused of before you, my hearty approbation of every sentiment contained in this little book; promising here, in the face of the world, to publish them upon every suitable occasion amongst that part of the community within the reach of my precept, influence and example. If there be any more prosecutors of this denomination abroad among us, they know how to take advantage of these declarations. (1:167, 169)

Erskine was almost always extremely brave, but in this instance courage was combined with cleverness. Given this challenge, how many people who knew of the popular acquittals he had won for Baillie and Keppel would dare to pronounce this simple dialogue a seditious libel, knowing that the state would then be obliged to extend the punishment designed for Shipley to the famous young barrister? And at a time, moreover, when William Pitt the Younger was himself campaigning for parliamentary reform.

Erskine followed this personal manifesto by enunciating a series of principles: first, the liberty of the press (*Speeches*, 1:169); second, that the jury could not be restricted to finding only on the fact of publication (1:183); third, that "the subject has a right to petition for what he thinks beneficial" (1:188); fourth (wielding as his authority Locke's *Two Treatises on Government*), that the tenor of the dialogue is purely speculative, "comprehending all the modes by which a government may be dissolved" (1:192); fifth, in direct denial of prosecutor Bearcroft's assertion that such topics were not fit for wide dissemination, that political education is the best political stabilizer. "'But,' says Mr. Bearcroft, again and again, 'are the multitude to be told all this?' I say as often on my part, yes. I say that nothing can preserve the government of this free and happy country . . . but its excellence and its wisdom being known . . . to the great body of the people, by disseminating among them the true principles on which it is established; which show them, that they are not the hewers of wood and drawers of water to men who avail themselves of their labor and industry; but that government is a trust proceeding from themselves; . . . that they are governed because they desire to be governed, and yield a voluntary obedience to the laws, because the laws protect them in the liberties they enjoy" (1:203–4). But towards the end of his speech he returned to the question of whether the jury had the right to decide whether the pamphlet was seditious, in addition to whether Shipley was responsible for its reprinting. Addressing the jurors themselves, he explained the legal paradox that Bearcroft, the prosecuting attorney, was attempting to maintain. (That it happened also to be the doctrine of Lord Mansfield should not be forgotten.) "[I]f you are only to find the fact of publishing, which is not even disputed, and the judge is to tell you, that the matter of libel being upon the record [i.e. in the indictment] he shall shut himself up in silence and give no opinion at all as to the libelous and seditious tendency of the paper, and yet shall nevertheless expect you to affix the epithet of guilty to the publication of a thing, the guilt of which you are forbid, and he refuses to examine, miserable indeed is the condition into which we are fallen!" (1:215). He explained to the jury that if they should be obedient to these instructions and vote Shipley guilty, then he, Erskine, would be prevented from moving for an arrest of judgement, since the word "guilty" had been pronounced. "Such is the way in which the liberties of Englishmen are by this new doctrine to be shuffled about from jury to court, without having any solid foundation to rest on. I call this the effect of new doctrines, because I do not find them supported by that current of ancient precedents which constitutes English law" (1:215–16).

In fact, as Erskine well knew, earlier history had provided far more precedents for the state's determination as to what constituted seditious libel than the opposite; and he then proceeded to argue both sides of the coin by giving a mini-history of legal practice under the Stuarts as an awful warning of where this new-old doctrine could lead. One famous whig case of which he reminded his audience was that of William Penn and Joseph Mead, two Quakers who in 1670 were indicted for seditious preaching:

> The Recorder of London . . . told the jury that they had nothing to do but to find whether the defendants had preached or not; for that, whether

the matter or the intention of their preaching were seditious, were questions of law and not of fact, which they were to keep to at their peril. The jury, after some debate, found Penn guilty of speaking to people in Gracechurch Street; and on the Recorder's telling them that they meant, no doubt, that he was speaking to a tumult of people there, he was informed by the foreman, that they allowed of no such words in their finding, but adhered to their former verdict. The Recorder refused to receive it, and desired them to withdraw, on which they again retired, and brought in a general verdict of acquittal; which the court considering as a contempt, set a fine of forty marks upon each of them and condemned them to lie in prison till it was paid. (*Speeches*, 1:220–21)

This led directly to the famous Bushel's case, whereby Edward Bushel refused to pay his fine, was imprisoned, and was issued a writ of habeas corpus which was granted in the Court of Common Pleas by Lord Chief Justice Vaughan, whose impressive decision, with its commonsense observation that this doctrine rendered the jury completely pointless, Erskine cited at length.

It is important to understand what Erskine was doing here. In fact, by the last quarter of the eighteenth century the doctrine that juries could determine matters of law as well as of fact—never very firmly established—had been eviscerated; as the editor of Erskine's speeches puts it, it "had been completely abandoned by all the profession except Mr. Erskine" (*Speeches*, 1:227).

John Almon had claimed that Mansfield was the originator of this reactionary move, but Erskine felt himself obliged to tell the jury that "Lord Mansfield was neither the original composer [of the new doctrines], nor the copier of them from these impure sources," despite the fact that they were imputed to him "in the libels of a few years past." This distinction neatly immunized Erskine from the famous *Letter Concerning Libels.* In delivering his charge to the jury, Mr. Justice Buller (who had been Erskine's own teacher at Lincoln's Inn) objected strenuously to Erskine's account of libel law, stating that "the question is so well settled that gentlemen should not agitate it again" (*Speeches,* 1:233). But Erskine's seminar in legal history had done its work. The jury promptly brought in a verdict of "Guilty only of publishing," thus echoing the jury in the case of *Rex v. Woodfall,* as Erskine was quick to point out (1:243). When Justice Buller attempted to bully the jury into dropping the word "only," Erskine insisted it be entered in the record. Erskine promptly moved in the Court of King's Bench to have the verdict set aside on the grounds of misdirection of the jury by the judge.

There is a slightly comic literary footnote to this phase. When declaring his reasons for refusing a new trial, Mansfield reviewed the history of libel cases in the reign of George II in order to show that Erskine had been overselective in his use of *Rex v. Woodfall.* One of the cases he mentioned, however, was the 1729 case in which the publisher of the *Craftsman* was acquitted on a libel charge, but not, or so Mansfield claimed, because the jury had decided on the criminality of the issue:

> I by accident (from memory only I speak now) rec-
> ollect one where the *Craftsman* was acquitted; and I
> recollect it from a famous, witty, and ingenious bal-
> lad that was made at the time by Mr. Pulteney; and
> though it is a ballad, I will cite the stanza I remem-
> ber from it, because it will show you the idea of the
> able men in opposition, and leaders of the popular
> party in those days. They had not an idea of assum-
> ing that the jury had a right to determine upon a

question of law, but they put it upon another and much better ground. The stanza I allude to is this:

For Sir Philip well knows
   That his innuendoes
Will serve him no longer
   In verse or in prose;
For twelve honest men have decided the cause,
Who are judges of fact, though not judges of laws.[8]

The scathing irony of the situation is that, in fact, Mansfield's memory had *not* served him (if we are not to suspect deliberate misquotation). In a pamphlet printed in 1754, the final couplet actually read: "For twelve honest men have decided the cause,/Who are judges alike of the facts, and the laws." In 1791, in his speech in the Commons supporting Fox's Libel Bill, Erskine himself produced the correct reading (*Speeches,* 4:449).

Erskine lost this stage of the duel between Mansfield and himself; later he explained that he never expected to win a new trial for Shipley but made the motion "from a fixed resolution to expose to public contempt the doctrines fastened on the public as law by Lord Chief Justice Mansfield, and to excite, if possible, the attentions of Parliament to so great an object of national freedom" (*Speeches,* 1:387). So much for his earlier diplomatic disclaimer that Mansfield was not the originator of these contemptible opinions! As far as Shipley was concerned, his conviction was removed by an arrest of judgement, and Mansfield himself agreed that the dialogue was not seditious. So honour was satisfied all round. Erskine, in the meantime, arranged for the speech he had delivered on November 15, immensely long as it was, to be published, in order to attract public attention to the libel bill which Charles James Fox was then preparing.[9] No doubt as part of the same publicity campaign and as a result of Erskine's new celebrity, his portrait was painted by Sir

Joshua Reynolds. As a new edition of the speech was appearing at the turn of 1785–86, so Erskine sat for Reynolds in January and February of the new year. And on May 6, 1786, there was also a print of the portrait engraved by John Jones (who had also engraved the 1784 manifesto portrait of Charles James Fox). Like the *Fox,* however, the portrait itself was exhibited merely as another "portrait of a gentleman," and was subsequently given to the Prince of Wales, who in 1783 had made Erskine attorney general to himself, a significant mark of approbation. The portrait remains in the Royal Collection (Figure 18).[10]

On June 1, 1792, Fox's Libel Act (32 Geo. III, c.60) was finally passed. Its first clause established that in any libel trial "where the king is a party, the jury may give a general verdict of guilty or not guilty, upon the whole matter . . . and shall not be required or directed by the judge . . . to find the defendant . . . guilty, merely on the proof of . . . publication." Thus the long struggle in which John Almon and Lord Camden had also enlisted themselves was finally resolved, in favor, surely we must admit, of the more progressive opinion.

But at the end of 1792, Erskine was not enjoying a triumph. On the contrary, he was facing perhaps the most difficult, thankless, and unprofitable task of his entire career. He was preparing to defend Thomas Paine, who was now himself safely in France, against the charge of seditious libel for having written the second part of the *Rights of Man.* Unusually for an eighteenth-century libel trial, it was now the author and not the publisher or distributor who was on trial, and there was not the slightest doubt about Paine's intentions in his book, nor any need to construe his meaning via innuendoes, since his challenges to the English Constitution and the social system were direct, outspoken, and absolute. One did not need to argue the implications of Paine's assertion that "[a]ll hereditary government is in its nature tyranny." The book had appeared at a moment when

COOL ARGUMENTS!!!

Figure 17. *Cool Arguments!!!: Thomas Erskine*. By Isaac Cruikshank. December 13, 1794. Courtesy of the Yale Center for British Art, Paul Mellon Collection.

Figure 18. *Lord Thomas Erskine.* By Sir Joshua Reynolds. 1786. The Royal Collection © 2001, Her Majesty Queen Elizabeth II.

English feeling against the French Revolution was at its height, having been enflamed by Edmund Burke's *Reflections*, written in 1790 when the changes in the French system seemed reasonably calm and auspicious, but with its dark prophecies seemingly vindicated by the violence in the interim. When it became known in London that Erskine would accept the brief for the defence, he was widely vilified in the press. As he remarked during the trial: "[T]he whole people of England, have been witnesses to the calumnious clamor, that, by every art, has been raised and kept up against me. . . . [D]ay after day my name and character have been the topics of injurious reflection. And for what? Only for not having shrunk from the discharge of a duty which no personal advantage recommended, and which a thousand difficulties repelled." But to refuse the case would have undermined the very principle of a free trial and the presumption of innocence until proved guilty. "From the moment that any advocate can be permitted to say that he will or will not stand between the Crown and the subject arraigned in the court where he daily sits to practice, from that moment the liberties of England are at an end" (*Speeches*, 1:474–75).

Erskine chose not to dispute any of the facts given in the information but to ground his case on the principle of the freedom of the press or, more precisely, on its nature and extent. He opened his defence with a ringing proposition:

> [T]hat every man, not intending to mislead, but seeking to enlighten others with what his own reason and conscience, however erroneously, have dictated to him as truth, may address himself to the universal reason of a whole nation, either upon the subject of governments in general, or upon that of our own particular country; that he may analyze the principles of its constitution, point out its errors and defects, examine and publish its corruptions, warn his fellow-citizens against their ruinous consequences, and exert his whole faculties in pointing out the most advantageous changes in establishments which he considers to be radically defective, or sliding from their object by abuse. All this every subject of this country has a right to do, if he con-

templates only what he thinks would be for its advantage, and but seeks to change the public mind by the conviction which flows from reasonings dictated by conscience. (*Speeches,* 1:479–80)

Erskine observed that Paine shared with the English nation the conviction that the rights of man are liberty, property, and security and that government is necessary to secure them; he merely believed that those rights were "better to be secured by a republican constitution" than by the current English one. Within that premise, he was, Erskine contended, just as law-abiding as the next man, and his book would be found, if read properly, "studiously and painfully to inculcate these great principles of government which [it] is charged to have been written to destroy" (*Speeches,* 1:482–83).

But the real heart of his defence was an argument crucial to my own and, like it, a commitment to the whig interpretation of history—"whig" here meant in the largest philosophical sense as someone who believes in progress. "Had it not been," Erskine continued, "for this unalienable right [the right to address the nation on the subject of its government] (thanks be to God and our fathers for establishing it!) how should we have had this constitution which we so loudly boast of?" And here comes his philosophy of political history: "If, in the march of the human mind, no man could have gone before the establishments of the time he lives in, how could our establishment, by reiterated changes, have become what it is? If no man had awakened the public mind to errors and abuses in our government, how could it have passed on from stage to stage, through reformation and revolution, so as to have arrived from barbarism to such a pitch of happiness and perfection, that the attorney-general considers it as a profanation to touch it further, or to look for any future amendment?" (*Speeches,* 1:483). The attorney general in question, Sir Archibald Macdonald, is then politely mocked: "In this manner power has reasoned in every age; government, in its own estimation, has been at all times a system of perfection; but a free press has examined and detected its errors, and the people have from time to time reformed them" (1:483–84). Thus Paine is identified not as a stirrer-up of sedition, but as one of those remarkable men who have "gone before . . . the time he lives in," that is to say, who thought the future, the then unthinkable.

The rest of Erskine's defence was a masterly juggling of great names from both sides of the political spectrum—Burke, Locke, Hume, Paley, Dr. Johnson, and, from the seventeenth century, Harrington and Milton. Of these, Burke and Milton are by far the most important. In Hume, Burke managed to find a paragraph in defence of freedom of the press, and he found another in Dr. Johnson, though a much more qualified one. Burke becomes simultaneously the antithesis of Paine and someone whose earlier publications, especially *Thoughts on the Causes of the Present Discontents*, propagated thoughts analogous, even identical, to Paine's; that is to say, he is shown to speak out of two sides of his mouth. Milton becomes the voice through which Erskine speaks most eloquently to his own time about the general issue of a free press. First, Burke—and here the strategy is dashing. Erskine needed to remind his audience, inside and outside the courtroom, that Paine did not volunteer his opinions unprovoked, but that both parts of the *Rights of Man* were written in answer to Burke's *Reflections*. This fact the attorney general had quietly suppressed. But Erskine did more than remind his audience—he created an astonishing analogy: "The just and awful principles of society are rarely brought forward but when they are insulted and denied, or abused in practice. Mr. Locke's *Essay on Government* we owe to Sir Robert Filmer, as we owe Mr. Paine's to Mr. Burke; indeed, between the arguments of

Filmer and Burke I see no essential difference, since it is not worth disputing whether a king exists by divine right or by indissoluble compact, if he exists whether we will or no" (*Speeches,* 1:519). To equate the new, reactionary Burke with the now indefensible Filmer, author of *Patriarcha,* was strong medicine, but Erskine strengthened the dose by commenting elegantly (and evasively) on Burke's change of direction:

> [P]leading, as I do, the cause of freedom of opinions, I shall not give offence by remarking that this great author has been thought to have changed some of his; and if Thomas Paine had not thought so, I should not now be addressing you, because the book which is my subject would never have been written. Who may be right and who in the wrong in the contention of doctrines, I have repeatedly disclaimed to be the question; I can only say that Mr. Paine may be right throughout, but that Mr. Burke cannot; Mr. Paine has been uniform in his opinions, but Mr. Burke has not; Mr. Burke can only be right in part; but, should Mr. Paine be even mistaken in the whole, still I am not removed from the principle of his defence. My defence has nothing to do with the rectitude of his doctrines. (*Speeches,* 1:498–99)

This was attack brilliantly disguised as respect, and worse was to follow. Having shown that Burke had shared with Paine exactly the same sentiments about the American Revolution, Erskine then accuses him of creating the climate of anti-French Revolution feeling. This panic, he claimed, would probably never have reached such a peak:

> [I]f it had not occurred to the celebrated person, whose name I must so often mention, voluntarily to

provoke the subject; a subject which, if dangerous to be discussed, he should not have led to the discussion of; for, surely, it is not to be endured that any private man shall publish a creed for a whole nation; shall tell us that we are not to think for ourselves—shall impose his own fetters upon the human mind—shall dogmatize at discretion—and yet that no man shall sit down to answer him without being guilty of a libel. I assert, that if it be a libel to mistake our constitution, to attempt the support of it by means that tend to destroy it, and to choose the most dangerous season for doing so, Mr. Burke is that libeler. (*Speeches*, 1:508)

Burke now discredited, Erskine introduces a normative figure, John Milton, with his mid-seventeenth-century plea for freedom of the press, *Areopagitica* (1644). Erskine's justification for introducing Milton is that resort to law cases is not useful in this trial, whose pretext has been raised to the level of a great principle, and "upon general subjects we must go to general writers." He therefore begins with Milton, one of those "whose works are classics in our language, taught in our schools, and repeatedly printed under the eye of government." The two possible objections against using this precedent are swiftly dealt with: "It may be said, indeed, he was a republican, but that would only prove that republicanism is not incompatible with virtue; it may be said too, that the work which I cite was written against previous licensing, which is not contended for to-day." This acknowledgement that the law was different now allowed Erskine to claim that licensing, whose lapse was universally seen as a social benefit, had actually been a less oppressive measure than current libel law in its application: for "if I present my book to a magistrate appointed by law, and he rejects it, I have only to forbear from the publication; . . . but, upon the argument of to-day, a man must print at his peril, without any guide to the principles of judgment, upon which his work may be afterwards prosecuted and condemned." Milton's arguments against the Licensing Act of 1643, Erskine therefore concluded, apply and "were meant to apply to every interruption to writing" which affects the freedom of the press and the public's access to debate (*Speeches*, 1:528-29). This is a point acknowledged much less frequently than it should be by those who today critique the *Areopagitica.*

And Erskine then proceeded to quote from *Areopagitica* at considerable length. First he mentioned Milton's visit to Galileo, imprisoned by the Inquisition "for not thinking in astronomy with the Franciscan and Dominican monks," a remark that allowed him to score another point about the march of the human mind, since a heliocentric system now stands "upon the foundation of mathematical truth . . . which but for Galileo we had never known" (*Speeches*, 1:531). (Here is a riposte to Butterfield's dislike of the "but for Luther" theory of history, which is at its weakest on the issue of scientific discovery.) Erskine then quoted Milton's appeal to the Long Parliament not to panic at the flood of publication that followed the abolition of the Star Chamber, but to see it as a welcome symptom of a new era:

> If it be desired to know the immediate cause of all this free writing and free speaking, there cannot be assigned a truer, than your own mild, and free, and humane government. It is the liberty, lords and commons, which your own valorous and happy counsels have purchased us; liberty, which is the nurse of all great wits. . . . Ye cannot make us now less capable, less knowing, less eagerly pursuing the truth, unless ye first make yourselves, that made us

so, less the lovers, less the founders of our true liberty. We can grow ignorant again, brutish, formal, and slavish, as you found us; but you then must first become that which ye cannot be—oppressive, arbitrary, and tyrannous—as they were from whom you have freed us. . . . Give me the liberty to know, to utter, and to argue freely according to conscience, above all liberties.[11] (*Speeches,* 1:532–33)

The ventriloquized first-person singular here has, as it had originally, the emotive force of personal witnessing, the sense that the speaker is willing to put his own beliefs on the line and take the consequences for them; and in his own peroration, Erskine would return to Milton's, making its applicability to Georgian England unavoidable. He also, however, proposed (and this was an extraordinarily daring move) that the free society Milton dreamed of, which was never permitted during the first revolution and was emphatically outlawed by the Restoration, might still come to pass in England—the current trial being one of its harbingers:

Gentleman, what Milton only saw in his mighty imagination, I see in fact; what he expected, but which never came to pass, I see now fulfilling; *methinks I see* this *noble and puissant nation, not degenerated* and *drooping to a fatal decay, but casting off the wrinkled skin of corruption* to put on again the vigor of her youth. And it is because others as well as myself see this, that we have all this uproar. France and its constitution are the mere pretences. It is because Britons begin to recollect the inheritance of their own constitution, left them by their ancestors; it is because they are awakened to the corruptions which

have fallen upon its most valuable parts, that for-
sooth the nation is in danger of being destroyed by
a single pamphlet. (*Speeches*, 1:567)

In this paragraph the italicized phrases are direct quotations
from *Areopagitica*;[12] but Erskine's rhetoric as a whole, from the
near-silent invocation of the ancient constitution (as distinct
from that of 1688–89) to the irony of the last clause, is Miltonic.
And Erskine closed *his* prophecy by mentioning the "exertions
for the public" of Fox, while those who had initiated such exertions (the younger Pitt, among others) not only deserted the
cause but created this false, hysterical alarm. It is they, not the
Presbyterians in the Long Parliament, who are now recognisable
as the "timorous and flocking birds . . . that love the twilight . . .
and in their envious gabble would prognosticate a year of sects
and schisms."[13] This was far more than literary polish. It was
unembarrassed utopianism, looking to the forward thinking of
the past to rebuke the reactionary present.

None of it had the slightest effect on the special jury, who
did not even do Erskine the courtesy of waiting for the attorney
general's reply to enter their verdict of guilty. Not that this mat-
tered to Paine, who was safely and defiantly in France. It would
be comforting, therefore, to end this chapter with Erskine's successful and far more important defence of Thomas Hardy and
John Horne Tooke in the Treason Trials of 1794, since those men
were in serious danger of execution. Alas, the argument of *Nobody's Perfect* instead requires us to confront Erskine's dreadful
lapse in the 1797 trial of Thomas Williams, an obscure bookseller who had been apprehended distributing Paine's *Age of
Reason*. Erskine was retained as the prosecutor by the Society
for the Suppression of Vice and Immorality, and not only did
he accept the brief, he proceeded to have the case tried in the
Court of King's Bench before not a common London jury but a

special one, arguing quite unpersuasively that the case required unusual treatment. Why would he thus abandon his often stated commitment to the common jury, whether grand or petit, as one of the bulwarks of English liberties? And, as Stryker marked more of the contradictions, "Erskine . . . was now prosecuting the seller of a book whose author he had formerly defended, and was opposed by one [Stewart Kyd, a co-defendant in the Treason Trials] whose life he had once saved." [14] At this point Erskine's modern admirers quickly become his apologists. James High, the editor of the *Speeches,* claimed that "whatever inconsistencies are manifest . . . may perhaps be reconciled by considering [the Paine trial] as the effort of an advocate, bound to use his best endeavour in behalf of his client, while the latter expresses his views as a man" (*Speeches,* 1:571). Stryker himself declared that Erskine had no relish for the task, "but such was his true zeal for the Christian faith that, little as he liked the work, he threw himself with his accustomed fervor into the case. It was the *Age of Reason* rather than the indicted Williams whom he prosecuted" (p. 357).

I fear, however, that there may have been other motives. Erskine was probably still resentful of having lost his post as attorney general to the Prince of Wales (he had mentioned it in his defence of John Horne Tooke in November 1794), and he may very well have been angry with Paine for creating such trouble from the immunity of voluntary exile. [15] He was certainly self-conscious that the charge of inconsistency, or worse, would be made against him and began with a defiant defence of himself: "I shall not be found today to express a sentiment, or to utter an expression, inconsistent with those valuable principles for which I have uniformly contended in the defence of others. Nothing that I have ever said, either professionally or personally, for the liberty of the press, do I mean to-day to contradict or counteract" (*Speeches,* 1:573). The strategy on which Erskine had to fall back, however, was to adopt the wriggler's position: that "this freedom, like every other, must be limited to be enjoyed, and . . . may be defeated by its abuse" (1:573–74). The abuse, he argued, consisted both in the virulence of Paine's attack on Christianity (he had failed to observe "common decorum") and in the attack itself, since in England "the Christian religion is the very foundation of the law of the land" and hence underpins the trial then in process, not only with its oaths but with its sanctions.

Like Milton's, Erskine's idea of freedom of speech had its exceptions. Milton had written into *Areopagitica* an escape clause, "I mean not tolerated popery and open superstition . . . [nor] that also which is impious or evil absolutely against faith or maners,"[16] thereby giving modern readers an excuse to discount his larger ideals.[17] And now Milton was dragged into *this* case, not as the author of *Areopagitica* but as the author of *Paradise Lost*, to testify to the compatibility of faith and reason. The results of Milton's inquiry into "the ways of God to man," wrote Erskine, were very different from Paine's: "The mysterious incarnation of our blessed Saviour, which [Paine] blasphemes in words so wholly unfit for the mouth of a Christian, or for the ear of a court of justice, that I dare not, and will not, give them utterance, Milton made the grand conclusion of his *Paradise Lost*, the rest from his finished labors, and the ultimate home, expectation and glory of the world" (1:586–87). And then he quoted seventeen lines of the archangel Michael's prophecy (book 12, ll. 368–71, 575–87) of the birth and ultimate kingdom of Christ as an example of the way, over time, men, "though divided by distant ages, and by clashing opinions," were yet capable of "joining as it were in one sublime chorus, to celebrate the truths of Christianity." Erskine would have been horrified to learn of the discovery of Milton's heterodox treatise, *De Doctrina Christiana*, discovered in manuscript in 1823, the year of Erskine's death.

By modern liberal standards of judgement, Erskine made a big mistake in citing public order as the rationale for an established religion. While he could not deny the propriety of enlightened discussions of theology and conceded that we might all become Deists eventually (*Speeches,* 1:590), he strongly implied that such discussions should be withheld from the general public. Why? Because it was essential that England remain a Christian nation: "The religious and moral sense of the people of Great Britain is the anchor, which alone can hold the vessel of the state amidst the storms which agitate the world; and if the mass of the people were debauched from the principles of religion . . . I would retire to the uttermost corners of the earth, to avoid their agitation" (1:591).

So Erskine bracketed all the superb statements he had made in defence of Shipley and Paine and of the public's right to education. He would not admit the equally Miltonic argument that the general public might learn critical thinking from Paine's desire to shock in the *Age of Reason* and reject it for themselves. The melodramatic story told by Stryker of how Erskine met the impoverished Williams (who was inevitably convicted) and his smallpox-ridden children, how he was filled with remorse and appealed to the Society for the Suppression of Vice for leniency, how when the society ignored his advice he returned the retainer and dropped the case—all this rather underlines than mitigates the temporary collapse of his principles. And if self-interest were an ingredient, the prosecution of Williams worked; shortly afterwards the Prince of Wales sent for Erskine and appointed him to the newly revived office of chancellor to himself. Meanwhile, Erskine's speech for the prosecution of Williams was published, in 1797, in three separate editions.

There was still a long way to go in whig and liberal thought before there could be enunciated, in 1929 and in another country, the *unlimited* principle of "freedom for the thought that we hate." That principle was enunciated by Justice Oliver Wendell Holmes in *Schwimmer v. United States*.[18] Meanwhile, Erskine would extend and complicate his public career by writing about England as if it were another country. In 1817 he published *Armata*, which qualifies as a utopian fiction only by the slenderest of devices: the premise of the traveller who, having sailed from New York in September 1814, was shipwrecked in a part of the world quite unknown—the island of Armata. Very little happens. Most of the first part consists of a conversation between the narrator and a distinguished citizen of Armata named Morven, who himself was shipwrecked there with his parents and personally saved by the famous dog with which this chapter began. During the conversation, the evolution of Armatan government, its recent international wars (with Hesperia/America and Capetia/France), and its current financial crises (largely caused by those wars) are described in terms that leave absolutely no doubt that it is England that is being so anatomized and criticized; both speakers, however, continue to insist that the problems of Armata have nothing to do with the far more enviable condition of England. In the second part of *Armata*, published as a sequel, the narrator acquires a new, younger guide, visits the capital city, observes the local customs (with a satirical perspective), and turns towards the end to a long discussion of what is wrong with the Armatan legal system, including the disintegration of libel law into virtual censorship. At this point the narrator observes that since his return to England, his perception of the value of Fox's Libel Law has been dramatically enhanced by seeing the sad state of a country that has not discovered that reform. The utopian perspective is thus complex— Armata itself, as England in the first decades of the nineteenth century, constitutes instead a dystopia. Yet the remedies which the narrator proposes to Morven in the first part for the crushing national debt and for the impoverishment of the people are

utopian in that they offer specific reforms—in taxation, in agri-
culture, in restricting the import of wool, in the treatment of
the poor. In particular, we might be struck with the still timely
quality of his recommendations for reducing the public's depen-
dence on welfare: "Humanity cannot pronounce that the poor
shall receive no alms when they can work, *if there be no work for
them*.[19]

Why take this route to communication? The author provokes
this question by heavily ironizing his own claim to be telling
a real history, describing a real place—which in a sense he is,
though the narrative, such as it is, is entirely fictional. He claims,
however, that had he written "a romance, and not a real history,
I must be a lunatic not to blazon it in the largest characters even
in the title-page of my work," since the only works that were
sure to sell those days were novels: "High reputation, indeed,
(a rare phenomenon!) with the aids of hot-pressed foolscap, a
broad margin and expensive engravings, may force a passage for
history through the libraries of the great, but *Novels* alone are the
books of universal sale. The only actual historians are the Editors of Newspapers, and bankruptcy would soon overtake even
their most favoured proprietors, if they were fettered in their
columns by truth" (p. 15). Therefore, so the ingenious argument
goes, since he is claiming to be writing that most unmarketable
of works, a true history, he must be telling the truth.

One obvious answer to the choice of method is that it gave
Erskine deniability, in case anyone in high places objected to
his account of recent Georgian political history. An alternative
answer is that the book, despite his disclaimer, would recommend itself to the readers of romances as unpalliated political
history never could. But without abandoning either of those two
possibilities, it seems likely that Erskine was also engaging in
a meditation on utopianism itself—its origins (especially in Sir
Thomas More's fictional island), its strategies (the typical con-

fusion or ironization of authorial perspective, as in Swift's *Gulliver's Travels*), and above all its governing premise, that there is such a thing as an ideal polity, to which the ones we have may approximate closely or distantly. The point of utopian (or dystopian) writing is to upset complacency, especially on this last conception.

That this was part of Erskine's thinking seems evident from *Armata's* opening paragraphs, which return us to a familiar cluster of persons and ideas:

> When Galileo discovered the phases of Venus through his telescope, he was cast into prison by the tribunal of the Inquisition. He was cast into prison, as Milton in his *Areopagitica* has well described it, only for differing in astronomy from the Franciscan and Dominican monks. Imperfect as the state of science was in the age of that great philosopher, it was nevertheless believed to be at its fullest maturity, and it has always been so considered, from Noah's flood to the present hour: the pride of man will scarcely enable him to accept the most manifest evidence of his senses, when brought into collison with the most manifest errors which time has sanctioned; and until ignorance shall be fairly pushed from her stool by the main force of truth, she will continue to sit staring like an idiot, worshipping the shapeless phantoms of her own blind creation. (pp. 1–2)

Thus Erskine enunciates a theory of progress in which scientific advance does not so much lead the way as provide the assurance that forward movement is both possible and necessary. To call this a rebuttal of Butterfield avant la lettre might be slightly overstating it; but when in part 2 the new tour guide describes his own failed attempt to introduce a bill for animal rights in both houses of the Armatan legislature, he not only speaks for Erskine's failed attempt in 1809, he adds a consolation for this and all other failed reforms: "The good seed has been sown, and, as often happens in the natural world, lies dormant for a future and perhaps not a distant harvest" (p. 35).

But to see how Erskine might, in his own way, be attempting a new whig interpretation of history in the aftermath of Hume's *History of England* and on a very different model from Catharine Macaulay's, we need to look more closely at the narrative itself. First, Morven describes an ancient history of resistance to arbitrary monarchy, followed by "a grand and glorious struggle to put an end to [it]" (the Revolution of 1688), which in turn was followed by an era of corruption, since the *"centrifugal force was lost"* (*Armata,* p. 42; italics original), an interesting theoretical tweak here being given to mainstream whig interpretation. Second, because the principle of the balance of power has long been departed from (p. 67), the remedy for constitutional drift is parliamentary reform. In proportion as Parliament is now effectively the ruling body, "they should be, *as far as can be made safely practicable,* in the choice and under the controul of the great body of your people" (p. 68; italics original). Third, he does not hesitate to attribute the problems in Armatan/English foreign policy to the influence of individuals; William Pitt the Younger, and Edmund Burke, both of whom, though of course not named, are clearly recognizable from the descriptions given of them. This is a brilliant, inverse development of the habit of "innuendoes" or elliptical naming that renders tiresome so much of eighteenth-century writing today. Thus Pitt is introduced as the son of "*another* man who had justly acquired a great reputation . . . by superior eloquence," who had risen "to so premature an eminence . . . by treading in his father's steps, pleading the cause of public reformation," but who "turned short round on a sudden, and not only renounced his former opinions, but sounded

the alarm when others persevered in sentiments they had im-
bibed from his own lips" (p. 94; italics original). Burke is, likewise, visible not only as the "warning voice" that had sounded
in the war with the American colonies (p. 97), but also as "the
trumpet of war" (p. 98) in relation to the French Revolution,
the Treason Trials in England, and the actual war with France
that followed. In fact, Erskine provided a summary of the central
constitutional arguments of Burke's *Reflections*, including actual
quotations or near quotations: "He set out by truly and perhaps
seasonably observing, 'that men were not the insects of a summer, . . . that they should therefore look upwards with pious
reverence to their fathers, and downwards with anxious care to
their posterity—that when they had accomplished a structure
sufficient to maintain social order . . . it was more convenient to
repair it when time had defaced it, . . . than to tumble it down
in a moment to its foundations'" (pp. 101-2). And through his
mouthpiece, Morven, he argued that Burke's *Reflections*, even
when their prophecies seemed fulfilled, were "only an exquisite
and in many parts a sublime exposure" of what had happened
in France, largely because England had earlier refused to help
her. In contrast, *Armata* expresses a surprising admiration for
Napoleon (pp. 107-14), whose major fault, it is claimed, was
in making himself an emperor rather than helping to free the
peoples of Europe from their "uncontrouled and justly incensed
kings" (p. 113). In so doing, he was no longer furthering but "opposing the progression of a world which, in spite of all obstacles,
will advance" (p. 113), a statement remarkably close to outright
republican yearnings.

Finally, towards the end of the second part, Erskine returned
to his own province, the English legal system, and in particular the reactionary developments in libel law that he pretended
had taken place only in Armata, whereas England had remained
immune. I cite this passage at length, not only because it consti-

tutes, in a sense, a retraction of Erskine's speech for the prosecution and his general tactics in the case of Williams, but also because it enunciates the whig historiographical belief, so berated by Butterfield, that there are always forces at work to turn back the advances of enlightenment and to substitute for the slow progress towards increasing civil rights and democratic structures the deliberate step backwards:

> [The Armatans] were, from the most ancient times, . . . an integral part of the courts; more independent indeed than the highest judges, whose decisions might be reviewed by superior tribunals, *but no tribunal could ever touch an acquitting sentence by the equals of the accused.* This had been the life's blood of popular freedom through all ages, yet a few years only had passed since it was running out like water in Armata, and she was dying without attending to her complaint. Her Judges, following one another, had, it seems, settled, as they called it, by a series of decisions, that *writings* forming an anomaly in criminal proceedings, were to be left to *their* censureship, and that it was for *them alone to decide,* even when no rights of individuals were affected, in what language the opinions of mankind *upon every possible subject* was to be expressed; assuming to themselves the sole judgment of *intention* whilst they shut themselves up from all testimony by which alone it could, in many cases, be ascertained. — This blind and presumptuous pretension . . . gave the fixed magistrate, appointed by the crown, the power of controuling the press, which is but another name for AN ABSOLUTE DOMINION OVER THE PEOPLE. (pp. 125–26; italics original)

Because he does not use the term "juries" with respect to Armata, substituting for it the ethically loaded "themselves," it is clear that Erskine now believed there was a direct structural connection between trial by jury and genuine popular representation in Parliament. Indeed, he stretched his utopian thinking now to include religion, and in a final dialogue with an "old man" who defended the Anglican articles of belief, he leaves his interlocutor (another version of himself, perhaps) "ashamed of what he had said" (p. 191). The narrator himself departs with a wish—the purest sign of utopian intentions: "Though I sincerely honour the Church of England, and hold by her doctrines, as the purest, and the best, yet I wish that our national religion, as well as our civil state, should be balanced by a popular constitution, and that the free spirit of the dissenters should continue" (p. 195).

7

Two Steps Forward,
One Step Backwards

WILLIAM WORDSWORTH'S REVISIONISM

In this final brief chapter, I return to the subject of human imperfection as instanced not momentarily by Thomas Erskine
but on the grand scale by William Wordsworth, who made that
topic the nerve center of his great autobiographical poem, *The
Prelude,* in which he explained to posterity (although he never
published the explanation in his lifetime) how he lost his early
enthusiasm for the French Revolution and for democratic principles in general. From Erskine's utopian prose romance, in fact,
we can make an effective and legitimate transition to Wordsworth's dystopic epic poem, most of whose contents and motives
were directly connected to the anti-Jacobin reaction expressed
in the Treason Trials and the Treasonable Practices Act that followed. This takes *Nobody's Perfect* into the nineteenth century,
since Wordsworth's poem was begun at the turn of the century
and revised at least through the 1830s. In the course of this push
forwards, however, we shall meet with a flurry of names and persons who appeared earlier in this book, so that the chapter, if
it cannot provide a conclusion (as, indeed, in attempting to re-
deem the theory of progress, it would not desire one) can at least
offer a leave-taking.

One of the two enlightened readers of this book for Yale
University Press observed that it was rather odd to introduce
Thomas Erskine as most famous for his defence of Hardy,
Tooke, and Thelwall in the Treason Trials of 1794 and then to

omit those trials from a review of his career. Odd indeed; but the omission makes sense in the broad new light of John Barrell's *Imagining the King's Death,* the most magisterial account of the Treason Trials so far.[1] Because Barrell deals exhaustively with the political circumstances and the legal issues involved— he devotes separate chapters to the trials of Thomas Hardy and of John Horne Tooke and John Thelwall—it would be otiose to do more here than refer the reader to his discussion. As his title indicates, these men, arrested for political organisation in the interests of extending the franchise, were tried under the ancient statute of 25 Edward III, where treason was defined as "imagining the king's death"; but the old language had been wrested from its intended meaning by the government lawyers, so that a supposed attack on the king's authority was interpreted as endangering his natural person. As Barrell explains, Erskine concentrated on establishing two simple principles: "that the person of the king was not to be conflated with his sovereignty, his authority, his government; and that in a charge of imagining the king's death, it is the traitorous intention, not the overt acts, that constitutes the crime, and is a matter of pure fact, *to be determined by the jury.*"[2]

Barrell also explains how Erskine had, in effect, trained for this momentous occasion by wrestling, over two decades, with what had come to be called the Mansfield doctrine, which (as we have seen in the story of John Almon) restricted the role of the jury to matters of fact (Did such and such actually occur? Did the defendant in fact publish or sell the pamphlet in question?) and reserved all matters of law to the judges. But he also reminds us, in grave detail, that Erskine's triumph was shortly rendered unrepeatable, if not nugatory, by the passage of the Treasonable Practices Act, which, along with the Seditious Meetings Act, was introduced into Parliament in November 1795. The Treasonable Practices Act, originally stated to last only as long as the life of George III, whose protection was its ideological gloss, remained in force until 1848. Hidden in the language of the Treasonable Practices Act was not only a protection against Erskine's reliance on the proof of treasonous intention, but the cover for a whole series of potential new treasons, which the Whig writers of the day were quick to excoriate and mock. Erskine, of course, attacked the bill in Parliament. Thelwall delivered a seriocomic lecture on what might now be included in the category of treason—if a brewer's cart broke down in front of the king's coach, thereby "restraining his Majesty's person," for example. William Godwin published (anonymously) a pamphlet entitled *Considerations on Lord Grenville's and Mr. Pitt's Bills,* explaining that under the new law David Hume would have been a traitor for writing his abstractly republican "Idea of a Perfect Commonwealth"; and Godwin also reinstated the original preface to his novel *Caleb Williams,* withdrawn in the spring of 1794 because, as the second preface tells us, "Terror was the order of the day." Samuel Taylor Coleridge, still himself on the side of the radicals, published an attack on the bill, suggesting that any theoretical argument in favor of republicanism could now be regarded as treasonable. Entitled *The Plot Discovered,* an allusion to the subtitle of Thomas Otway's Restoration tragedy, *Venice Preserved,* Coleridge's pamphlet connected with the October production of the play by Richard Sheridan and John Philip Kemble, a production intended to reclaim a royalist text for the opposite side, ideologically speaking.[3] Thus literature, as conventionally understood, reenters the Whig interpretation of history with a vengeance.

The interpenetration of literature and politics was inevitable, if you think about it, at a moment when the relation between principle and interest was on everyone's mind. In December 1794, Coleridge had sent a series of eleven, or perhaps twelve, sonnets on "Eminent Characters" to the *Morning Chronicle,* which published them one at a time, from December 1 through January 31, 1795.[4] The first of the series was addressed "To the honourable Mr. Erskine"; it was obviously part of the celebrations that followed the acquittals of Hardy and John Horne Tooke, the second of which took place on November 22. So, too, in a different tone of voice, was no. 6, entitled curtly "Pitt." The other "Eminent Characters" included Edmund Burke, Joseph Priestley, Lafayette, Koskiusko, W. L. Bowles, the actress Sara Siddons (though this one was probably written by Charles Lamb), William Godwin, Robert Southey, Richard Brinsley Sheridan, and Earl Stanhope. Of these, Priestley, Godwin (identified in his sonnet as the "Author of *Political Justice*"), Southey, Sheridan, and Stanhope were all known English radicals, while Koskiusko and Lafayette were international heroes. Sheridan had been a witness for the defence in the trials of Hardy and Tooke. On January 5, 1795, two weeks before the sonnet to him appeared in the *Morning Chronicle,* he had proposed in the Commons the repeal of Pitt's Habeas Corpus Suspension Act. In addition to *Political Justice,* Godwin had published, on October 21, an attack on the interpretation of treason law provided by Lord Chief Justice Eyre.[5] Priestley, a leading dissenting minister in Birmingham, had had his house and laboratory sacked and burned by a loyalist mob in July 1791, and Coleridge referred to that episode in the opening lines of his sonnet. Earl Stanhope had protested in the Lords against the treatment of the Scottish "martyrs" Skirving, Margarot, and Gerrald, the first victims of anti-Jacobin legal innovation. His sonnet is subtitled "On Reading His Late Protest in the House of Lords." On February 4, Stanhope would address a crowd of more than nine hundred celebrants of the remarkable turn of affairs against Pitt's government. Southey (though you would never know it from Coleridge's title, which acknowledges Southey as "Author of the *Retrospect* and other poems") was in 1794 writing his revolutionary drama *Wat Tyler,* which would remain, however, prudently in manuscript until William Hone published an unauthorized edition in 1817.

The marquis de Lafayette and Thaddeus Koskiusko were both presented by Coleridge as victims of tyranny abroad; though the *Morning Chronicle* observed in a note that the sonnet to Lafayette was written "antecedently to the joyful account of the Patriot's escape from the Tyrant's Dungeon" (p. 82). The reference is to Lafayette's imprisonment, after a failed attempt to rescue Louis XVI, in various Prussian and Austrian prisons. The career of Lafayette represents a curious mixture of allegiances, to the American Revolution on the one hand and to Louis XVI on the other, though in France Lafayette seems to have played the role of a liberal reformer. There is no such corrective note attached to the sonnet to Koskiusko, perhaps because Coleridge seems to have believed he was dead. "They saw beneath a Hireling's sword/Their Koskiusko fall!" Koskiusko was a Polish patriot who served on the side of the Americans in the Revolutionary War. In 1793, when Poland was partitioned between Russia and Prussia, he led the Polish freedom forces but was wounded, captured, and sent prisoner to Russia, where he remained until 1796. In all, the little collection of sonnets had a function not unlike that of the list of subscribers to Edward Thompson's edition of Marvell's works; the listing of some of the friends of Liberty; some of her erstwhile friends; and some in more equivocal positions.

Coleridge was, with a few mysterious marvels as the exception, a dreadful poet; but he was somewhat better at blame than praise. Whereas Thomas Erskine, hero of the hour, was offered flatulent tribute as the "hireless Priest before the insulted shrine [of Liberty]" whose light will shine "beyond the tomb" (Erskine cannot have appreciated this premature anticipation of his death thirty years later), Pitt is described as the "dark Scowler":

Who with proud words of dear-lov'd Freedom came—
More blasting than the mildew from the South!
And kiss'd his country with Iscariot mouth
(Ah! foul apostate from his Father's fame!).

(p. 83)

The word "apostate" appears again in the sonnet to Sheridan, again attached to Pitt, as Sheridan's "patriot Rage and Indignation high" are imagined to have pierced to the heart "The Apostate by the brainless rout ador'd / As erst that elder Fiend beneath great Michael's sword." Thus Milton's *Paradise Lost* reenters the picture on the side of the whig interpretation of history.

The sonnet to Pitt is the only hostile tribute in the series; though we must pause to consider the ambivalent presence of Burke in this company. Coleridge acknowledges that Burke, too, like Pitt, has turned his coat. The figure of Freedom rises to lament that reversal:

Great Son of Genius! sweet to me thy name,
Ere in an evil hour with alter'd voice
Thou bad'st Oppression's hireling crew rejoice.

(p. 80)

Freedom consoles herself, however, about Burke's motives, which she acknowledges were "Pity . . . and proud Precipitance of soul," rather than ambition or material corruption. But Coleridge later, in 1796, added a severe correction. "When I composed this line ('Yet never, Burke! thou drank'st Corruption's bowl,') I had not read the following paragraph in the *Cambridge Intelligencer* (of Saturday, November 21, 1795): *When Mr. Burke first crossed over the House of Commons from the Opposition to the Ministry, he received a pension of £1200 a year charged on the Kings Privy Purse*" (p. 80). Burke's pension was commented on adversely in the Lords on November 13, 1795, by the duke of Bedford and the earl of Lauderdale, and in the Commons on November 16 by John Curwen. On February 14, 1796, Burke published a long defence of his pensionary status, "Letter to a Noble Lord," using the occasion to insult Bedford and to claim as an ally the now dead Admiral Keppel, invoking with sentiment Keppel's portrait, as painted by Sir Joshua Reynolds, which he had received as a gift for helping with Keppel's defence in his court-martial in 1779. As one Foxite Whig pointed out, this was to enrol a dead hero in support of a government that had "conspired against his honour and his life," to force Keppel into posthumous complicity with Burke's own political turncoatism.[6] Burke seemed to think that old friendships could not be spoiled by political apostasy, and perhaps they should not be. Keppel's portrait, he remarked, "was painted by an artist worthy of the subject, the excellent friend of that excellent man from their earliest youth, and a common friend of us both, with whom we lived for many years without a moment of coldness . . . or of jar, to the day of our final separation."[7] How far he himself had travelled since 1778, however, was also marked in the *Letter* by what must be one of the last and the most unintentionally ironic of Burke's citations from Milton. Still obsessing about the French Revolution, he wrote: "Had the portentous comet of the rights of man (which 'from its horrid hair shakes pestilence and war,' and 'with fear of change perplexes Monarchs') had that comet crossed upon us in that internal state of England, nothing human could have prevented our being irresistibly hurried . . . into all the vices, crimes, horrours and miseries of the French revolution."[8] The unintentional irony comes from our knowing, as probably Burke did not, that it was this second description of the comet that almost prevented the licensing of *Paradise Lost*, since it seemed to hint that Milton's epic was still, in some sense, an old revolutionary's testimony.

With what further irony, then, must the admirers of Coleridge observe that by 1817, during the scandal caused by the appearance of *Wat Tyler*, Coleridge himself had become, avowedly, an apostate from the radical cause.⁹ At the end of his book, John Barrell resurrects the sad old questions as to how and when Coleridge abandoned his radical principles. Similar questions will continue to be asked about Wordsworth, perhaps forever; but here I want us to reconsider the *Prelude* in its various stages of composition, not as a key to when Wordsworth, too, abandoned the radical cause; but, more radically, whether he ever did.

Coleridge wrote his sonnets at a moment of exuberance, when Erskine's triumphs in the court had seemed to make progress possible or at least to discountenance the forces of regression. The euphoria did not last. Like Coleridge, Wordsworth experienced embarrassment, when in 1797, John Thelwall, on the run from his persecutors, sought temporary shelter with them in Somerset, and panic, when a government spy invaded their pastoral and literary enclave, sending the Wordsworths into temporary exile in Germany. Coleridge clearly believed he had successfully persuaded his friend to convert his allegiance to political liberty, now so politically incorrect, into philosophical claims for transcendence and the freedom only of the individual mind. Most subsequent Wordsworth critics have agreed. After all, Wordsworth described that process of conversion at length in the poem. But are we supposed to take him entirely at his word? We should not forget that the poem remained in manuscript until Wordsworth's death in 1850. Why, if he had rendered it politically harmless or actually conservative, did he not see to its publication in 1843 to celebrate his appointment as Poet Laureate? Or in 1849, when his *Poetical Works* were issued with his final revisions? Because, I suggest, its whig allegiances were far from definitively neutralized. In fact, whereas Wordsworth has usually been described as revising the poem in a tory and orthodox Christian direction over the long period—almost half a century—of its quiescence between 1805 and his death, it is surprising to note how little he censored out its whiggish dreams and premises. Instead, he conflated political history with autobiography, making the story of a revolution that failed to live up to its idealistic beginnings ("when the whole earth,/The beauty wore of promise") both the model and the cause of a life gone astray. As Wordsworth himself tells us, his tale was one of "juvenile errors," loss of direction, and temporary cynicism. He lived—and understood himself to have lived—one of the arguments of *Nobody's Perfect*: that human progress is erratic, that the very idea of progress has to be reformed, the road to reform being personal experience.

> Oh! who is he that hath his whole life long
> Preserved, enlarged, this freedom in himself?
> For this alone is genuine Liberty:
> Where is the favoured being who hath held
> That course unchecked, unerring, and untired,
> *In one perpetual progress smooth and bright?*
> —A humbler destiny have we retraced,
> And told of lapse and hesitating choice,
> And backward wanderings along thorny ways.
>   (italics added)

Of these lines, 130–38 of the new book 14 which was separated off as a conclusion during the revisions of the 1830s, only the first three were carried forward from the 1805 stage of composition; the rest were a product of very late understanding.

In the *Prelude,* in the second stage of composition that took place in 1804, well after the panic of 1797, Wordsworth looked back at the history of the French Revolution and his own involvement with it. He reviewed what took place in France, and in England, and in his own mental life during the years from 1789 to the turn of the century. And, given Coleridge's claim that the Treasonable Practices Act made it treason to argue, however theoretically, for republicanism, it is no coincidence that Wordsworth frequently inserted into his poem the term "Republic"—four times, to be precise, always in an idealistic context—and that he did not later demean it. In book 3, Wordsworth remembered his time at Cambridge as the period that gave him an idealist's commitment not only to learning for its own sake, but also to "a seemly plainness, name it what you will,/Republican or pious" (3:400–401). In book 9, Wordsworth looked back at that same education as that which first gave him a concept of human equality:

> . . . nor was it least
> Of many benefits, in later years
> Derived from academic institutes
> And rules, that they held something up to view
> Of a Republic, where all stood thus far
> Upon equal ground.
>
> .   .   .   .
> . . . It could not be
> But that one tutored thus should look with awe
> Upon the faculties of man, receive
> Gladly the highest promises, and hail,
> As best the government of equal rights
> And individual worth.
>
> (9:222–43)

In book 10, he turns to his experience in France to note that the revolutionary "state" had "assumed with joy/The body and the *venerable* name/Of a Republic" (10:40–41; italics added), a far from casual statement, fully supported by the Roman republican iconography of the new regime. Between 1805 and his death in 1850, Wordsworth removed the "joy" and added a negative view ("spiteful gratitude," "proud haste") of France's motives in declaring a republic at that stage of the war—on September 22, 1792, after the French victory at Valmy forced the retreat of Austrian and Prussian troops—but he retained the "venerable name of a Republic" to keep the classical ideal itself untarnished.

The fourth instance occurs later in book 10, or in book 11 in Wordsworth's revised version, when he considers the message the French Revolution has for English reformers. Having already seen much to horrify him in French revolutionary practice, he nevertheless declares (in a passage heavily worked over after 1805) his continued faith both in the French example and in its English potential: "I knew that wound external could not take/Life from the young Republic" (10:582; 11:13-14), Wordsworth declared, and this confidence in the future of France led him to expect "Triumphs of unambitious peace at home,/And noiseless fortitude" 10:591-92; 11:220-21). "Noiseless fortitude" is Wordsworth's version of Milton's "better fortitude" in the invocation to his book 9 and is perhaps not unrelated to Milton's definition of fortitude *after* the failure of the English revolution of the mid-seventeenth century—that is to say, "patience and heroic martyrdom" in the face of a punitive and censoring regime. This fourth mention of republicanism occurs just before Wordsworth's most explicit condemnation of Pitt's anti-Jacobin legislation:

> Our shepherds . . . at that time
> Thirsted to make the guardian crook of law
> A tool of murder. They who ruled the state
>
> . . . .
>
> Giants in their impiety alone,
> But in their weapons and their warfare base

As vermin working out of reach, they leagued
Their strength perfidiously to undermine
Justice, and make an end of liberty.

(10:653–56)

Again, though Wordsworth marginally toned down this passage after 1805—the government now "acted, or seemed at least to act, like men/Thirsting to make the guardian crook of law/A tool of murder" (11:63–65)—the central indictment remains. What Wordsworth had in mind, surely, were not only the 1794 Treason Trials, but also the new repressive legislation introduced after the acquittals.

In *The Plot Discovered,* Coleridge had carried Pitt's intentions to their logically absurd conclusion: "To promulgate what we believe to be a truth is indeed a law beyond law; but now if any man should publish, nay, if even in a friendly letter or in social conversation any should assert a Republic to be the most perfect form of government . . . he is guilty of High Treason."[10] Would this also be true of a long philosophical poem? I think this casts a new light not only on Wordsworth's decision not to have the *Prelude* published until after his death, but also, more importantly, on the fact that the political books of the poem were all written at a time when it was still highly imprudent to be writing about such matters.

Even when he most vividly described his fall into disillusion with the French Revolution during the Terror, Wordsworth evoked Milton, and Milton's own reprise of his career in *Samson Agonistes,* the tragedy of the warrior-hero blinded and in servitude to the Philistines, but ultimately, of course, completely victorious over them. In book 10, where Wordsworth described his psychological crisis and the nightmares that accompanied it, he recalled how night after night he:

> strove to plead
> Before *unjust tribunals*, with a voice
> Labouring.
>
>   (book 10, ll. 411-13)

The words I have italicized are quoted from what had become by then a culturally overdetermined passage. The Chorus, commenting on the collapse of Samson's heroic career, complains that God seems careless towards his chosen deliverers:

> Yet toward these, thus dignifi'd, thou oft
> Amidst their height of noon,
> Changest thy count'nance.
>
> . . . .
>
> Oft leave'st them to the hostile sword
>
> . . . .
>
> *Or to th'unjust tribunals under change of times.*
>
>   (italics added)

These lines had previously been read, first, as an allusion to the trials of the regicides in the opening years of Charles II's restoration, and, second, as a prophecy of the juridical assassination of Algernon Sidney in 1683 (a point made in the Hollis edition of Sidney's *Works* in 1763);[11] and they were now being adapted to the nightmare world of government terrorism, not only in France, but in England also.

But what then, the reader will be asking, are we to make of another late addition to the *Prelude*, the famous or notorious insertion into book 7, "Residence in London," of the panegyric to Edmund Burke? Perhaps by subjecting it to very close reading, both intertextual and contextual. The "Genius of Burke" passage appeared in its earliest form in Wordsworth's manuscripts in 1832, when the poet was fifty-two. The passage arrives with an apology for its belatedness and, with its opening echo of Coleridge's sonnet to Burke of 1794 (and of his retraction of 1796), an apology, too, for Coleridge. Coleridge had begun his sonnet "Great Son of Genius" with the statement that Burke's name was sweet to him "Ere in an evil hour" (an echo also of *Paradise Lost*, book 9, ll. 1067: "O Eve, in evil hour thou didst give ear/To that false Worm") he changed his tune and encouraged "Oppression's hireling crew." In 1804, Wordsworth had, into his description of a visit to Parliament, introduced Burke without naming him, though by way of commenting on the significance of his name:[12]

> . . . Oh, the beating heart,
> When one amid the prime of these rose up,
> One of whose name from childhood we had heard.
>
> (ll. 524–27)

A quarter of a century later, he added:

> Genius of Burke! forgive the pen seduced
> By specious wonders, and *too slow to tell*
> Of what the ingenuous, what bewildered men,
> Beginning to mistrust their boastful guides,
> And wise men, willing to grow wiser, caught,
> Rapt auditors! from thy most eloquent tongue
> . . . but some-
> While he forewarns, denounces, launches forth,
> Against all systems built on abstract rights,
> Keen ridicule; the majesty proclaims
> Of Institutes and Laws, hallowed by time;
> Declares the vital power of social ties
> Endeared by Custom; and with high disdain,
> Exploding upstart Theory, insists

Upon the allegiance to which men are born—
Some—say at once a froward multitude—
Murmur.

(ll. 512–32; italics added)

If Wordsworth heard Burke speak in Parliament, it must have been during the seven months that he spent in London in 1793, after his return from France as an enthusiastic supporter of the revolution, at the age of twenty-four. Burke retired from Parliament in the summer of 1794, and Wordsworth would not return to London until February 1795. If he sat in the Visitors' Gallery in 1793, he could have heard Burke speak (on February 28) in the debate on Sheridan's motion "relative to the Existence of Seditious Practices," on the second reading (March 21) of the Traitorous Correspondence Bill, and again, to the same purpose, on April 9; and he could have listened to Burke opposing Fox's motion for peace with France on June 17.[13] On every one of these occasions Burke took exactly the opposite stance from what we know were Wordsworth's opinions at the time; but what he did *not* do was deliver a speech of the equality and color described in Wordsworth's later addition. He had his opportunity—indeed, the provocation. On May 6, Charles, Earl Grey, one of the founder members of the Whig Association of the Friends of the People, introduced a motion for parliamentary reform which attempted to provide an umbrella for the numerous petitions to this effect from the radical societies. The motion was brilliantly seconded by Erskine, who ironically quoted in its defence Burke's own words in his *Thoughts on the Causes of the Present Discontents;*[14] but the man who rose to reply, and to close down the debate, leading to the motion's disastrous defeat by a majority of 282 to 41, was not Burke, but Pitt, who indeed ridiculed "all systems built on abstract rights," proclaimed "the majesty . . ./Of Institutes and Laws, hallowed by time," and insisted

"Upon the allegiance to which men are born." His mantra was the British Constitution, its antiquity, its rationality, its place in the patriotic heart.[15] The speech was a classic statement of conservative political thought, delivered in simple but powerful language. In absolute contrast, Wordsworth in these months was writing his never-to-be-published "Letter to the Bishop of Llandaff . . . by a Republican" and a full year later was writing to William Matthews about their joint plan for a new periodical (perhaps to be called *The Philanthropist*) to counter the repressive tendencies of the day and to avert, if possible, revolution by "gradual and constant reform."

In order to establish the terms of such a collaboration, Wordsworth set out his own political principles. He did not mince his words. "You know perhaps already that I am of that odious class of men called democrats, and of that class I shall for ever continue."[16] And in the next letter he explained in considerable detail what that must mean in the 1790s: "I disapprove of monarchical and aristocratical governments, however modified. Hereditary distinctions, and privileged orders of every species, I think must necessarily counteract the progress of human improvement: hence it follows that I am not amongst the admirers of the British Constitution." And, turning to the purpose of the proposed journal:

> A writer who has the welfare of mankind at heart should call forth his best exertions to convince the people that they can only be preserved from a convulsion by economy in the administration of the public purse, and a gradual and constant reform of those abuses which, if left to themselves, may grow to such a height as to render even a Revolution desirable. . . . He should let slip no opportunity of explaining and enforcing those general principles of

the social order, which are applicable to all times and to all places; he should diffuse by every method a knowledge of those rules of political justice, from which the further any government deviates the more effectually must it defeat the object for which government was ordained. A knowledge of these rules cannot but lead to good; they included an entire preservative from despotism.

Since Pitt had particularly scorned the idea of general rights or principles that transcended national boundaries, these comments seem particularly bold; especially as Wordsworth went on to remind Matthews of Pitt's recent suspension of the habeas corpus act,[17] that event protested, we remember, by the reissue of Barry's print *The Phoenix*.

As for the imagined *Philanthropist*, each issue was to begin with a political editorial, to be followed by essays on manners and morals, on taste and criticism. It should include a little poetry, both old and new; reports of parliamentary debates; and short biographies of "eminent men, particularly those distinguished for their exertions in the cause of liberty, as Turgot, Milton, Sydney, Machiavel, Bucaria, &c &c &c." In other words, the *Philanthropist* was to be constructed on the model of Almon's *Political Register!* Finally, in late December, he wrote again to Matthews, rejoicing with him on the acquittal of Hardy, Tooke, and Thelwall and suggesting that the "late occurrences" will "abate the insolence and presumption of the aristocracy by shewing it that neither the violence nor the art of power can crush even an unfriended individual, though engaged in the propagation of doctrines confessedly unpalatable to privilege."[18] Thus Wordsworth completed his self-definition as a reformist whig of the old style. What could have, must have, gone through his mind then, when he added to the ageing text of the *Pre-*

lude those lines that seem to reject absolutely these brave confidences—brave even in a private correspondence.

But note that this belated eulogy (which is also an elegy, since Burke is "now for ever mute in the cold grave") is framed by two versions of Wordsworth himself at twenty-five: the first (written in 1804), a person capable of ennui and even of suspicion ("Words follow words, sense *seems* to follow sense . . . till the strain . . . Grows tedious even in a young man's ear"), and the second, reimagined in the 1830s, apparently wholeheartedly admiring.

> . . . Could a youth, and one
> In ancient story versed, whose breast had heaved
> Under the weight of classic eloquence,
> Sit, see, and hear, unthankful, uninspired?

Of course, it is possible to answer those rhetorical questions in the negative; as the retention of the first young man by his now elderly and revisionary self might encourage us to do. The result would be a moment as convoluted in its values [19] as Wordsworth in the 1830s must have known himself to be, keeping scrupulously alive in the manuscript of the *Prelude* (though keeping it private) the tale of "lapse . . . and backward wanderings" which was his own whig interpretation of history. This understanding of how political history moves, two steps forward and one step backwards, is our best response to early Butterfield, who, like Wordsworth, recanted his earlier position, although in the opposite direction.

By the end of the eighteenth century in England, and even more so by 1850, when Wordsworth died, it must have looked as though accommodation to the ancien régime was inevitable and permanent; but the structural results of whig and radical impulses were still to come. As Albert Goodwin put it in 1979:

The welfare state, the deep-seated concern for social justice, civic and legal equality, full religious toleration, the continuing insistence on human rights, the right of association, public meeting and free speech, national self-determination, the freedom of trade unions from state regulation or legal repression, the solidarity of the working class in industrial disputes and across national frontiers, the right to protest and participate, female emancipation and the right to strike—all these policies and principles had been conceived and pioneered by the eighteenth-century "friends of liberty." As Thelwall had anticipated, the harvest sown by the democratic impulse, postponed in his own day, was at length safely gathered in.[20]

And how does this list look now, I ask the reader, whenever this book may be read?

NOTES

Introduction: Historiography and Method

1. Annabel Patterson, *Early Modern Liberalism* (Cambridge, 1997).
2. Horace Walpole, *Memoirs of the Reign of King George III*, ed. Sir Denis Le Marchant, 4 vols. (London, 1845), 2:94–95.
3. Memorandum (1772), Royal Archives, Windsor, RA 15672, printed in Herbert Butterfield, *George III, Lord North and the People, 1779–80* (London, 1949), p. 3.
4. For an account of the mid-century shift in historiography which informs my own, but evaluates it differently, see Vincent Carretta, *The Snarling Muse: Verbal and Visual Political Satire from Pope to Churchill* (Philadelphia, 1983), pp. 211–26. Carretta points out that in 1763, Hume complained to Gilbert Elliott that he had made mistakes in his Stuart volumes "from the plaguy Prejudices of Whiggism, with which I was too much infected when I began this Work," citing *New Letters of David Hume,* ed. Raymond Klibansky and Ernest C. Mossner (Oxford, 1969), p. 69. Among the alterations he made to his work, not incidentally, was a revision to his statement of historiographical method. In place of the judicious sentence distinguishing the two main branches of political principles, the 1759 version, cited by Carretta, read: "And because the ruling party had obtained an advantage over their antagonists in the philosophical disputes concerning some of their general principles, they thence assumed a right to impose on the public their account of all particular transactions, and to represent the other party as governed entirely by the lowest and most vulgar prejudices."
5. See Craig Walton, "Hume and Jefferson on the Uses of History," in *Hume: A Re-Evaluation,* ed. Donald Livingston and James King (New York, 1976), pp. 389–403. For a recent account of Hume's historiography which defines Baxter's as "the crudest form of ancient constitutionalism" and celebrates Butterfield's, see Donald W. Livingston, "Hume's Historical Conception of Liberty," in *Liberty in Hume's History of England,* ed. Nicholas Capaldi and Donald W. Livingston (Dordrecht, 1990),

especially pp. 148–51. Livingston equates whig historiography with "liberal progressive ideology generally," including feminism, and appeals to the "good humoured, reconciling genius of the Humean imagination" to heal a society "poisoned by twentieth-century liberal reenactment of nineteenth-century whig historical alienation."

6. David Hume, *The History of England, from the Invasion of Julius Caesar to the Revolution in 1688 . . . to Which Is Prefixed a Short Account of His Life, Written by Himself,* 8 vols. (London, 1807), 1:xi. All citations from this edition.

7. Hume, *History of England,* 8:323.

8. Victor Wexler, *David Hume and the History of England* (Philadelphia, 1979), especially pp. 1–25.

9. Nicholas Phillipson, *Hume* (London, 1989), pp. 59–60.

10. Sir Lewis Namier, *The Structure of Politics at the Accession of George III* (London, 1929, 2d ed. 1963), p. 16.

11. John Brewer, *Party Ideology and Popular Politics at the Accession of George III* (Cambridge, 1976), p. 30.

12. Herbert Butterfield, *The Whig Interpretation of History* (London, 1931), pp. 11–12; italics added.

13. Herbert Butterfield, *The Englishman and His History* (Cambridge, 1944), p. 2.

14. Burke's *Thoughts* attacked the "King's Friends" (for which read Bute) for having substituted for parliamentary government rule by private cabal. Macaulay, in her *Observations on a Pamphlet, Entitled Thoughts on the Cause of the Present Discontents,* which went through three editions before the end of 1770, expressed the views of more radical Whigs who did not believe that the Rockingham faction—like themselves, an aristocratic cabal—were any better than the Ministry, and were likely to hinder structural reform.

15. Edmund Burke, *Observations on a Late State of the Nation,* in *The Writings and Speeches of Edmund Burke,* ed. Paul Langford, vol. 2 (Oxford, 1981), pp. 211–12. Langford calls this response to William Knox's *State of the Nation* Burke's "first major foray into party polemics" (2:102).

16. Mark Philp, "The Fragmented Ideology of Reform," in *The French Revolution and British Popular Politics,* ed. Mark Philp (Cambridge, 1991), pp. 50–77.

17. Herbert Butterfield, *George III and the Historians* (London, 1957, rev. ed. 1959), pp. 207–8.

18. Catharine Macaulay, *History of England from the Accession of James I to the Elevation of the House of Hanover* (London, 1763–71), p. xii.

19. Joseph Towers, *Tracts on Political and Other Subjects,* 3 vols. (London, 1796), 3:10–11.

20. *The Writings and Speeches of Edmund Burke,* ed. W. M. Elofson with John A. Woods, vol. 3 (Oxford, 1996), pp. 120–21.

21. Brewer, *Party Ideology,* pp. 208–26.

22. Pitt's suspension of habeas corpus immediately followed the arrest of Hardy, Tooke, and Thelwall in May 1794. It was enacted by statute (34 Geo. III, c.54). The following year the implications of its suspension were made clear by the passage of the Treasonable and Seditious Practices Act (36 Geo. III, c.7), which extended the law of treason to spoken and written words, precisely that extension which had been used in the case of Algernon Sidney; and the Seditious Meetings Act (36 Geo. III, c.8), restricting public meetings and political lectures.

23. James T. Boulton, *The Language of Politics in the Age of Wilkes and Burke* (London, 1963).

24. Kathleen Wilson, *The Sense of the People: Politics, Culture and Imperialism in England, 1715–1785* (Cambridge, 1995).

CHAPTER I
John Almon: More Than a Bookseller

1. This slightly overstates Almon's modern obscurity. He had the honor of being featured at the opening of Simon Maccoby's *English Radicalism, 1762–1785* ([London, 1955], p. 15), a blow-by-blow account of the fortunes and misfortunes of the Opposition in the reign of George III. And references to Almon are scattered throughout Robert Rea's important study, *The English Press in Politics, 1760–1774* (Lincoln, Nebr., 1963).

2. Deborah Rogers, *Bookseller as Rogue: John Almon and the Politics of Eighteenth-Century Publishing* (New York, 1986). Rogers had been preceded, however, by Rea's *English Press in Politics,* in which Almon is a ubiquitous figure.

3. Lucyle Werkmeister, *The London Daily Press, 1772–1792* (Lincoln, Nebr., 1963).

4. For the Darbys, see my *Early Modern Liberalism* (Cambridge, 1997), pp. 133, 205–7; for the Baldwins, see ibid., pp. 205–6; and Lena Rostenberg, "English 'Rights and Liberties': Richard and Anne Baldwin, Whig Patriot Publishers," in Rostenberg, *Literary, Political, Scientific, Religious and Legal Publishing, Printing and Bookselling in England, 1551–1780,* 2 vols. (New York, 1965), 2:369–431. For Smith, see Tim Crist, "Francis Smith and the Opposition Press in England, 1660–1688" (Ph.D. diss.,

Cambridge University, 1977). See also mentions of Smith and Baldwin in Melinda Zook, *Radical Whigs and Conspiratorial Politics in Late Stuart England* (University Park, Pa., 1999); and Adrian Johns, *The Nature of the Book* (Chicago, 1998).

5. John Almon, *Review of Mr. Pitt's Administration* (London: George Kearsley, 1762); this pamphlet ran to five editions and was translated into French and German. Not missing a beat, Almon followed up his success with *An Appendix to the Review of Mr. Pitt's Administration by the Author of the Review,* which appeared under his own imprint in 1763.

6. Peter Thomas, *John Wilkes: A Friend to Liberty* (Oxford, 1996), pp. 27–56.

7. Rea, *English Press in Politics,* p. 111; the first advertisement, in the *Public Advertiser,* was dated October 19; the actual date of publication was November 29.

8. Rogers, *Bookseller as Rogue,* p. 23. Walpole's comment, which was not quite what Rogers reported, is worth quoting for its evaluative content: "About the same time was published a pamphlet, perhaps the ablest ever written, called, an 'Inquiry into the Doctrine concerning Libels.' It severely took to pieces the arbitrary maxims of Lord Mansfield and Norton, who were roughly handled, as well as the late Lord Hardwicke. Dunning, a rising lawyer, was supposed the principal author, assisted by the Lord Chief Justice Pratt, and one or two others." See Horace Walpole, *Memoirs of the Reign of King George III,* ed. Sir Denis Le Marchant, 4 vols. (London, 1845), 2:37.

9. John Almon, *Biographical, Literary, and Political Anecdotes, of Several of the Most Eminent Persons of the Present Age,* 3 vols. (London, 1797), 1:244. Rogers erroneously cites p. 80 as the source of Almon's attribution, where, however, Almon had instead stated that "the real author was a late master in Chancery; he had much assistance from Lord Camden." Rea (*English Press in Politics,* p. 113) prefers the Dunning hypothesis, on the unlikely grounds that he would subsequently defend it in court.

10. John Almon, *Memoirs of a Late Eminent Bookseller* (London, 1790; reprint, New York, 1974), p. 18.

11. For a more detailed account of these proceedings and their connection to the intervening debate in Parliament on the question of general warrants, see Rea, *English Press in Politics,* pp. 110–21.

12. For a clear and disinterested account of the emergence of the Rockingham Whigs, see John Brewer, "From Old Corps to Rockinghamite Whigs: The Emergence of a Party," in his *Party Ideology and Popular Politics at the Accession of George III* (Cambridge, 1976), pp. 77–95.

13. Horace Walpole has a rather different account of these events. See *Memoirs of the Reign of King George III*, 2:66–68: "Almon, an active and officious printer for the Opposition, and attached to Lord Temple and Wilkes, having been prosecuted for publishing the excellent letter on libels, appeared on February 6th, [1765] in the King's Bench, to show cause why an attachment should not be issued. As Lord Mansfield would not openly appear in this cause (he himself being severely treated in that pamphlet), as Judge Denison had resigned, and the new judge had not taken his seat, Wilmot, the remaining judge in that court, said, 'It would be too much for him to take upon himself.' The Attorney-General moved to have Almon bound over to the next term. His counsel desired he might be heard, or dismissed; but he was bound over. This suit was afterwards dropped, when Mr. Grenville found it convenient to have libels written *against* the Administration."

14. For a brief account of Jones and his early career as a caricaturist, see Jürgen Döring, *Eine Kunstgeschichte der frühen englischen Karikatur* (Hildesheim, 1991), p. 211 n. 25: "Seit 1765 arbeitete er regelmassig for Zeitschriften wie das *Oxford Magazine* und das *Political Register*." For 1765 we should read 1767, when Almon started the *Political Register*, and the *Oxford Magazine* followed his lead in January 1768.

15. Walpole, *Memoirs of the Reign of King George III*, p. 47.

16. M. Dorothy George, *English Political Caricature to 1792* (Oxford, 1959), p. 141.

17. Herbert M. Atherton, *Political Prints in the Age of Hogarth: A Study of the Ideographic Representation of Politics* (Oxford, 1974), pp. 262–63.

18. See the description by F. G. Stephens in *Catalogue of Political and Personal Satires in the British Museum*, 11 vols. (1883; reprint, London, 1978), 4:417–18, where the print is catalogued as no. 4179; but its artist remains unidentified, as is the case with all the prints from the *Political Register*.

19. This piece has sometimes been attributed to Wilkes on the basis of its appearance in *English Liberty: Being a Collection of Interesting Tracts, from the Year 1762 to 1769, Containing the Private Correspondence, Public Letters, Speeches, and Addresses of John Wilkes, Esq.* (1769). In fact, only a section of this account appears in *English Liberty*, as a long footnote attached to a letter to Wilkes from Charles Churchill, dated August 3, 1763, pp. 366–68. The footnote was evidently added by the editor of the volume.

20. For Hollis's edition of Sidney, see my *Early Modern Liberalism* (Cambridge, 1997), pp. 44–47.

21. Rea, *English Press in Politics*, p. 138: "The ostensible connection between

the magazine and the Grenvilles was thus broken." Rea had been following Almon's attempts to serve several of the Opposition factions through the *Register*.

22. Rogers, *Bookseller as Rogue*, pp. 43–44.

23. Almon subsequently complained in his *Memoirs*, p. 62, that "even in striking the special jury, there was an obvious partiality; for although the king was party, several servants of the King's household, and gentlemen in the public offices, were allowed to be of the forty-eight."

24. Rogers, *Bookseller as Rogue*, pp. 49–52; perhaps this conviction was the effect of her training as a literary scholar.

25. Ibid., p. 54 n. 11.

26. See *Another Letter to Mr. Almon, in a Matter of Libel*, p. 141: "I do not, Mr. Almon, understand it, although I dare say you do, and will for that reason be unwilling to publish what I say. However, it will do you no harm." And see the postscript, p. xxviii: "The very nobility are not so blind as not to see what occasioned the contemptible upshot of the proceedings in your case, Mr. Almon, some years ago," and p. xxxi: "I forget now what happened in your case, Mr. Almon. There was some blunder, I believe, in the title of the affidavit; and the court not caring for any further proceeding in so clamorous a business, took advantage of that circumstance to let it drop."

27. The satire is dated June 13, 1770, and appears facing p. 121 of the *Register*. See Stephens, *Catalogue of Political . . . Satires*, 4:614–25, no. 4392, artist unidentified.

28. Thomas, *John Wilkes*, pp. 125–40.

29. Werkmeister notes that the price of paper, and hence newpapers, doubled during this period. In July 1776 the tax on paper increased from 1d. to 1 1/2d., so that newspapers cost 3d. In Pitt's budget of June 1789 the tax on paper increased to 2d. The *Star* charged that the purpose was "to diminish the number of Newspapers, and thereby withhold . . . information from the people." See Werkmeister, *London Daily Press*, pp. 5–6.

30. *An Appeal to the Justice and Interests of the People of Great Britain, in the Present Disputes with America, by an Old Member of Parliament*. (London: John Almon, 1774).

31. Werkmeister, *London Daily Press*, pp. 114–47.

32. Ibid., pp. 131–49; Rogers, *Bookseller as Rogue*, pp. 97–98.

33. Almon, *Biographical, Literary, and Political Anecdotes*, 1:360–66.

34. John Almon, *Anecdotes of the Life of the Right Hon. William Pitt, Earl of Chatham*, 2 vols. (London: J. S. Jordan, 1792).

35. In Joseph Towers's report on this case in his own *Observations on the*

Rights and Duty of Juries in Trials for Libel, originally published in 1784, and republished in his collected works (London, 1796), it is stated that Hamilton, a Philadelphia lawyer who went to New York to defend Zenger pro bono, was therefore given the freedom of the city of New York, "for his generous defence of the rights of mankind, and the liberty of the press" (2:124).

36. Watt, in his *Bibliotheca Britannica; or, A General Index to British and Foreign Literature* (4 vols; Edinburgh, 1824) does not mention this title; he does attribute to Almon *Free Parliaments; or, A Vindication of the Parliamentary Constitution of England, in Answer to Certain Visionary Plans of Modern Reformers* (1772).

37. Rea, *English Press in Politics,* p. 8; though Rea does cite a single Public Record Office document concerning a possible subsidy.

CHAPTER 2
Reading the *Letter:* A (Short) Chapter of Its Own

1. Candor, *A Letter to the Public Advertiser* (London, 1764), p. 11.

2. *A Defence of the Majority in the House of Commons, on the Question Relating to General Warrants* (London, 1764).

3. For an extended and scathing account of this debate, see Horace Walpole, *Memoirs of the Reign of King George III,* ed. Sir Denis Le Marchant, 4 vols. (London, 1845), 1:361–65. As the *Defence* complained, this issue threatened to "revive the Distinctions of Party; wantonly to sound the Alarm of Privilege and Prerogative, of Whig and Tory, when the Wisdome and Goodness of the common Father of his People had perfected the happy Union of his Subjects" (p. 51).

4. Walpole, *Memoirs of the Reign of King George III,* 1:365.

5. John Almon, *Biographical, Literary, and Political Anecdotes of Several of the Most Eminent Persons of the Present Age,* 3 vols. (London, 1797), 1:79.

6. Almon's ignorance of Lloyd's authorship of *The Defence of the Majority* may account for his being the publisher of two of Lloyd's pamphlets, an attack on Pitt in 1766 and his *Conduct of the Late Administration* in 1767. These were but two more symptoms of the divisiveness of the Whigs.

7. These sentences in quotation marks are not, as one might suppose, transcribed from the *Defence*'s opening, but are a paraphrase of a late passage summarizing Townshend's tactics (p. 43).

8. "Foolish Ligurian, vainly glorying in pride of heart, you have tried your slippery native tricks to no end, nor shall cunning get you safely home to lying Aunus." The Ligurian (*Ligus* in the original), son of Aunus, who has

tried to escape the warrior-maiden Camilla by a trick (challenging her to fight on foot and then, when she dismounts, rushing away on horseback) is here condemned both for his cunning and his cowardice.

9. See Milton, *Complete Prose Works*, ed. D. M. Wolfe et al., 8 vols. (New Haven, 1953–82), 2:535.

10. Ibid., p. 515; John Almon, *Memoirs of a Late Eminent Bookseller* (London, 1790; reprint New York, 1974), pp. 73–75.

11. The first set accompanied the first edition of the *Postscript to the Letter on Libels, Warrants, &c.* (London, 1765); the second set accompanied the second edition of the same. In the latter case, Almon preceded the "Additions" with the following note emphasizing their importance: "Although the following Additions (made at different times to the *Letter on Libels, &c.*) were printed with the former Edition of the *Postscript*, yet there as is reason to believe several Gentlemen who bought the *Second* or *Third* Editions of the Letter have not had these Additions, they are again reprinted; in order that they may still have an Opportunity of making their Copies as complete as if they were to buy the Book now."

12. See "Epistle for the Lord Lovel to Lord Chesterfield by Mr. Pultney, Afterwards Earl of Bath," *New Foundling Hospital for Wit*, 3d. ed., vol. 4 (London, 1771), p. 129.

13. *A Second Postscript to a Late Pamphlet* . . . (London, 1770), p. 38.

CHAPTER 3
Inventing Postcolonialism: Burke's and Barry's
Paradise Lost and *Regained*

1. Isaac Kramnick, *The Rage of Edmund Burke: Portrait of an Ambivalent Conservative* (New York, 1977).

2. David Bromwich, ed., *On Empire, Liberty, and Reform: Speeches and Letters of Edmund Burke* (New Haven, 2000), p. 10. Bromwich also suggests, however, that Burke had been horribly alarmed by the Gordon Riots in London in 1780. A loftier statement of this position is by J. G. A. Pocock, "Burke and the Ancient Constitution: A Problem in the History of Ideas," in *Politics, Language, and Time* (New York, 1973), pp. 202–3.

3. Thomas W. Copeland, *Our Eminent Friend Edmund Burke* (New Haven, 1949), pp. 73–76.

4. The full title is *The Speech of Edmund Burke, Esq., on Moving His Resolutions for Conciliation with the Colonies, March 22, 1775.*

5. One valuable exception is the reprinting of the speech in Bromwich's *On Empire*, pp. 66–134.

6. E. M. Sowerby, ed., *Catalogue of the Library of Thomas Jefferson*, 5 vols. (Charlottesville, 1983), 3:259, #3097.

7. The exception is a brief discussion in Frans de Bruyn, *The Literary Genres of Edmund Burke: The Political Uses of Literary Form* (Oxford, 1996), pp. 138–42. While de Bruyn notes one of the central allusions to Milton in *On Conciliation,* his account of its function virtually upends what Burke, as I shall show, intended.

8. F. P. Lock, *Edmund Burke,* 2 vols. (Oxford, 1998), 1:539.

9. Whereas the sale catalogue indicates Paris as the place of publication, volume 1 was first published in London in 1729, and both volumes together in London in 1735.

10. For the significance of both Thomas Hollis and Richard Baron in the Whig publishing program, see my *Early Modern Liberalism* (Cambridge, 1997).

11. See the catalogue of his library sale in 1833, in *Sale Catalogues of Libraries of Eminent Persons,* ed. Seamus Deane, vol. 8 (London, 1973), pp. 14, 16, 18, 21.

12. Knox's proposal included a similar proposal to raise one hundred thousand pounds a year by taxing Ireland, a notion which may have first attracted Burke's attention, leading to his interest in the American issue.

13. For these figures, the context of the speech, and the speech itself, see *The Writings and Speeches of Edmund Burke,* ed. Paul Langford, vol. 2 (Oxford, 1981), pp. 406–63. See especially Langford's remark that, "considering that Rockingham had taken particular pains to rally the forces of his party for that day, this represented a crushing defeat for the opposition" (p. 463).

14. This construction metaphor had a long history, originating in the account of the building of Solomon's temple, where he had the stones cut to size before being brought to the construction site so that the quiet of the holy place would not be disturbed. During the English revolution, this was interpreted by Thomas Hill, a conservative divine, to mean "that no noise of contentions and schismes . . . might be heard, . . . and that in his house wee might all thinke and speake the same thing" (*The Good Old Way, Gods Way* [London, 1644], p. 39). In *Areopagitica,* Milton reversed this interpretation: "as if, while the Temple of the Lord was building, some cutting, some squaring the marble, others hewing the cedars, there should be a sort of irrationall men who could not consider there must be many schisms and many dissections made in the quarry . . . ere the house of God can be built. And when every stone is laid artfully together, it cannot be united into a continuity, it can but be contiguous in this world; neither

can every peece of the building be of one form; nay rather the perfection consists in this, that out of many moderat varieties and brotherly dissimilitudes that are not vastly disproportionall arises the goodly and the gracefull symmetry that commends the whole pile and structure." See Milton, *Complete Prose Works*, ed. D. M. Wolfe et al., 8 vols. (New Haven, 1953–82), 2:555.

15. Lucan, *The Civil War*, trans. J. D. Duff (Cambridge, 1977), pp. 518–19.

16. Lock, *Edmund Burke*, p. 300; earlier Lock had noted Burke's peculiar analogy between Conway and Satan as serpent, but without making the connection between it and this constant animosity. Hence his interpretive wavering: "In *Paradise Lost*, however, the crest that is elevated and brightened is Satan's. . . . Had the phrase become entirely detached from its context, or did E. B. mean his hearers to think of Conway as a fallen angel?"

17. *The Parliamentary History of England, from the Beginnings*, 25 vols. (London, 1816), 18:441.

18. *The Writings and Speeches of Edmund Burke*, ed. W. M. Elofson with John A. Woods, vol. 3 (Oxford, 1996), p. 105; italics added.

19. Addison's *Cato* was first staged in 1713. Though mostly written a decade earlier, it was immediately read as a political allegory by the Whigs, who chose to see Marlborough as Cato. The Tories responded by seeing Marlborough as Caesar. It was revived several times during the period of Wilkite radicalism. See Kathleen Wilson, *The Sense of the People: Politics, Culture, and Imperialism in England, 1715–1785* (Cambridge, 1995), p. 219. Wilson cites performances in Bristol in 1769, in Newcastle in April 1770, and in Hull in December 1770. The lines Burke remembered are from act 5, scene 1, ll. 13–14: "The wide, th'unbounded prospect, lyes before me;/But shadows, clouds, and darkness, rest upon it."

20. See Hester Thrale, *Thraliana*, ed. K. C. Balderson, 2 vols. (Oxford, 1942), 1:194.

21. [Samuel Johnson], *Taxation No Tyranny: An Answer to the Resolutions and Address of the American Congress* (London, 1775).

22. *Parliamentary History of England*, 18:440–41.

23. Thrale, *Thraliana*, 1:194.

24. De Bruyn, *Literary Genres of Edmund Burke*, pp. 138–39.

25. See *Correspondence of Edmund Burke*, ed. Thomas Copeland, 10 vols. (Cambridge, 1958–78), 6:164–67.

26. There may be little Miltonic echoes in the whaling eulogy which pull the whalers back to the world of the fallen angels; when Sin and Death create the bridge between earth and Hell in Book 10 of Milton's epic, they do

so "as when two Polar Winds blowing adverse/Upon the Cronian Sea, together drive/Mountains of Ice" (10:290–92). And when they actually create the horrific weather which is the consequence of the Fall, they let loose the winds:

> Now from the North
> Of Norumbega, and the Samoed shore
> Bursting their brazen Dungeon, arm'd with ice
> And snow and hail and stormy gust and flaw,
> Boreas and Caecias and Argestes loud.
>
> (10:695–99)

"Norumbega" was the term, in Milton's culture, for all of northern New England; and this very same catalogue of Northern winds would later be conjured up (inaccurately remembered) by Burke in an attack on decayed English courts and palaces that no longer deserved to be maintained. See his speech on economic reform, delivered on February 11, 1780, and published by Dodsley: "Our palaces are vast inhospitable halls. There are bleak winds, there, 'Boreas, and Eurus, and Caurus, and Argestes loud,' howling through the vacant lobbies, appal the imagination, and conjure up the grim spectres of departed tyrants" (*Writings and Speeches*, 3:510).

27. Wilson, *Sense of the People*, pp. 241–42; see also Solomon Lutnick, *The American Revolution and the British Press, 1775–1783* (New York, 1967); Colin Bonwick, *English Radicals and the American Revolution* (Chapel Hill, 1977).

28. For the propaganda efforts of Burke, the earls of Abingdon and Effingham, and the duke of Richmond, see *Correspondence of Edmund Burke*, 3:223–35.

29. The print, an etching and aquatint, executed in brown ink, measures 43.1 by 61.3 centimetres.

30. See William Pressly, *The Life and Art of James Barry* (New Haven, 1981), pp. 179–80.

31. Ibid., p. 81; this letter exists in manuscript in Yale University's Beinecke Library.

32. William Pressly, *James Barry: The Artist as Hero* (London, 1983).

33. Pressly, *Life and Art*, p. 268.

34. Ibid., p. 78.

35. This was discovered by Chester Greenough in 1918. See his "Algernon Sidney and the Motto of the Commonwealth of Massachusetts," in *Collected Studies* (Cambridge, Mass., 1940; repr. from *Massachusetts Historical Society Proceedings*, vol. 51, 1918), pp. 68–88.

36. For more on this story of direct transmission, see my *Early Modern Liberalism;* for the presence of Samuel Adams in this list, see my next chapter, on the subscribers to Captain Edward Thompson's 1776 edition of Marvell's *Works.*

37. Pressly, *Life and Art,* p. 214 n. 31.

38. Pressly, *James Barry,* p. 75.

39. Lock, *Edmund Burke,* 1:404; the public apology was the *Letter to the Sheriffs of Bristol.*

40. This interpretation would consist with F. P. Lock's reading of *Ulysses and a Companion,* which Lock finds governed not by the friendship between Burke and Barry, but by their recent quarrel, in the summer of 1774, over a portrait of himself that Burke wanted and Barry declined to paint. Lock's theory is that *Ulysses* is itself "decidedly ambiguous," since readers of Homer well knew that Odysseus was responsible for the landing on Polyphemus's island and that he would be the only survivor of this rashness. See *Edmund Burke,* 1:367.

41. Pressly, *Life and Art,* p. 214 n. 35.

42. See Bromwich, *On Empire,* p. 147.

CHAPTER 4
The Meaning of Names: Thompson's Marvell and the Whigs

1. Edmund Burke, *The Correspondence of Edmund Burke,* ed. John A. Wood (Cambridge, 1970), 9:411.

2. Andrew Marvell, *The Works of Andrew Marvell, Esq.: Poetical, Controversial, and Political,* ed. Captain Edward Thompson, 3 vols. (London, 1776).

3. Robert Rea, *The English Press in Politics, 1760–1774* (Lincoln, Nebr., 1963), pp. 182–83.

4. Recorded in the *Annual Register* for 1773, vol. 16, pp. 100, 178–82.

5. Andrew Marvell, *Poems and Letters,* ed. H. M. Margoliouth, rev. Pierre Legouis, 2 vols. (Oxford, 1971), 2:325. This letter is inscribed "To a Friend in Persia," taken by Marvell's editors to mean Popple.

6. One manuscript version, including only the first eleven stanzas, was dated May 1670. A much expanded version, ascribed to Marvell but brought up-to-date to cover later events, was printed in *Poems on Affairs of State* (London, 1697). For the text, attribution, and textual problems, see Marvell, *Poems and Letters,* 1:173–75 and 2:374–76.

7. Thomas Cooke, *The Works of Andrew Marvell, Esq.,* 2 vols. (London, 1726), dedication.

8. J. G. Nichols, *Literary Anecdotes of the Eighteenth Century*, 6 vols. (London, 1812), 2:449.

9. For the most recent attempt to take Thompson's advice and include the *Second* and *Third Advices to the Painter* in Marvell's canon, see my *Andrew Marvell: The Writer in Public Life* (Harlow, 2000)

10. Harvard's copy of the edition of 1726 (15463.47*) was donated to that library by Thomas Hollis in 1765 and honoured by one of his splendid red morocco bindings, with a liberty cap on the spine. It is also there miscatalogued online as having been published in 1720.

11. For a telling sketch of Oppositional disarray at the end of 1775, see Horace Walpole, *Journal of the Reign of King George the Third, from the Year 1771 to 1783*, ed. John Doran, 2 vols. (London, 1859), 1:526. "This month [November] ended triumphantly in Parliament for the Ministers, not only from the corruption of that assembly, from the predominance of Toryism, and from the frenzy of the nation against America, but from the want of abilities and from the factions in the Opposition. The Duke of Richmond, whose health was bad, disgusted with ill success, had been gone a fortnight into the country: so was the Duke of Grafton, and many other young men, for their hunting and sports attached them more than their principles; and as Lord Camden said well, *it was impossible to command an army of volunteers.* Formerly the obstinacy of the Jacobites and Tories had kept them together better than the troops of the Court; now . . . the incapacity of Lord Rockingham, the Cavendishes, and Burke, and the factions in Opposition, reduced them to nothing. Lord Shelburne, Barré, and Dunning were so dissatisfied with the Rockinghams, that they declared it should be long before they voted with them again. Wilkes obstinately pursued his own ideas, and was therefore shunned by all those lordly leaders."

12. Pierre Legouis, *André Marvell: Poète, puritain, patriote, 1621–1678* (Paris, 1928); abridged and translated as *Andrew Marvell: Poet, Puritan, Patriot, 1621–78* (Oxford, 1965), p. 230.

13. *The Parliamentary History of England, from the Beginnings*, 25 vols. (London, 1816).

14. John Almon, *Biographical, Literary, and Political Anecdotes of Several of the Most Eminent Persons of the Present Age*, 3 vols. (London, 1797), 2:145. Almon also explained that one paragraph had been deemed a libel by Charles Yorke, the attorney general, but that Grenville, using more common sense (and believing Sir George Savile to have been the author), decided to avoid confrontation.

15. See Lucyle Werkmeister, *The London Daily Press, 1772–1792* (Lincoln, Nebr., 1963), p. 120.

16. Horace Walpole, *Journal of the Reign of King George the Third*, ed. J. Doran, 2 vols. (London, 1759), 1:482.

17. See James Thomson, *Liberty, the Castle of Indolence, and Other Poems*, ed. James Sambrook (Oxford, 1986), p. 39: "Occasional 'prospects' and land-scapes in art and nature . . . serve only to remind us that in the greater part of *Liberty* the poet of *Seasons* misdirected his talent." It is striking that Sambrook never mentions the relation between *Liberty* and Thomson's preface to the edition of *Areopagitica* produced as a warning against the Stage Licensing Act of 1737.

18. Thomson, *Liberty*, p. 122, ll. 1058–1063, 1096–1102.

19. For this archaic use of "independence," see Thomson, *Liberty*, part 3, ll. 135, 341; part 4, l. 529; and part 5, l. 121, in its original context.

CHAPTER 5

The Two Snuffboxes: Recovering the Whig in Reynolds

1. Sir Joshua Reynolds, *Discourses on Art*, ed. Robert R. Wark (New Haven, 1975), p. 70.

2. Blake's comment was one of a series of marginal notes he wrote in his own copy of the 1798 edition of the *Discourses*, now in the British Library.

3. Sir Joshua Reynolds, *The Works of Sir Joshua Reynolds*, ed. Edmond Malone, 3 vols. (London, 1798), 1:ci–cvi.

4. This mistake is still in place in Wark's edition of the *Discourses*, p. 290.

5. See John Dryden, *Absalom and Achitophel*, ll. 51–56.

6. The evidence seems to be limited to Reynolds' caricature of Voltaire as one of the demons of error in *The Triumph of Truth*, his allegorical por-trait of Dr. James Beattie, and Fox's daughter's anecdote of a "dinner conversation at Holland House . . . in which, sitting next Sir Joshua, she burst out into glorification of the Revolution, and was grievously chilled and checked by her neighbour's cautious and unsympathetic tone." See Charles Leslie and Tom Taylor, *The Life and Times of Sir Joshua Reynolds*, 2 vols. (London, 1865), 2:544. At this point Reynolds was sixty-six.

7. Nicholas Penny, ed., *Reynolds* (London, 1986); the catalogue is, however, invaluable for the biographical information it includes.

8. John Barrell, *The Political Theory of Painting from Reynolds to Hazlitt: "The Body of the Public"* (New Haven, 1986).

9. Reynolds, *Discourses*, pp. 140–41; Barrell, *Political Theory of Painting*, pp. 141, 146–53.

10. For the *Ironical Discourse,* see Frederick Hilles, *Portraits by Sir Joshua Reynolds* (New York, 1952), pp. 139–42.

11. Barrell, *Political Theory,* p. 340.

12. David Solkin, *Painting for Money: The Visual Arts and the Public Sphere in Eighteenth- Century England* (New Haven, 1993), p. 1.

13. For the most detailed account of the affair of *North Briton,* no. 45, see Peter D. G. Thomas, *John Wilkes: A Friend to Liberty* (Oxford, 1996), pp. 27–56.

14. For the portraits of Fox, Shelburne, Secker, and Drummond, see David Manning, *Sir Joshua Reynolds: A Complete Catalogue of His Paintings* (New Haven, 2000), nos. 679, 525, 1439, and 1598. It is worth noting that Reynolds painted Shelburne again in 1766 and that his appointment as secretary of state occurred on July 23 of that year.

15. See Thomas, *John Wilkes,* pp. 81, 246 n. 53.

16. See Penny, *Reynolds,* p. 24.

17. Reynolds, *Discourses,* p. 73.

18. This evidence conflicts, however, with Peter Thomas's statement that in 1766, Wilkes did not carry out his threat of a secret visit to England until May 12, "when he secretly lodged in London with Lauchlin Macleane, having told no one of his intention," and that he left for Paris again on May 31. See Thomas, *John Wilkes,* p. 64.

19. Ibid., p. 62.

20. See Paul Langford, *The First Rockingham Administration, 1765–1766* (Oxford, 1973), p. 2.

21. See Alison Gilbert Olson, *The Radical Duke: Career and Correspondence of Charles Lennox, Third Duke of Richmond* (Oxford, 1961), p. 169.

22. Horace Walpole, *The Last Journals of Horace Walpole,* ed. A. Francis Steuart, 2 vols. (London, 1910), 2:219. The woman he had seduced with promise of marriage, Walpole adds, preferred to die in childbirth, leaving illegitimacy to her baby as its inheritance, rather than claim the solution of marriage that Thurlow had previously reneged on. "She died protesting she would not marry so black a villain."

23. See N. A. M. Rodger, *The Insatiable Earl: A Life of John Montague, Fourth Earl of Sandwich, 1718–1792* (London, 1993), pp. 240–41: "The real difficulty [with Keppel] was what he had been doing" during the fifteen years since his last naval engagement. "He had become more or less a full-time politician. He and his friend Saunders were leaders of the Rockingham Whigs, distinguished throughout the 1760s and 1770s by the strength, or at least the immoderation of their views. . . . Keppel had learnt, or been taught, to judge even professional matters by political criteria." For Wal-

pole's ideologically opposite view, see his *Last Journals,* 2:223–25, 234–37, 241, 247–49.

24. See Penny, *Reynolds,* p. 183: "The artist noted in his pocket-book on 11 April 1759, 'Commodore Keppell speak about print,' which suggests, although it does not prove, that the print was made on the painter's initiative."

25. See Leslie and Taylor, *Life,* 2:235.

26. For a clear and good-humoured account of these events, see Edward Lascelles, *The Life of Charles James Fox* (Oxford, 1936), pp. 110–33.

27. See Charles James Fox, *Speeches of the Right Honourable Charles James Fox in the House of Commons,* 6 vols. (London, 1815), 2:436. An unveiled but impotent threat, "that it has anciently been the practice of this House, to withhold supplies until grievances were redressed," was evidently intended to remind George III of seventeenth-century parliamentary history.

28. See Sir Joshua Reynolds, *Letters of Sir Joshua Reynolds,* ed. Frederick Hilles (Cambridge, 1929), pp. 101–2.

29. Walter Armstrong, *Sir Joshua Reynolds* (London, 1900), p. 41.

30. James Northcote, *Memoirs of Sir Joshua Reynolds . . .* (London, 1813), p. 235.

CHAPTER 6
Thomas Erskine: The Great Defender

1. Thomas Erskine, *The Speeches of Lord Erskine,* ed. James L. High, 2 vols. (Chicago, 1876; reprint, Birmingham, Ala., 1984), 1:1.

2. Lloyd Paul Stryker, *For the Defense: Thomas Erskine, the Most Enlightened Liberal of His Times, 1750–1823* (New York, 1947).

3. John Hostettler, *Thomas Erskine and Trial by Jury* (Chichester, England, 1996).

4. The most striking and relevant exceptions here are two books on the 1794 Treason Trials: Alan Wharam's *Treason Trials, 1794* (Leicester, England, 1992), and John Barrell's *Imagining the King's Death* (Oxford, 2000); but see also Richard Helgerson, "Writing the Law," a masterly resurrection of the figure of Sir Edward Coke, in his *Forms of Nationhood: The Elizabethan Writing of England* (Chicago, 1992); and David Harris Sacks, "The Promise and the Contract in Early Modern England: Slade's Case in Perspective," in *Rhetoric and Law in Early Modern Europe,* ed. Victoria Kahn and Lorna Hutson (New Haven, 2001).

5. Erskine, speech in defence of John Stockdale, in *Speeches,* 2:68–69.

6. This is the only meaning of "strangury," the condition from which Hargrave suffered, that the dictionaries allow. Why it inhibited his speaking remains a mystery.

7. Stryker, *For the Defense*, p. 69.

8. The Sir Philip in question was Philip Yorke, solicitor-general, afterwards Lord Chancellor Hardwicke, a minor target of the *Letter Concerning Libels*. William Pulteney, made earl of Bath in 1742, was earlier an active member of the whig or Patriot opposition to Walpole and was himself a contributor to the *Craftsman*. There is considerable confusion about the occasion of this ballad. It was printed (twice) in 1729 as *The Honest Jury; or, Caleb Triumphant*, and the poem is self-dated as referring to a case of "the year Twenty-nine." Yet W. W. Wilkins, who prints it in *Political Ballads of the Seventeenth and Eighteenth Centuries*, 2 vols. ([London, 1860], 2:232–36), dates it 1732; the *Dictionary of National Biography* article on Hardwicke mentions the case but gives no date. Mansfield himself had no other record of the case than his memory of that one stanza of the ballad and stated that there were no legal notes of it.

9. Thomas Erskine, *The Rights of Juries Vindicated; In the Arguments of the Hon. Thomas Erskine and W. Welch, Esq., in the Court of King's Bench, Westminster; In the Case of the King against the Dean of St. Asaph on Wednesday, November 15, 1784, in Support of the Motion for a New Trial*, 2d ed. (London, 1785–86).

10. See David Manning, *Sir Joshua Reynolds: A Complete Catalogue of His Paintings* (New Haven, 2000), no. 586.

11. See John Milton, *Complete Prose Works*, ed. D. M. Wolfe et al., 8 vols. (New Haven, 1953–82), 2:559–60.

12. Ibid., 2:557–58.

13. Ibid., 2:558.

14. Stryker, *For the Defense*, p. 358.

15. See Erskine, *Speeches*, 2:134. "I, who now speak to you, was threatened with the loss of office, if I appeared as his advocate. . . . I did defend him, and I did lose my office."

16. Milton, *Complete Prose Works*, 2:565.

17. See, for example, Stanley Fish, "There's No Such Thing as Free Speech and It's a Good Thing Too," *Boston Review* 17, no. 3 (1992):23–26.

18. See G. Edward White, *Justice Oliver Wendell Holmes: Law and the Inner Self* (Oxford, 1993), pp. 446–48.

19. [Thomas Erskine], *Armata: A Fragment*, 2d ed. (London, 1817), part 2, p. 164. The two parts were separately paginated. Italics added.

CHAPTER 7

Two Steps Forward, One Step Backwards:
William Wordsworth's Revisionism

1. John Barrell, *Imagining the King's Death: Figurative Treason, Fantasies of Regicide, 1793-1796* (Oxford, 2000); but see also Albert Goodwin, *The Friends of Liberty: The English Democratic Movement in the Age of the French Revolution* (London, 1979), on which Barrell could draw for his detailed history of the radical organisations; and Alan Wharam, *The Treason Trials, 1794* (London, 1992), which offers a barrister's view.

2. Barrell, *Imagining*, pp. 343-44; italics added.

3. Ibid., pp. 567 n. 105, 575-76, 587-88.

4. See *The Poetical Works of Samuel Taylor Coleridge*, ed. Ernest Hartley Coleridge (London, 1912), pp. 79-89.

5. [William Godwin], *Cursory Strictures on the Charge Delivered by Lord Chief Justice Eyre to the Grand Jury, October 2, 1794* (London, 1794).

6. See *The Writings and Speeches of Edmund Burke*, ed. William B. Todd (Oxford, 1991), 9:145.

7. Burke, "Letter to a Noble Lord," in *The Writing and Speeches of Edmund Burke*, 9:181.

8. Burke, "Letter to a Noble Lord," 9:151; Milton, *Paradise Lost*, 1:597, 2:707.

9. See Nicholas Roe, *Wordsworth and Coleridge: The Radical Years* (Oxford, 1988), p. 4. Indeed, Roe cites a much earlier apostasy by Coleridge, and a mendacious one at that. "In his letter to Sir George and Lady Beaumont of 1 October 1803 . . . Coleridge announced that during the 1790s he had been 'utterly unconnected with any party or club or society. . . . All such Societies, under whatever name, I abhorred as wicked Conspiracies.'"

10. Ibid., p. 149.

11. See Patterson, *Early Modern Liberalism* (Cambridge, 1997), pp. 90, 134.

12. Mary Moorman unaccountably states that "in the early text Burke is not mentioned at all"; see *William Wordsworth, A Biography: The Later Years, 1803-1850* (Oxford, 1965), p. 506.

13. *The Parliamentary History of England, from the Beginnings*, 36 vols. (London, 1816), 30:550-56, 611, 639-46, 1008-13.

14. Ibid., 30:826-27.

15. Ibid., 30:890-902.

16. *Early Letters of William and Dorothy Wordsworth (1787-1805)*, ed. E. de Selincourt (Oxford, 1935), pp. 114-17; letter dated Friday, May 23 (1794).

17. Ibid., pp. 119-22; letter dated Sunday, June.

18. Ibid., p. 129.
19. For Wordsworth's movements during this period, see Mary Moorman, *William Wordsworth: A Biography* (Oxford, 1957), pp. 209–70.
20. Goodwin, *Friends of Liberty,* p. 499.

Dunning, John, later baron Ashburton, 44-47, 96, 183, 184, 187,
189, 195-96, 208, 260nn. 8, 9,
269n. 11

East India Bill, 70, 191-94
Echard, Laurence, historian, 2
Edgecumbe, Lord, 171, 187
Edward III, treason law of, 147,
239
Effingham, Thomas Howard,
earl of, 117, 155, 187
Elliott, Gilbert, 257n. 4
Erskine, Thomas, 1, 2, 19, 23, 25,
34, 156-57, 201-37, 238, 252;
Almon's defence, 70, 201, 209;
Almon's prosecution, 72; *Armata*, 201-2, 231-37; Baillie's
defence, 206-7; Coleridge's
sonnet on, 202, 242; Cruikshank cartoon of, 218; defending
dean of St. Asaph, 185, 209-
14; Keppel's defence, 187, 189;
Lord George Gordon's defence,
207-9; and jury trials, 214-16,
237; Paine's defence, 217-27,
273n. 1; portrait of, 217, 219;
prosecuting Williams, 227-28;
and Sir Joshua Reynolds, 205,
217; and Treason Trials *(1794)*,
201, 202, 209, 238-41, 245
Exclusion Crisis, 166
Ex officio informations, 90-93, 95
Eyre, Sir James, Lord Chief
Justice, 241

Filmer, Sir Robert, 222-23
Fish, Stanley, 273n. 17
Fisher, Edward, engraver, 189

Fisher, Kitty, courtesan, 173, 175
Fitzmaurice, Thomas, sheriff, 210
Fitzroy, Mrs., 172
Foote, Samuel, actor, 156
Fox, Charles James: 18, 22, 26, 70,
125, 128, 133, 137, 170-72, 185,
187, 197, 200, 207, 271n. 27; car-
toons of, 191-92; East India Bill,
191-93; Fox's Libel Act *(1792)*,
22-23, 195, 209, 216-17, 227, 231;
Reynolds's portrait of, 189-97
Fox, Henry, Lord Holland, 6, 49,
172, 174-75
Frankland, Thomas, historian,
83-84
Franklin, Benjamin, 68, 125, 130-
31, 134
Fuller, Rose, M.P., 104

Galileo, Galilei, 125, 233
Gardiner, S. R., 2
Garrick, David, actor, 150, 156
Gazeteer, 40, 137
General Advertiser, 69-70
general warrants, 23, 41, 42, 78, 94,
173, 260n. 11
Gentleman's Magazine, 44, 198
George I, 170
George II, 159-60, 215
George III, 3, 11, 112, 134, 137,
170, 176, 177, 192, 196, 240,
272n. 27; and Almon, 59, 74,
94; and America, 98, 101; antiparty policy, 5-6, 18, 41, 140,
153, 263n. 3; and Hume, 6, 10,
22; madness of, 72-73; and Reynolds, 177, 183, 184, 195; satires
on, 5-7, 51, 64, 130-31, 144,
161-62

Machiavelli, Niccolo, 254
Macintosh, Sir James, 18
Macleane, Lauchlin, 271n. 18
Macpherson, James, 125
Magna Carta, 8, 26, 28, 49, 54, 64, 79, 90
Mainwaring, Sir Philip, 181
Malone, Edmund, 163–67, 171, 196
Manchester, George Montagu, fourth duke of, 117
Manning, David, 180
Mansfield, William Murray, earl of, 4, 141, 160, 208; duel with Almon, 43, 44–46, 59–60, 71, 74, 78–82, 86, 94, 96–98, 159, 260n. 8, 261n. 13; and Thomas Erskine, 157, 204–6, 215–16; and habeas corpus, 26; Reynolds portrait of, 185
Mansfield doctrine (on juries), 22–23, 60, 214–16, 239, 273n. 8
Margarot, Maurice, Scots "martyr," 241
Marlborough, John Churchill, earl of, 115, 266n. 19
Marvell, Andrew, 1, 29, 130–31; *Account of the Growth of Popery*, 140, 145, 160; *Advices to the Painter*, 143; *Last Instructions*, 143; *Rehearsal Transpros'd*, 144; *Royal Resolutions*, 144, 161; Thompson's edition of, 139–62, 187, 201, 242
Mason, William, 198
Massachusettts Government Bill *(1774)*, 151
Massacre of St. George's Fields, 56, 67
Matthews, William, 253–54
Matthias, Vincent, 150

Maudit, Israel, 125
May, Thomas Erskine May, historian, 1, 11
McNally, Leonard, 72
Mead, Joseph, Quaker, 212–13
Melville, Herman, 121
Meredith, Sir William, 78, 155, 157
Millar, Andrew, publisher, 56, 84, 149
Miller, John, 64–65, 86
Milton, Deborah, 198
Milton, John, 1, 83, 85, 130–31, 204–5, 222, 254; *Areopagitica*, 23, 38, 76, 86, 87, 105, 224–27, 229, 233, 265–66n. 14, 270n. 17; Burke's holdings of, 103–4; *De Doctrina Christiana*, 229; *Eikonoklastes*, 103; and Galileo, 225, 233; *Life of* (Toland), 103; *Paradise Lost*, 101, 102, 108–10, 114–19, 124, 131, 136–37, 205, 229, 243, 244, 248, 251, 266–67n. 26; *Paradise Regained*, 110, 114, 131, 205; portrait of, 198; *Samson Agonistes*, 51, 249–50; sonnet, 57
Moby Dick, 121
Molesworth, Lord Robert, 56, 67
Molesworth family, 171
Molineux, Crisp, 156
Monmouth, James Scott, duke of, 197–98
Moorman, Mary, 274n. 11
More, Sir Thomas, 232
Morning Post, 69

Namier, Sir Lewis, 2, 11–13, 21
Namierism, 29, 104, 170
Napoleon Bonaparte, 235
Nettleton, Robert, 149–50
New Daily Advertiser, 137

Priestley, Joseph, 241
prints, political, 6–7, 29, 48–51,
    261n. 18. *See also* Barry, James
Public Advertiser, 59, 119, 139
Public Ledger, 40
Pulteney, William, 95, 170, 215,
    273n. 8

Quicke, Andrew, 169, 195

Raikes, Thomas, 149, 150
Raikes, William, 150
Ralph, James, historian, 2
Rapin de Thoyras, Paul, historian,
    2, 8
Rea, Robert, 44, 45, 75, 259nn. 1, 2,
    261–62n. 21
Reform Bill *(1832)*, 25
Revolution, French, 18, 20, 24, 25,
    137, 164–67, 203, 219, 235, 238,
    246, 248, 249–50. *See also* Burke,
    Edmund; Wordsworth, William
Revolution of *1688*, 6, 49, 94, 137,
    145, 158, 198
Reynolds, Sir Joshua, 28, 163–200;
    Discourses on Art, 163–64, 167–
    68, 173, 175, 178, 194–95, 198,
    200; and Thomas Erskine, 205;
    and Charles James Fox, 171,
    189–95; and George III, 183,
    184; *Ironical Discourse*, 168; and
    Dr. Johnson, 171, 196–97; and
    Augustus Keppel, 171, 187–89,
    244; and Rockingham, 171, 179–
    82; *Triumph of Truth*, 270n. 6;
    and Wilkes, 171, 178–79, 199
Richmond, Charles Lennox, third
    duke of, 25, 117, 182, 187, 207,
    269n. 11
Richmond, duchess of, 172

Rigby, Richard, 4, 158
Rockingham, Charles Wentworth,
    second marquis of, 18, 40, 47, 67,
    68, 107, 117, 135–36, 157, 163, 173,
    177, 183, 187, 265n. 13, 269n. 11;
    assessments of, 179–80; death
    of, 99, 101; Reynolds portraits
    of, 179–82
Rockingham, Lady, 172
Rockingham Whigs, 19, 20, 24, 68,
    100–101, 104, 155, 196, 197, 258n.
    14, 260n. 12, 269n. 11; secession
    from parliament, 133–36, 151
Rogers, Deborah, 39, 44, 45,
    60–61, 69, 73, 260n. 9
Rolli, Paolo, 103
Romney, George, painter, 183
Royal Academy, 169, 183
Rushworth, John, historian, 2, 11,
    85–86
Russell, Conrad, 2
Russell, Lord John, 25
Russell, Lord William, 11, 25, 43,
    141

Sacheverell, Henry, 135
Sacks, David Harris, 272n. 4
Sackville, Lord George, 40
St. James's Chronicle, 141
Sambrook, James, 270n. 17
Sandes, Lady, 172
Sandwich, John Montague, fourth
    earl of, 42, 186, 206, 207
Saunders, Sir Charles, 179
Savile, Sir George, 78, 80, 133, 152,
    155, 207, 208, 269n. 14
Say, Charles Green, publisher, 40,
    61
Sayers, James, cartoonist, 101,
    191–92

Index/285